Perspectives on Thinking, Learning, and Cognitive Styles

The Educational Psychology Series

Robert J. Sternberg and Wendy M. Williams, Series Editors

Perspectives on Thinking, Learning, and Cognitive Styles

Edited by

Robert J. Sternberg
Yale University

Li-fang Zhang
University of Hong Kong

2001

LAWRENCE ERLBAUM ASSOCIATES, PUBLISHERS
Mahwah, NJ   London

Lawrence Erlbaum Associates, Inc., Publishers
10 Industrial Avenue
Mahwah, NJ 07430

Cover design by Kathryn Houghtaling Lacey

Library of Congress Cataloging-in-Publication Data

Perspectives on thinking, learning, and cognitive styles / edited
    by Robert J. Sternberg, Li-fang Zhang.
            p.   cm. — (The educational psychology series)
        Includes bibliographical references and index.
    ISBN 0-8058-3430-3 (cloth : alk. paper)
    ISBN 0-8058-3431-1 (pbk. : alk. paper)
1. Cognitive styles. 2. Thought and thinking. 3. Human
    information processing. 4. Learning, Psychology of.
I. Sternberg, Robert J.   II. Zhang, Li-fang.   III. Series.
BF311 .P375 2001
153—dc21   00-059606
                                                        CIP

Books published by Lawrence Erlbaum Associates are printed on
acid-free paper, and their bindings are chosen for strength and
durability.

Printed in the United States of America
10   9   8   7   6   5   4   3   2   1

Contents

Preface

Traditionally, many psychologists and educators have believed that people's successes and failures are attributable mainly to individual differences in abilities. For the past few decades, however, investigators have been studying the roles of thinking, learning, and cognitive styles in performance with both academic and nonacademic settings. Although these three kinds of styles may be viewed as overlapping historically, they have been conceptualized in different ways. Consider, for example, a topic in school such as the Civil War in the United States.

Learning styles might be used to characterize how one prefers to learn about the Civil War. Would one rather learn about it visually (by reading) or auditorily (by lectures)? Or perhaps one would prefer an active form of learning (simulating it) versus a passive form (reading or listening to material about it).

Thinking styles might be used to characterize how one prefers to think about material as one is learning it or after one already knows it. For example, would one rather think about global issues or local issues? Would one prefer to evaluate what one has learned or to go beyond what one has learned?

Cognitive styles might be used to characterize ways of cognizing the information. For example, does one tend to be a splitter, seeing each battle as a distinct entity, or as a lumper, viewing many or all of the battles as similar acts of war? Does one tend to be impulsive in jumping to conclusions about the war or to be reflective? The cognitive styles tend to be closer to personality than are the other types of styles.

In general, abilities refer to things one can do, such as to execute skills or skill combinations (strategies). Styles refer to preferences in the use of abilities. For example, in one theory (Witkin, Dyk, Faterson, Goodenough, & Karp, 1962), people with a field-dependent style tend to be unable to separate things to which they attend from the context in which they attend to these things, where people with a field-dependent style are able to make such a separation. In another well-known theory, a deep-processing strategy is to use one's abilities to the utmost in processing material to a great depth, whereas a surface-processing strategy may involve the use of the same abilities, but to process material to be learned in a more superficial way (Marton & Booth, 1997). In yet another theory, a person with a legislative style likes to use his or her abilities to generate new ideas, whereas a person with a judicial style prefers to use his or her abilities to analyze existing ideas (Sternberg, 1997). Research styles has indicated that styles account for individual differences in performance that go well beyond abilities.

Theory and research on styles went out of fashion for a number of years. Several reasons contributed to this lapse of interest (see Sternberg & Grigorenko, 1997). First, some of the early theories presented styles that were not clearly distinguishable from abilities, on the one hand, or personality, on the other. Second, many of the early theories were of isolated styles that made little contact with other psychological literature. Third, the quality of some of the early empirical research was variable. But styles have reemerged as an area of interest because new theories better differentiate styles from abilities and make more contact with the other psychological literature. Recent research is also, in many cases, more careful and conclusive than some of the older research.

Styles are of interest to educators because they predict academic performance in ways that go beyond abilities (Marton & Booth, 1997). They are also of interest because when teachers take styles into account, they help improve both instruction and assessment. Moreover, teachers who take styles into account can show sensitivity to cultural and individual diversity that is so often absent in the classroom.

For example, there is quantitative evidence that teachers tend to think students are better matches to their own styles than the students really are. Perhaps as consequence, the teachers evaluate more positively students who match their own style of thinking, regardless of the students' abilities or achievements. It also has been found that styles predict academic success incrementally better than do ability tests (Grigorenko & Sternberg, 1997); Sternberg, 1997; Sternberg & Grigorenko, 1995).

Our student populations are more diverse than ever before, so the issue of thinking and learning styles has become important as it never has been before. What can we do in the face of such diversity to maintain the quality of the education we provide students? One thing we can do is to take into account students' diverse styles of thinking and learning.

Although styles are primarily of interest in education, they are also of great interest in business, and the Myers-Briggs Type Indicator (Myers & McCaulley, 1985) is one of the leading tests used in business for selection and placement.

To prepare this book, we asked leading worldwide experts in the field of styles to contribute chapters on the topics of thinking, learning, and cognitive styles. We had an overwhelmingly positive response, enabling us to bring together the leaders in this field. We asked only people who have contributed serious theory and published empirical data, or both, not individuals whose work is primarily commercial, or who implement the theories of others but who have not proposed theories or collected data of their own. We have also sought and achieved international representation so as to include many of the major leaders in the field of styles.

The goal of this book is to present the most recent theory and research on styles in a way that (a) represents diverse theoretical perspectives, (b) includes solid empirical evidence testing the validity of these perspectives, and (c) shows the application of these perspectives to school as well as situations involving other kinds of organizations.

The book will be of interest, we believe, to diverse audiences. Educators will be interested in the book for ideas as to how to improve their teaching and assessment of student performance. Psychologists will be interested in the book because it represents an important area of psychology at the interface of cognition and personality. It is an area that has interested psychologists not only in these two fields, but in the fields of educational psychology, industrial and organizational psychology, clinical psychology, consulting psychology, and developmental psychology. Managers in business may be interested in the book because it will be relevant to the issue of effective supervision. And lay people may be interested in learning more about their own styles and how these styles affect their lives.

ACKNOWLEDGMENTS

We are grateful to Sai Durvasula for her assistance in the preparation of the manuscript and to Grant R206R950001 from the United States Office of Educational Research and Improvement, U.S. Department of Education, which has funded Robert Sternberg's work on styles. The findings and opinions expressed in this book do not reflect the positions or polices of that agency.

—Robert Sternberg
—Li-fang Zhang

REFERENCES

Grigorenko, E. L., & Sternberg, R. J. (1997). Styles of thinking, abilities, and academic performance. *Exceptional Children, 63*, 295–312.

Marton, F., & Booth, S. A. (1997). *Learning and awareness*. Mahwah, NJ: Lawrence Erlbaum Associates.

Myers, I. B., & McCaulley, M. H. (1985). *Manual: A guide to the development and us of the Myers-Briggs type indicator.* Palo Alto, CA: Consulting Psychologists Press.

Sternberg, R. J. (1997). *Thinking styles.* New York: Cambridge University Press.

Sternberg, R. J., Grigorenko, E. L. (1995). Style of thinking in school. *European Journal of High Ability, 6*(2), 1–18

Sternberg, R. J., & Grigorenko, E. L. (1997). Are cognitive styles still in style? *American Psychologist, 52,* 700–712.

Witkin, H. A., Dyk, R. B., Faterson, H. F., Goodenough, D. R., & Karp, S. A. (1962). *Psychological differentiation.* New York: Wiley.

1

A Capsule History of
Theory and Research on Styles

Robert J. Sternberg
Yale University
Elena L. Grigorenko
Yale University and Moscow State University

Most mathematicians would make lousy accountants. But why? Do they lack mathematical ability? Obviously not. For the most part, they are at or near the top of the scale on any test of mathematical ability that anyone can come up with. Moreover, they were able to become mathematicians only by virtue of high levels of achievement in mathematics, so they are not people whose abilities simply go unrealized. Rather, they seem to differ stylistically from accountants in major ways. The kinds of problems they like to work on are completely different. For example, few mathematicians would want to learn tax codes, but few accountants would want to spend their time doing mathematical proofs. Accountants and mathematicians may or may not have the abilities to do each others' jobs; what is clear is that stylistically, the requirements of the jobs are worlds apart.

Interest in the notion of styles developed in part as a response to the recognition that conventional ability tests provide only part of the answer to why people differ in their performance, whether that kind of performance is in mathematics or something else. If abilities are only part of the answer to understanding how and why people differ in their performance, what might the rest of the answer be?

One possibility, of course, would be personality. Someone with personal difficulties might well be at risk for various kinds of performances, in school or on the job. But personality has not seemed to be the entire answer either. For example, two people might be equally conscientious, but find they want to be conscientious in different domains and in different ways. Theorists interested in styles have sought an answer at the interface between abilities, on the one hand, and personality, on the other.

More and more, people are recognizing the importance of this interface. The concept of emotional intelligence is one example of this interface. The concept of social intelligence is another. In the case of styles, though, we believe it is important to maintain the distinction between abilities and styles. Emotional intelligence may or may not represent a set of abilities. Styles do not represent a set of abilities, but rather a set of preferences. The distinction is important because abilities and preferences may or may not correspond, as we find in the case of someone who wants to be a creative writer but who just can't come up with the ideas.

If we want to start with an understanding of the work that has been done on styles, perhaps as good a place as any to start is the dictionary. According to *Webster's Dictionary* (1967), "A style is a distinctive or characteristic manner . . . or method of acting or performing" (p. 873). In psychology, the idea of style was formally introduced by Allport (1937) when he referred to style as a means of identifying distinctive personality types or types of behavior. Allport's understanding of styles was rooted in Jung's (1923) theory of psychological types. Since Allport's time, the term has been modified and imbued with different meanings, but the core definition of style–that is, its reference to habitual patterns or preferred ways of doing something (e.g., thinking, learning, teaching) that are consistent over long periods of time and across many areas of activity—remains virtually the same.

The more specific term, *cognitive style*, refers to an individual's way of processing information. The term was developed by cognitive psychologists conducting research into problem solving and sensory and perceptual abilities. This research provided some of the first evidence for the existence of distinctive styles.

More recently, attention has turned to styles in learning and teaching. Goldman (1972), for example, classified students' study practices into two styles: "logical" and "mnemonic." Reissman (1964) also argued for the concept of styles in learning, defining a learning style as a "more wholistic (molar) or global dimension of learning operative at the phenomenal level" (p. 485).

But support for the notion of styles has not been limited to cognitive psychology. The broad and flexible nature of the concept of style has made it attractive to researchers in widely differing areas of psychology and related fields. For example, Conway (1992), in discussing the philosophy of science, stated that philosophical differences among psychologists may be related to individual differences in their personality factors and cognitive styles.

Fortunately, the increasing volume of published material on styles has included a number of excellent review papers. Vernon (1973) examined the historical roots of cognitive styles in early 20th-century German typological theories and then critically analyzed contemporary approaches. Bieri (1971), Goldstein and Blackman (1978), and Kagan and Kogan (1970) considered the diverse theoretical orientations that have distinguished the cognitive style domain. Kogan (1976) offered a review of research on cognitive styles from the point of view of their implications for intellectual functioning and academic achievement. Wardell and Royce (1978) analyzed problems related to the definition of style in the current literature.

Although there is fairly extensive disagreement throughout these reviews on preferred approaches to and measurement of styles, there is considerable agreement as to the empirical and conceptual problems related to the concept of style (e.g., Goldstein & Blackman, 1978; Kogan, 1976; Wardell & Royce, 1978).

The most often-mentioned empirical problems is that of the empirical generalizability of findings. Most findings in the field appear to be "instrument bound." In other words, whatever is measured by a particular test or questionnaire is called a "style of . . . ," and there are only a few examples in the literature of replications in which the same latent constructs have been studied with measures created by different authors.

The conceptual problems stem from difficulties related to defining style as a theoretical construct. Specifically, there are two crucial issues in constructing such a definition. The first is related to differentiation between the concepts of styles and strategies (Luchins & Luchins, 1970). Each concept has different theoretical foundations and encompasses functional differences. Cognitive styles are adaptive control mechanisms of the ego that mediate between needs and the external environment (Wallach & Kogan, 1965). "Strategies" usually imply operations followed to minimize error during the decision-making process. At a basic level styles and strategies can be distinguished by the "degree of consciousness" involved. Styles operate without individual awareness, whereas strategies involve a conscious choice of alternatives. The two terms are used interchangeably by some authors (Cronbach & Snow, 1977), but, in general, strategy is used for task- or context-dependent situations, whereas style implies a higher degree of stability falling midway between ability and strategy.

The second issue is related to the nature of styles themselves. Many theorists locate styles at the interface of intelligence and personality, in a sense placing them in both domains, but there are exceptions. Gustafson and Kallen (1989), for example, distinguished cognitive styles from personality styles, and Myers (1988) referred to a hierarchy of styles of cognition (e.g., perceptual, verbal, and cognitive styles) and assumed personality is a source of individual variability within styles. As noted, much of this confusion is due to the nature of styles, because although styles have been viewed primarily in the context of cognition, as cognitive styles they have always included a heavy element of affect.

In the 1970s, the concept of style was further developed as it gained popularity among educators. As a result, the notion of styles developed in two directions through research in educational and vocational psychology. The first direction was primarily one of application. Investigators attempted to apply traditional cognitive styles to school settings, seeking explanations for students' individual differences in achievement and performance via styles. The second direction was an effort to create new frameworks for studying learning and teaching styles based on empirical observations rather than theoretical background. These researchers produced several domain-specific theories of styles, including theories of learning styles (Dunn & Dunn, 1978; Gregorc, 1979, 1985; Renzulli & Smith, 1978), teaching styles (Fischer & Fischer, 1979), and even styles relevant to choosing career opportunities (Holland, 1973).

Styles have received much less attention than they deserve, given their importance to people's functioning. Both successes and failures that have been attributed to abilities are often due to styles. We should give styles their proper due, if only because preferences can be so much easier to mold than abilities. So what have theorists and researchers learned about styles?

COGNITION-CENTERED STYLES: THE COGNITIVE STYLES MOVEMENT

A movement came into prominence in the 1950s and early 1960s with the idea that styles could provide a bridge between the study of cognition (e.g., how we perceive, how we learn, how we think) and the study of personality. A small group of experimental psychologists set out to explore and describe individual differences in cognitive functioning (for more history of the field, see Cantor & Kihlstrom, 1987; Kagan & Kogan, 1970). Collectively, these efforts led to a school of thought in cognitive psychology, designated the "new look," which developed several stylistic constructs, all of which seemed closer to cognition than to personality.

Field Dependence–Field Independence

Did you ever notice that some people seem to be able to find objects that are temporarily misplaced, whereas others cannot? One person can be looking right at missing earrings, for example, and the earrings seem to blend in with the table on which they are lying. Another person immediately sees the earrings against the background of the table. In general, the first type of person cannot see inconspicuous things right in front of his or her nose, whereas the second type of person can see them. In a war, it may well pay off for an infantryman to be the second kind of person, if he wants to distinguish the enemy's camouflage from the background. But at other times, such as in appreciating a painting, noticing things sticking out from their background may be a nuisance. Just what is the difference between the two kinds of people and how they perceive things?

Witkin (1973) suggested that people could be categorized in terms of the degree to which they are dependent on the structure of the prevailing visual field. Some people are highly dependent on this field; others are not.

The kind of person who is more field independent is the person who, when on an airplane, can sense whether the plane is level with the ground or flying at an angle, without looking down at the ground; the field-dependent person needs to look out the window to figure out the plane's orientation relative to the ground. The field-independent person also can look at a complex drawing and find embedded within it a figure or a shape, such as a hidden triangle. The field-dependent person has more trouble separating the hidden form from its surrounding context. Thus, the field-independent person is the one who sees the earrings as standing out from the table, and the enemy's camouflage against its natural background.

Witkin and his colleagues actually developed two major tests of field independence-dependence, measuring the construct in much the ways described earlier. The two tests are different both with respect to the way in which they are given and with respect to what the test taker needs to do.

In the *Rod and Frame Test* (RFT; Witkin, Dyk, Faterson, Goodenough, & Karp, 1962), the individual must ignore a visual context to locate a true vertical. In particular, a rod must be oriented vertically to the ground rather than to a frame that is situated at an angle to the ground. Because the room is dark except for the lighted frame and rod, and because the person is seated at the same angle as the frame, the person cannot use the ground as a visual context cue. Thus, the person must ignore the distracting context (field) of the frame to locate the rod properly relative to the true vertical.

In the *Embedded Figures Test* (EFT; Witkin, Oltman, Raskin, & Karp, 1971), the test taker must locate a previously seen simple figure within a larger, more complex figure that has been designed to obscure or embed the simpler figure. This is a test-like analogue of the situations involving the earrings and the camouflage.

The field-independent person is able to locate the true vertical, despite the position of the frame, and the embedded figures. The field-dependent person has more trouble with these tasks, presumably because he or she experiences the field of vision as more fused, so that it is difficult to separate one particular object from the field in which it is placed.

Is the style of field independence versus field dependence a style, or is it an ability? For a construct to be classified as a style, it has to be distinct from an ability. If styles and abilities amount to the same thing, the construct of a style would be superfluous. The research of Witkin and his colleagues suggested their measures are different in what they measure from verbal abilities, as measured by a standard intelligence test, but there does appear to be a confounding with abilities.

One becomes suspicious of the relation between a style and an ability when one of two complementary styles always seems to be better. As mentioned earlier, one style may be better than another in a given situation, but on average, styles should not be better or worse, but rather differentially good fits to different environments.

In the case of field dependence and field independence, field independence almost always seems to be the preferable style. You are certainly better off if you can orient yourself in a given environment: It's hard to imagine a situation in which you would be at a disadvantage in having better orientation. If you are an airplane pilot, you want better orientation for sure! Similarly, you are likely to be better off if you can find things that blend in the environment, whether they are keys lost in the house, earrings that fell onto the ground, or the proverbial needle in the haystack, for that matter. If one so-called style is always better, then the style seems to have the properties of an ability rather than of a style.

Finally, the tests used to measure field dependence–independence have the whiff of ability tests: There are right and wrong answers, and the "difficulty" of an item can be computed as a function of the number of problems the test taker answers correctly. It certainly sounds like an ability! In fact, the preponderance of the data support this interpretation.

A review of 20 studies (Goldstein & Blackman, 1978) suggested that field independence is consistently correlated with both verbal and perform- ance aspects of intelligence, and that the correlations are moderate (.40 to .60 on a scale where 0 is low, indicating no relation, and 1 is high, indicating a perfect relation). MacLeod, Jackson, and Palmer (1986) provided evi- dence that field independence is essentially indistinguishable from spatial ability—the kind of ability you need to rotate objects mentally in your head, to find your way around a new town, or to fit the suitcases into the trunk of your car.

In an attempt to differentiate field dependence–independence from fluid intelligence, researchers investigated heritability (i.e., the proportion of genetic variance in the overall phenotypic variance) of this cognitive style (Del Miglieo, Paluzzi, Falanga, & Talli, 1996; Egorova, 1987; Grigorenko, LaBuda, & Carter, 1992). Overall, the estimates were about 50%, that is, virtually identical to the estimates researchers have obtained for heritability of intelligence (e.g., Plomin & Petrill, 1997). Given high correlations between field dependence–independence and intelligence, it is plausible that a significant portion of the genetic variance in field dependence–independence (up to 60%; Bergman, Norlin, Borg, & Fyrö, 1975) is explainable by genetic variation in intelligence. Thus, the preponderance of evidence at this point suggests that field independence is tantamount to fluid intelligence.

Equivalence Range

Some people tend to see things that are different as almost alike; other people see things that are similar as very different. Several names have been given to describe this difference in categorizing behavior (Bruner, Goodnow, & Austin, 1956; Gardner, 1953; Gardner & Schoen, 1962). One name, the one we use here, is equivalence range. Another is leveling (seeing things as similar) versus sharpening (seeing things as different), and still another is conceptual differentiation (narrow versus wide). Some people tend to have a relatively broad equivalence range, whereas others may have a narrower equivalence range. The advantage of having a broad equivalence range is seeing things as related where other people might not see the relation; the disadvantage is not seeing important differences that distinguish one thing from another.

The *Free Sorting Test* (Gardner, 1953) has been used to measure equivalence range. In the test, people are given the names of 73 common objects and are instructed to sort into groups the objects that seem to belong together. Objects that do not seem to belong with any others can be placed into groups by themselves. The subject's score is the total number of groups formed, with lower scores implying broader equivalence range and higher scores implying narrower equivalence range. Other scores can be derived as well.

The equivalence range construct seems to be a legitimate style, so long as it is used to measure preference rather than ability. Virtually all psychologists believe that as people grow older and become cognitively more mature, their ability to make differentiations increases. For example, what is a "doggie" to a very young child may include not only dogs, but also cats and other small domesticated animals.

Moreover, as people become expert in an area, they can make distinctions that they could not make before. For example, what would all appear to be wildflowers to a novice would appear as a wide variety of different types of wildflowers to an expert; similarly, what would look like any old chess position to a novice would likely be a specific and nameable chess position to an expert. Thus, equivalence range appears to be a style so long as it measures preference rather than some kind of cognitive complexity.

Category Width

What is the range in amounts of annual rainfall over ten years? How about the range in the widths of windows in colonial houses? How about the range in the lengths of whales? No one is likely to know the answers to any of these or similar questions. But to a theorist of cognitive styles, the accuracy of responses is not what is at issue, anyway. Rather, what is of interest is the breadth of the ranges proposed for various objects, such as windows and whales. When people are asked to estimate ranges, some of them consistently tend to give broad estimates, whereas others give narrow estimates. The tendency to estimate high or low is used as an estimate of category width.

Items such as those just described are found on the *C-W Scale* (Pettigrew, 1958), which is a measure of category width. The idea is to measure the extent to which people tend to see categories as being relatively broader or relatively narrower.

People are not wholly consistent in their category width, as would be expected, because styles can vary across tasks and situations. Thus, time and the emotional condition of the individual can affect the responses the individual makes. But often the consistencies are more salient than the differences.

Category width has particularly interesting implications when one goes beyond estimates of ranges of lengths of physical objects to estimates of ranges of psychological variation. For example, what is the range of *Scholastic Assessment Test* (SAT) scores at the University of Vermont; how about at the University of Florida; at Yale? Perhaps even more interesting would be the possibility that people with broader category widths not only perceive wider variation, but also perceive wider variation as permissible; for example, they believe that students with a wider range of SAT scores could do the work at the University of Vermont, the University of Florida, or Yale. This aspect of category width bears investigation.

Conceptual Style

Of the following three things, which two best go together: whale, shark, tiger? Which two of the following three best go together: airplane, bird, train? Obviously, there is no right answer to quiz questions like these.

Kagan, Moss, and Sigel's (1963) *Conceptual Style Test* (CST) is supposed to measure not right answers, but rather one of three "conceptual styles." The difference between the test and the rendition here is that we use words to describe objects, whereas the test uses pictures.

People with an *analytic-descriptive* style tend to group together pictures on the basis of common elements (e.g., airplane and bird because they both have wings, or two people who both are wearing socks). People with a *relational* style tend to group things together because of functional, thematic relations (e.g., both whales and sharks swim). People with an *inferential-categorical* style tend to group objects together because of an abstract similarity that can be inferred but usually not directly observed in the picture (e.g., that both a whale and a tiger are mammals).

As a measure, the CST is probably confounded with abilities. Indeed, in most theories of cognitive development, inferential–categorical thinking, as defined here, is seen as more sophisticated than is relational thinking, which is in turn seen as more sophisticated than is the analytic–descriptive style.

For example, on the vocabulary tests of the Wechsler or the Stanford–Binet intelligence scales, more credit is given for a categorical than for a functional definition. Thus, a child who defines an automobile as a vehicle of conveyance will receive more credit than will one who defines the automobile as something that uses gasoline. Similarly, in the theory of Piaget (1972), a child is viewed as cognitively more advanced if he or she can use formal operations (logical thinking) than if he or she can only see concrete relations between things of the kind required by, say, the descriptive style.

Cognitive Controls

Klein (1951, 1954) introduced the term *cognitive control* to refer to a hypothetical construct that directs the expression of need in socially acceptable ways, as required by the situation. Gardner and Long (1962) noted that cognitive controls were conceived within the framework of psychoanalytic ego psychology. According to the authors, controls are viewed as enduring cognitive structures that emerge in the course of development from the interaction of genetics and experience.

The evolution of terms used to denote this set of styles parallels the evolution of the construct itself. Gardner (1962) noted that, in early work, Klein and his associates used the term *perceptual attitudes*. This term was later replaced by the terms *cognitive attitudes* and *cognitive system principles*. The terms *cognitive controls* and *cognitive control principles* were then adopted to denote the idea that a delaying, controlling function was involved in cognition.

Gardner, Jackson, and Messick (1960) differentiated cognitive controls from cognitive style. According to these authors, the former term refers to the specific dimensions, including leveling–sharpening, scanning, field articulation, conceptual differentiation, and constricted–flexible control. In contrast, cognitive style refers to the organization of these dimensions within an individual. However, as Kagan and Kogan (1970) noted, the distinction between cognitive control and cognitive style has not been strictly adhered to by other researchers investigating these concepts.

Reflection–Impulsivity

Do you remember when, as a child, you had to solve rows or even pages of arithmetic problems as fast as you could? The idea was to burn the arithmetic facts into your mind so you would never forget them. Or did you ever take a keyboarding class and have timed typing exercises? In both these situations, the common element is that you had more to do than you could do well in the time that was allotted. This kind of situation leaves you with a choice: Should you complete less of the task, but do what you do flawlessly? Or should you complete as much as you can, recognizing that you will make errors?

Kagan (1966) pointed out that people tend to have a fairly consistent style on tasks like these. Kagan called the style *impulsivity–reflectivity*. The impulsive person completes a lot of the task, but allows himself or herself to make mistakes. The reflective person completes less of the task, but is more careful not to make mistakes in what he or she completes. The individual usually does not make a conscious choice; he or she does what feels natural. Some students rush so much in their keyboarding competitions that they make a tremendous number of mistakes, even though their total word count is high. Similarly, some students rush to arrive to the solution of an interesting math problem, but end up making simple computational errors along the way.

The test most frequently used to measure impulsivity versus reflectivity, the *Matching Familiar Figures Test* (MFFT), requires people to select, from among several alternatives, the picture that exactly matches a standard picture (Block, Block, & Harrington, 1974; Butter, 1979; Kagan, 1966). Test takers are measured both for how quickly they finish the test and for the number of errors they make.

The rationale of the MFFT is that impulsive people will tend to complete many problems, but with a relatively high error rate; reflective people will tend to complete fewer problems, but with a relatively low error rate. Two other categories of scorers, of less interest to cognitive styles researchers, are those who finish many items accurately (who are labeled as quick) and those who finish few items but make a lot of errors nevertheless (who are labeled as slow (Eska & Black, 1971).

This test, like the EFT, has the feeling of an ability test, and its content is practically identical to that found on certain tests of perceptual–motor or clerical ability. What distinguishes this test from the abilities tests is the type of data of interest. Here, the investigator is interested in the pattern of response times versus error rates, and he or she looks only at people who trade off accuracy for speed in one way or another. The quick and slow people are not exhibiting a cognitive style at all, but rather a skill. Whether the same test is well used when it measures both abilities and styles is an open question, but such a test seems on its face to be nonideal.

Although there seem to be relations between impulsivity–reflectivity and various personality attributes, the kind of impulsivity measured by the MFFT appears to be different from the kind of impulsivity measured by personality tests (Furnham & Kendall, 1986). For example, one study found that scores on the test were related to attentional deficit, but not to any of 11 other behavioral problems, including aggressiveness, social withdrawal, and delinquency (Achenbach & Edelbrocker, 1983).

Several studies of the reflectivity–impulsivity construct showed that it is relatively stable over time and tasks. Moreover, if one equates reflective and impulsive children for age and verbal ability, one finds that impulsive children make more errors in reading prose, make more errors of commission on serial recall tests (i.e., asked to recall a string of numbers in order, they are more likely to say a number that is wrong or out of order), and more often offer incorrect solutions on problems requiring inductive reasoning or visual discrimination. In contrast, reflective children make fewer errors in word-recognition tests, serial learning, and inductive reasoning.

There also seem to be personality differences between reflective and impulsive individuals. Impulsive people tend to have minimal anxiety over committing errors, have an orientation toward quick success rather than toward avoiding failure, have relatively low standards for their perform-ance, have low motivation to master tasks, and pay less attention to monitoring of stimuli.

Other Cognitive Styles

Several other cognitive styles have been proposed. One style is *compartmentalization*, which is the extent to which a person tends to compartmentalize ideas or things in discrete categories (Messick, & Kogan, 1963). A compartmentalizer likes to put things in a box with a label.

Compartmentalization can help people organize their world, but it can also result in their becoming rigid. In negotiations, for example, compartmentalization often results in talks that stall. As long as Israelis saw Palestinians more or less uniformly as the bad guys, or Palestinians saw Israelis in the same way, negotiations between the two groups could go nowhere. The same was true in the negotiations regarding the indepen-dence of former republics of Former Yugoslavia. Yale University and its unions negotiate every few years, and as is often in the case in such negotiations, it is difficult for the two sides not to start believing their own posturing. But as soon as one side is compartmentalized, it becomes almost impossible to progress toward solutions.

A second style is *conceptual integration*, which is a person's tendency to relate or hook up parts or concepts to each other to make meaningful wholes (Harvey, Hunt, & Schroder, 1961). Perry Mason was a conceptual integrator, so was Sherlock Holmes, and so are doctors who try to put symptoms into a meaningful pattern so they can form a diagnosis. But many people have no great need to make the parts fit together. They can go through their lives with what Feuerstein (1979) called an episodic grasp of reality, content to let different concepts and events occur without concern for their relation to one another. Note that here we are talking about style, not ability. The question is not how well the person puts together the parts, but how much he or she wants to put them together.

A third cognitive style is *tolerance for unrealistic experiences* (Klein, Gardner, & Schlesinger, 1962). This style refers to the extent to which a person is willing to accept and report experiences at variance with the conventional experiencing of reality as we know it. This style can take several of concrete forms. For example, some people with this style would welcome the effects of an hallucinatory drug, whereas other people, low in this style, would beg off. Some people eagerly embrace virtual-reality experiences that plug them into a world of fantasy dimensions, whereas other people have no use for such experiences.

Finally, a fourth additional style is *scanning*, which, according to Gardner and Moriarty (1968), is the extent to which an individual attempts to verify the judgments he or she makes. Scanning, as defined by Gardner and Moriarty, is a style rather than an ability—it refers to seeking verification, not to the quality of verification. But this is a case where a high score on a measure of the style is better than a low score, so that the construct is more like an ability than most styles. We all stand to gain when we verify our judgments.

Evaluation of the Cognition-Centered Theories

The theories of cognitive styles were a first attempt, and an impressive one, to find an interface between abilities, on the one hand, and personality, on the other. Many of the studies were done some time ago, and it is difficult to judge earlier research by contemporary standards. Yet, today, interest in the kinds of cognitive styles described previously has waned, and it is worthwhile to try to understand why. At the same time, the theories have to be viewed in their historical context and with the realization that it is much easier to criticize theories than it is to propose them. No psychological theory is beyond criticism, even those that have had the most impact on the field of psychology.

The main problem is that styles seem too close to abilities. Isn't it almost always better, say, to be field independent rather than field dependent, or reflective rather than impulsive? Kogan (1973) suggested that we might be able to deal with this problem by dividing styles into three types, depending on how close they are to the abilities domain Type I styles are closest to the abilities domain and Type III are farthest away from this domain). But the taxonomy seems more to recognize that a problem exists than to solve the problem. When styles become like abilities, it is inevitable that one style will be viewed as better than another overall, which seems to carry us away from the whole notion of what a style is supposed to be about.

A second problem is that the classifications of individuals into categories sometimes seem to be arbitrary, and not cleanly dichotomous, as some theorists suggested. People are impulsive or reflective to degrees, rather than just showing one style or the other. Investigators can place people into categories by splitting scores down the middle, but using such a split to categorize people does not eliminate the individual differences that exist within the two groups.

A third problem is the absence of any organizing theory or model for understanding the styles in relation to each other. Each set of styles is a separate entity unto itself, without any unifying framework that relates, say, field independence to category width, or category width to reflectivity. In this respect, the literature on styles diverges from most psychological literatures, where there has been an attempt to specify a relatively more complete taxonomy, say, of abilities or of personality traits.

PERSONALITY-CENTERED STYLES

A second movement also has attempted to understand styles, but in a way that resembles the conceptualization and measurement of personality more than of cognition. We consider two of the main theories.

Theory of Psychological Types

The first theory derives from the work of Carl Jung as interpreted by Myers and Myers (1980). In this theory, four basic distinctions are made. The first is with regard to our attitudes in dealing with people we encounter. *Extraversion* characterizes people who are outgoing, with an interest in people and the environment; *introversion* describes people who are more inwardly focused. The second distinction is with regard to perceptual functions. An *intuitive* person perceives stimuli holistically and concentrates on meaning rather than details, whereas a *sensing* person perceives information realistically and precisely. The third distinction is with regard to judgment. *Thinking* people are logical, analytical, and impersonal in their judgments; whereas *feeling* people are more oriented toward values and emotions in their judgments. The fourth distinction is with regard to interpretation of information. *Perceptive* people are more dependent on information in the environment, whereas *judging* people are more willing to go beyond the information in the environment to make interpretations.

This theory is one of the most elaborated, in that each of the 16 combinations of types that make up the four distinctions is alleged to produce a different overall personality type. Consider, for example, two types.

Sensing types who are introverts and who show thinking with judging are alleged to be serious, quiet, and to earn success by concentration and thoroughness. They are believed to be practical, orderly, matter of fact, realistic, and dependable, and to live their outer life more with thinking but their inner life more with sensing. In contrast, intuitives who are extroverts with thinking and judging are believed to be hearty, frank, decisive, and leaders in activities. They feel real concern for what others think and want, and try to handle things with regard for other people's feelings. They live their outer life more with feeling but their inner life more with intuition.

Styles in this theory are measured via the *Myers–Briggs Type Indicator* or (MBTI; Myers & McCaulley, 1985), which is a published and widely available test that looks a lot like a personality inventory. People respond to statements about themselves in a way that ultimately classifies them as belonging to one category or another.

This theory has probably been the most widely applied of all of the theories of styles. It has been used in settings such as business and education. How valid the theory and measure is for these purposes is open to question. A recent review of the uses of the test suggested the test is not valid for the purposes for which it is used.

Energic Theory of Mind Styles

Gregorc (1982, 1984, 1985) suggested a different and simpler theory of styles, which is based on the notion that people differ in the ways they organize space and time. With regard to space, people are classified as either *concrete* or *abstract*. As the names imply, concrete people prefer dealing with the physical expression of information, abstract people with more metaphorical expression. With regard to time, people are classified as either *sequential* or *random*. A sequential person likes things to be presented in a step-by-step, orderly manner, whereas a random person likes things presented in a more haphazard way.

Gregorc devised a measure of the styles, and, like Myers, characterized what people are like who have each of the four possible combinations of styles. For example, a concrete–sequential person likes the ordered, the practical, and the stable. Individuals in this category focus their attention on concrete reality and physical objects, and validate ideas via the senses. In contrast, an abstract–random person prefers emotional and physical freedom. Individuals in this category focus their attention on the world of feeling and emotion. They also validate ideas using inner guidance.

Gregorc's (1982) measure of styles, the *Gregorc Style Delineator*, consists of 40 words arranged in 10 sets of 4 words, with 1 word in each set corresponding to each style. Individuals rank the 4 words from the least to the most descriptive of themselves. The total score for each of the 4 style subscales is the sum of the ranking of the 10 words composing the subscale. Joniak and Isaksen (1988) found that despite the appeal of Gregorc's four-category approach, there appeared to be little empirical support for their internal-consistency reliability and construct validity. It was also shown that although the four scales meet minimal requirements for factor definition and may have some practical utility, only three of the four can be considered defensible measurement models (O'Brien, 1990).

Evaluation of the Personality-Centered Theories

The personality-centered theories, like the cognition-centered theories, have received various criticisms. Again, remember that all theories can be criticized, no matter how good or useful they are.

The personality-based theories are more comprehensive than the cognition-based theories, but statistical analyses of the structure underlying the data from the tests used to measure the constructs provide only mixed support for the theories. Thus, attractive though the theories may be, the validations of their structures have not been as promising as one might have hoped.

Second, just as the cognitive styles come close to abilities, the styles in the personality-based theories come close to personality traits. Indeed, one might be hard-pressed to distinguish the MBTI from a conventional, paper-and-pencil personality inventory.

Third, although the theorists recognize that styles can vary across tasks and situations, these theories tend to "type" people, as the name of the MBTI suggests. Both theories describe people who are certain types and classify people into groups. Realistically, though, people cannot be as easily pigeon holed as psychologists often seem to like them to be. Most people, at least, are more flexible than psychological theories give them credit for.

ACTIVITY-CENTERED STYLES

Activity-centered theories of styles are more action oriented than are cognitive- or personality-centered theories. They are more centered around kinds of activities people engage in at various points in their lives, such as schooling and work.

Learning Styles

Theories of learning styles deal with how people like to learn. Two theories are described here.

Kolb (1978) proposed a theory of learning styles that is intended primarily to apply in school settings. The theory comprises four basic types of learning styles: converging, diverging, assimilating, and accommodating.

Convergers are abstract conceptualizers and are interested in active experimentation. They like to use deductive reasoning and to focus it on specific problems. *Divergers* are in some respects the opposite. They prefer concrete experience and reflective observation, they are interested in people, and they are imaginative and emotional in their dealings with things and with people. *Assimilators* are abstract conceptualizers and reflective observers. They like to create theoretical models and to use inductive reasoning to assimilate disparate observations into an integrated explanation. Assimilators are less interested in people than in abstract concepts. *Accommodators* like concrete experience and active experimentation, and they like to take risks. People's styles are determined through the *Learning Style Inventory* (LSI).

Another theory of learning styles widely used in education is the theory developed by Dunn and Dunn (1978). Dunn and Dunn's theory includes 18 styles divided into four main categories: environmental (sound, light, temperature, design), emotional (motivation, persistence, responsibility, structure), sociological (peers, self, pair, team, adult, varied), and physical (perceptual, intake, time, mobility). It is hard to say how the 18 styles were chosen, or even why they are called styles. They refer more to elements that affect a person's ability to learn than to ways of learning.

The theories of Kolb (1978) and of Dunn and Dunn (1978) have been used primarily in the educational world. A theory proposed by Holland has been used primarily in the occupational world. This theory, which serves as the basis of the *Strong Vocational Interest Blank* (SVIB), specifies five styles that people should take into account in making job choices: realistic, investigative, artistic, social, and enterprising. Scores on the styles help people narrow vocational choices to those that use the people's preferred styles.

Teaching Styles

The concept of teaching styles is especially important in light of the fact that different learners respond in different ways to different styles of teaching. What works well for one learner may not work well for another.

One theory of teaching styles is that of Henson and Borthwick (1984). They suggested six styles of teaching. In a *task-oriented* approach, planned tasks associated with appropriate materials are prescribed. In a *cooperative-planner* approach, an instructional venture is planned by teachers and students collaboratively, though the teacher is in charge. In a *child-centered* approach, the task structure is provided by the teacher and the students choose from options according to their interests. In a *subject-centered* approach, the content is planned and structured to the extent that students are nearly excluded from the process. In a *learning-centered* approach, equal concern is shown by the teacher for both the student and the subject content. Finally, in an *emotionally exciting* approach, the teacher tries to make his or her teaching as emotionally stimulating as possible. These styles are not mutually exclusive. They could be used in conjunction with each other and probably are most effective when they are so used.

Evaluation of the Activity-Centered Approaches

The strength of the activity-centered approaches is their relevance for the school setting. Yet, these approaches, like those discussed earlier, have their limitations.

First, the activity-centered framework lacks a clear definition of style. Thus, it is difficult to find a correspondence between different approaches developed in this framework, and it is even more difficult to relate them to work outside of the activity-centered tradition.

Second, activity-centered approaches do little about the development of styles. The fact that we can diagnose the learning style of a student does not tell us anything about how this style was developed or if a teacher can "revise" the learning style of a student. Cognition-centered and personality-centered theories, in contrast, do discuss the development of styles in the context of overall intellectual and personality development.

Finally, these approaches, unlike many of those considered earlier, are not integrated with more general theories of psychological functioning. The cognition-centered and personality-centered approaches are special cases of more general psychological theories. Of course, there is no a priori reason why a theory of styles should have to be a special case of a more general psychological theory. At the same time, it remains to be seen how the activity-centered approaches to styles can be related to more general theories of psychological functioning.

SUMMING UP

Interest in styles remains strong, at least in some circles. The reason is the sense people have that styles exist, that they account for variation in performance not accounted for by abilities, and that they may be important in various real-world settings, such as the school, the workplace, and even the home. No theory is going to answer every objection that might be lodged against it, but the theories described in this book attempt to address at least some of the criticisms that have been leveled against theories of styles in the past.

REFERENCES

Achenbach, T. M., & Edelbrocker, C. (1983). *Manual for the Child Behavior Checklist and Revised Child Behavior Profile.* Burlington, VT: University of Vermont.

Allport, G. W. (1937). *Personality, a psychological interpretation.* New York: Holt.

Bergman, H., Norlin, B., Borg, S., & Fyrö, B. (1975). Field dependence in relation to alcohol consumption: A co-twin control study. *Perceptual and Motor Skills, 41,* 855–859.

Bieri, J. (1971). Cognitive structures in personality. In H. M. Schroder & P. Suedfeld (Eds.), *Personality theory and information processing* (pp. 178–208). New York: Ronald Press.

Block, J., Block, J. H., & Harrington, D. M. (1974). Some misgivings about the Matching Familiar Figures Test as a measure of reflection–impulsivity. *Developmental Psychology, 11,* 611–632.

Bruner, J. S., Goodnow, J., & Austin, G. A. (1956). *A study of thinking.* New York: Wiley.

Butter, E. (1979). Visual and haptic training and cross-modal transfer of reflectivity. *Journal of Educational Psychology, 72,* 212–219.

Cantor, N., & Kihlstrom, J. F. (1987). *Personality and social intelligence.* Englewood Cliffs, NJ: Prentice-Hall.

Conway, J. B. (1992). A world of differences among psychologists. *Canadian Psychology, 33,* 1–24.

Cronbach, L. J., & Snow, R. E. (1977). *Aptitudes and instructional methods.* New York: Wiley.

Del Miglio, C., Paluzzi, S., Falanga, M., & Talli, M. (1996). Field dependence and characteristics of conceptualization in identical twins. *Acta Geneticae Medicae Gemellologicae, 45,* 449–460.

Dunn, R., & Dunn, K. (1978). *Teaching students through their individual learning styles.* Reston, VA: Reston Publishing.

Egorova, M. S. (1987). Genetic factors in interpersonal variance in field dependence–independence indicators. *Activitas Nervosa Superior, 29,* 19–22.

Eska, B., & Black, K. N. (1971). Conceptual tempo in young grade-school children. *Child Development, 45,* 505–516.

Feuerstein, R. (1979). *The dynamic assessment of retarded performers: The learning potential assessment device, theory, instruments, and techniques.* Baltimore, MD: University Park Press.

Furnham, M. J., & Kendall, P. C. (1986). Cognitive tempo and behavioral adjustment in children. *Cognitive Therapy and Research, 10,* 45–50.

Gardner, R. W. (1953). Cognitive style in categorizing behavior. *Perceptual and Motor Skills, 22,* 214–233.

Gardner, R. W. (1962). Cognitive controls in adaptation: Research and measurement. In S. Messick & J. Ross (Eds.), *Measurement in personality and cognition* (pp. 183–198). New York: Wiley.

Gardner, R. W., Jackson, D. N., & Messick, S. J. (1960). Personality organization in cognitive controls and intellectual abilities. *Psychological Issues, 2,* 7.

Gardner, R. W., & Long, R. I. (1962). Control, defence and centration effect: A study of scanning behaviour. *British Journal of Psycholog, 53,* 129–140.

Gardner, R. W., & Moriarty, A. (1968). Dimensions of cognitive control at preadolescence. In R. Gardner (Ed.), *Personality development at preadolescence* (pp. 108–118). Seattle: University of Washington Press.

Gardner, R. W., & Schoen, R. A. (1962). Differentiation and abstraction in concept formation. *Psychological Monographs, 76.*

Goldman, R. D. (1972). Effects of a logical versus a mnemonic strategy on performance in two undergraduate psychology classes. *Journal of Educational Psychology, 63,* 347–352.

Goldstein, K. M., & Blackman, S. (1978). *Cognitive style*. New York: Wiley.

Gregorc, A. F. (1979). Learning/teaching styles: Potent forces behind them. *Educational Leadership*, 36, 234–236.

Gregorc, A. F. (1982). *Gregorc Style Delineator*. Maynard, MA: Gabriel Systems.

Gregorc, A. F. (1984). Style as a symptom. A phenomenological perspective. *Theory into Practice*, 23, 51–55.

Gregorc, A. F. (1985). *Inside styles: Beyond the basics*. Maynard, MA: Gabriel Systems.

Grigorenko, E. L., LaBuda, M. C., & Carter, A. S. (1992). Similarity in general cognitive ability, creativity, and cognitive styles in a sample of adolescent Russian twins. *Acta Geneticae Medicae et Gemellologiae*, 41, 65–72.

Gustafson, R., & Kallen, H. (1989). Alcohol effects on cognitive and personality style in women with special reference to primary and secondary process. *Alcoholism: Clinical and Experimental Research*, 13, 644–648.

Harvey, O. J., Hunt, D. E., & Schroder, H. M. (1961) *Conceptual systems and personality organization*. New York: Wiley.

Henson, K. T., & Borthwick, P. (1984). Matching styles: A historical look. *Theory into Practice*, 23, 1, 3–9.

Holland, J. L. (1973). *Making vocational choices: A theory of careers*. Englewood Cliffs, NJ: Prentice-Hall.

Joniak, A. J., & Isaksen, S. G. (1988). The Gregorc Style Delineator: Internal consistency and its relationship to Kirton's adaptive-innovative distinction. *Educational and Psychological Measurement*, 8, 1043–1049.

Jung, C. G., (1923). *Psychological types*. New York: Harcourt Brace.

Kagan, J. (1966). Reflection-impulsivity: The generality and dynamics of conceptual tempo. *Journal of Abnormal Psychology*, 71, 17–27.

Kagan, J., & Kogan, N. (1970). Individual variation in cognitive processes. In P.A. Mussen (Ed.), *Carmichael's manual of child psychology* (Vol. 1, pp. 1273–1365). New York: Wiley.

Kagan, J., Moss, H. A., & Sigel, I. E. (1963). Psychological significance of styles of conceptualization. *Monographs of the Society for Research in Child Development*.

Klein, G. S. (1951). The personal world through perception. In R. R. Blake & G. V. Ramsey (Eds.), *Perception: An approach to personality* (pp. 328–355). New York: Ronald Press.

Klein, G. S. (1954). Need and regulation. In M. R. Jones (Ed.), *Nebraska symposium of motivation*. Lincoln, NE: University of Nebraska Press.

Klein, G. S., Gardner, R. W., & Schlesinger, H. J. (1962). Tolerance for unrealistic experience: A study of the generality of a cognitive control. *British Journal of Psychology*, 53, 41–55.

Kogan, N. (1973). Creativity and cognitive style: A life-span perspective. In P. B. Baltes & K. W. Schaie (Eds.), *Life-span developmental psychology: Personality and socialization* (pp. 145178). New York: Academic Press.

Kogan, N. (1976). *Cognitive styles in infancy and early childhood*. New York: Wiley.

Kolb, D. A. (1978). *Learning style inventory technical manual*. Boston: McBer & Co.

Luchins, A. S., & Luchins, E. H. (1970). Effects of preconceptions and communications on impressions of a person. *Journal of Social Psychology*, 81, 243–252.

MacLeod, C. M., Jackson, R. A., & Palmer, J. (1986). On the relation between spatial ability and field dependence. *Intelligence*, 10, 141–151.

Messick, S., & Kogan, N. (1963). Differentiation and compartmentalization in object-sorting measures of categorizing style. *Perceptual and Motor Skills*, 16, 47–51.

Myers, I. B., & McCaulley, M. H. (1985). *Manual: A guide to the development and use of the Myers–Briggs Type Indicator*. Palo Alto, CA: Consulting Psychologists Press.

Myers, I. B. & Myers, P. B. (1980). *Manual: A guide to use of the Myers-Briggs Type Indicator.* Palo Alto, CA: Consulting Psychologists Press.

Myers, P. L. (1988). Paranoid pseudocommunity beliefs in a sect milieu. *Social Psychiatry and Psychiatric Epidemiology, 23,* 252–255.

O'Brien, T. P. (1990). Construct validation of the Gregorc Style Delineator: An application of Lisrel 7. *Educational and Psychological Measurement, 50,* 631–636.

Pettigrew, T. F. (1958). The measurement of category width as a cognitive variable. *Journal of Personality, 26,* 532–544.

Piaget, J. (1972). *The psychology of intelligence.* Totowa, NJ: Littlefield Adams.

Plomin, R., & Petrill, S. A. (1997). Genetics and intelligence: What is new? *Intelligence, 24,* 53–78.

Reissman, F. (1964). The strategy of style. *Teachers College Record, 65,* 484–489.

Renzulli, J. S., & Smith, L. H. (1978). *Learning styles inventory.* Mansfield Center, CT: Creative Learning Press.

Vernon, P. (1973). Multivariate approaches to the study of cognitive styles. In J. R. Royce (Ed.), *Multivariate analysis and psychological theory* (pp. 125–141). London: Academic Press.

Wallach, M., & Kogan, N. (1965). *Modes of thinking in young children.* New York: Holt, Rinehart & Winston.

Wardell, D. M., & Royce, J. R. (1978). Toward a multi-factor theory of styles and their relationships to cognition and affect. *Journal of Personality, 46,* 474–505.

Webster's seventh new collegiate dictionary. (1967). Springfield, MA: Merriam Company.

Witkin, H. A. (1973). *The role of cognitive style in academic performance and in teacher–student relations.* Unpublished report, Educational Testing Service, Princeton, NJ.

Witkin, H. A., Dyk, R. B., Faterson, H. F., Goodenough, D. R., & Karp, S. A. (1962). *Psychological differentiation.* New York: Wiley.

Witkin, H. A., Oltman, P. K., Raskin, E., & Karp, S. A. (1971). *Embedded Figures Test, Children's Embedded Figures Test, Group Embedded Figures Test.* Palo Alto: Consulting Psychologists Press.

ACKNOWLEDGMENT

Preparation of this chapter was supported by Grant No. R206R950001 as administered by the Office of Educational Research and Improvement, U.S. Department of Education. Grantees undertaking such projects are encouraged to express freely their professional judgment. This chapter, therefore, does not necessarily represent the position or policies of the Office of Educational Research and Improvement or the U.S. Department of Education, and no official endorsement should be inferred.

2

Abilities, Interests, and Styles as Aptitudes for Learning: A Person-Situation Interaction Perspective

Joseph S. Renzulli
University of Connecticut
David Yun Dai
Central Missouri State University

Active learning or construction of knowledge entails information process-ing beyond passive responses to stimuli or encoding verbatim of whatever input has been provided. It also means that individuals differentially and selectively attend to and process learning materials based on their prior knowledge, understanding, values, attitudes, styles, and resultant motiva-tion. Thus, active learning is most likely when instructional programming and design take into account developmental and individual characteristics that have a direct bearing on how students learn and how well they learn under a specific learning condition.

Our main argument is that schools will fare much better if they place the act of learning at the center of the education process (Renzulli, 1992). An act of learning takes place when three major components of instructional settings interact with one another in such a way as to produce the intellectual or artistic equivalent of spontaneous combustion. These three components are a learner, a teacher, and the material to be learned (i.e., curriculum).

Each of these three major components, shown in Fig. 2.1, has its own important subcomponents. Thus, for example, when considering the learn-er, we must look at his or her *abilities* and present appropriate levels of

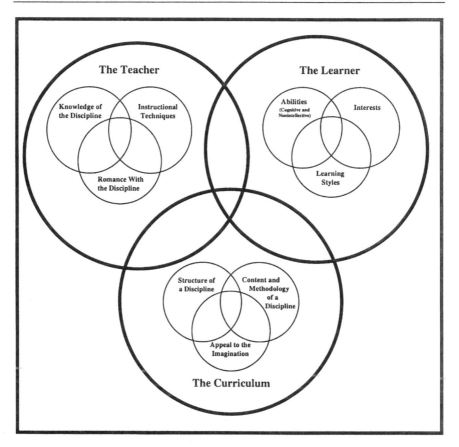

FIG. 2.1.   Figural representation of the Act of Learning.

challenges in a particular area of study, the learner's *interest* in the topic and ways in which we can enhance his or her interests or help him or her develop new interests, and the preferred *styles* of learning that will improve the learner's motivation to pursue the material being studied. Similarly, we must consider the teacher's role in instructional techniques and the extent to which the teacher has developed a "romance" with the material being taught. Finally, the curriculum must be examined in terms of the structure of the discipline, the content and methodology of the discipline, and the extent to which the material appeals to the imagination of the learner. At the core of this theory is the notion of dynamic person-situation interaction. To facilitate our discussion, we develop a model that includes (but does not exhaust) major components of the person–situation interaction in the instructional-learning process and desirable educational outcomes.

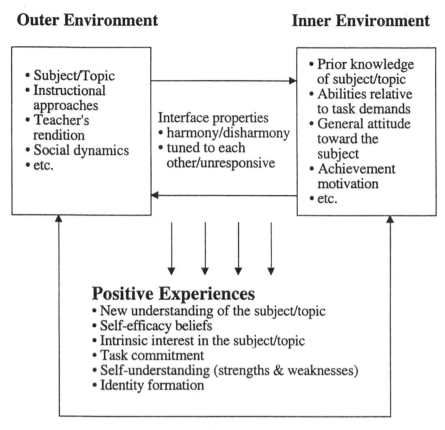

Outer Environment   **Inner Environment**

• Subject/Topic
• Instructional
  approaches
• Teacher's
  rendition
• Social dynamics
• etc.

Interface properties
• harmony/disharmony
• tuned to each
  other/unresponsive

• Prior knowledge
  of subject/topic
• Abilities relative
  to task demands
• General attitude
  toward the
  subject
• Achievement
  motivation
• etc.

Positive Experiences
• New understanding of the subject/topic
• Self-efficacy beliefs
• Intrinsic interest in the subject/topic
• Task commitment
• Self-understanding (strengths & weaknesses)
• Identity formation

FIG. 2.2 A schematic representation of the person-situation interaction in the instruction-learning process and positive experience.

As shown in Fig. 2.2, the outer and inner environments of the person–situation interaction represent a typical classroom condition in which components within each block are present and often operate simultaneously and interactively with one another. For the convenience of analysis, four components are specified for the outer environment and each has bearings on abilities, interests, and styles.

Subject content and topics involved in a curriculum unit determine task demands and task features. *Task demands* concern the difficulty levels of the material and complexity involved. It is reasonable to assume that, given a specific learning task, the zone of proximal development in terms of competence is different not only between but also within age groups. *Task features* involve affective and stylistic appeal of a domain or topic to individual students. Does a topic invite a more holistic, intuitive or an analytic, sequential approach, or is it presented in such a way that favors one approach over another? Is a topic mainly a pure intellectual game or does it involve rich human experiences and emotions? Subject content of a topic should be examined under such a task analysis to elucidate its ramifications for readiness and proneness of a person's inner environment.

Although various instructional approaches such as lecture, discussion, and role playing could be incorporated to make instruction effective, not all instructional approaches benefit students in the same way. Thus, given a challenging science topic, a less structured, highly involving presentation may excite highly able students but overwhelm less able students, for whom more scaffolding is needed (Snow & Lohman, 1984). By the same token, a student who prefers to follow rules (executive style, if you will) will feel secure in a highly structured, less involving instructional environment. However, the same environment will bore another student who prefers to create his or her own rules (legislative style; Sternberg, 1997). Clearly, a one-size-fits-all instructional approach does not serve students equally well.

Teacher's rendition refers to the way the teacher transforms content knowledge into highly accessible, exciting learning experiences for students. Shulman (1986) refers to this aspect of teaching skills as "*pedagogical content knowledge*," characterized by being loyal to the essential features of the subject taught while making them accessible to students of varied prior knowledge, motivation, and other characteristics. Renzulli (1988) named this aspect, "*artistic modification*," a personal rendition of teaching-learning materials not unlike conducting a symphony or directing a play in that the text material is interpreted and presented at a highly personal, intimate level. It is not hard to conceive that the same textbook materials can be turned into exciting, lively instructional-learning experiences in one teacher's hand but remain "dead," boring stuff, full of inert knowledge in another's (Phenix, 1987). Making learning materials accessible, interesting, and intellectually stimulating is clearly no small feat.

Social dynamics refers to teacher–student and peer interactions that create a classroom or school culture that makes some values and incentives more salient than others. Thus, a highly competitive, ego-involving academic environment may create an ethos that makes all students self-conscious about their relative ability and normative performance status, sometimes at the cost of learning goals and challenge-seeking behavior (Nicholls, 1989). An environment that emphasizes meaningful learning and mutual reciprocity among learners is likely to promote a group of identity among students as intentional learners (Brown, 1997). Social dynamics could also determine whether and to what extent students' conformity (or intellectual independence) is encouraged.

Although presented separately, it is useful to think of these components of the outer environment as orchestrated to produce an overall instructional environment, which is uniquely perceived and acted upon by each learner, with his or her unique configuration of the inner environment. The nature and quality of the person–situation interaction can be seen as a continuum with harmony on the one end and disharmony on the other. From a more dynamic perspective, the quality of the interaction depends on adaptivity of the two systems, ranging from the tendency for both the outer environment and the inner environment to tune into each other on the one end, and the tendency to remain unresponsive to, or even turn off, each other on the other end (Snow, 1992).

How do we judge, then, whether the instructional environment is optimized for a group of students or for individual students? Our answer is whether the interaction produces *positive experiences*, some of which are listed in Fig. 2.2. An underlying proposition is that when instruction is tuned to developmental and individual differences in terms of readiness and zones of proximal development, learners are more likely to have positive experiences with school learning, which is crucial for successful mastery and learning. The essence of seeking optimal personal–situation interactions is not simply to make students feel good about themselves but to help them find their own strengths, inner resources, and passion so that school learning becomes their own personal enterprise, rather than things they have to do to meet adults' expectations and approval. The arrow from positive experiences to the inner environment implies that positive experiences change the inner environment and transform the person into someone more confident about learning, more interested in learning, and more self-directed and future oriented, as well as someone who has newly acquired knowledge, skills, and cognitive apparatus. The arrow from positive experiences to the outer environment suggests that as new experiences and changes come along, instruction needs to aim at new levels of challenges, understanding, and technical precision. Thus, the person–situation interaction becomes reciprocal and optimized.

As this model suggests, cognitive and learning styles are but one of many components of the inner environment. Thus, instead of discussing exclusively cognitive and learning styles, we include interests and abilities, along with styles, as central developmental and individual difference constructs. In line with Snow (1992; see also Snow, Corno, & Jackson, 1996), we use the term *aptitude* to refer to psychological readiness or proneness, cognitively, affectively, or conatively, for a specific learning situation. We discuss the theoretical underpinnings of these constructs and their intricate relation with one another, particularly as they are brought to bear upon instructional conditions in terms of curricular materials and instructional approaches.

We further explore stability and changes of these learner characteristics. We then suggest ways we might design instruction to address these individual differences to optimize learning conditions for the individual students.

FROM ABILITIES TO STYLES: A CHANGING PERSPECTIVE

Abilities are the most talked about factor considered crucial for successful learning. There are many versions of theoretical accounts of the nature and origins of human abilities (Sternberg & Kaufman, 1998). Three traditions stand out as responsible for our current thinking. In the first, Piaget and neo-Piagetian views provide a developmental perspective of how human abilities are developed in a sequential fashion, as a result of both maturation and interaction with the environment in terms of direct experience and social transmission (Case, 1985; Piaget, 1967). In the second tradition, the psychometric approach explains human abilities in terms of individual differences (Carroll, 1993; Guilford, 1959). Finally, cognitive psychology attempts to elucidate elementary processes (e.g., encoding and retrieval) and components (e.g., short-term and long-term memory, executive function) involved in learning and performance (Newell & Simon, 1972, Sternberg, 1985). Of the three traditions, the most influential in education is the psychometric perspective on human abilities. Take the example of IQ testing, where an age-normed test score is interpreted as one's relative standing in a specific age population and is considered an indicator of how well a student will do compared with age peers in the future. Problems occur when the score is interpreted as indicating some fixed ability. Especially troublesome is a further inference that the ability is largely genetically determined (Herrnstein & Murray, 1994). Evidence, however, is far from supporting such a strong claim. First, the psychometric view of human abilities exaggerates individual differences at the expense of disguising enormous developmental gains in cognitive competence as children grow and are increasingly exposed to environmental stimuli (Lohman, 1993). As McCall (1981) pointed out, relying on the evidence of the high correlation of age-normed IQ scores over time amounts to focusing on the consistency of a difference of a few inches in the heights of trees from blossoming to maturity while ignoring how they grow to be hundreds of feet tall.

Second, many IQ tests that are supposed to measure natural ability are in fact measures of achievement, that is, developed or developing competencies (Anastasi, 1980; Lohman, 1993; Sternberg, 1998). Tests such as vocabulary, reading comprehension, and arithmetic problem solving typically found in IQ tests can be seen in part as measures of achievement. Thus, inferring the casual precedence of natural ability from the correlation of IQ measures and academic achievement becomes problematic. Because there has been no reliable and valid measure of individual differences in pure natural abilities (some doubt we will ever have one; e.g., Lohman, 1993), all ability tests are best treated as measures of developed or developing competencies.

Third, the claim of heritability of intelligence is based heavily on genetic studies of twins, which consistently found heritability estimates to be between .50 to .78; that is, half or more than half of the total variance in IQ scores is accounted for by genetic factors (Plomin & Petrill, 1997). Putting aside, for the moment, the methodological adequacy of teasing apart the effects of heredity and environment (see Sternberg & Kaufman, 1998), the fact that a large portion of variance remains unexplained by genetic factors assures us that genetics is not destiny. Remarkable increases in IQ scores found over the generations (Flynn, 1987, 1994, 1999) have led many researchers to look into various environmental factors for answers, such as better nutrition, more parental attention, and increased schooling (see Sternberg & Kaufman, 1998, for a review). Furthermore, increasing evidence suggests that intelligence may have nonintellective origins. For example, the quality of interaction between infants and their caregivers was found to be related to differences in cognitive abilities 2 years later (Lewis, 1989). Particularly illuminating is the implication that the seemingly natural abilities assessed at the ages of 2 and 3 years might well be the consequence of cognitive engagement and environmental exploration since infancy; the intensity of this cognitive activity is engendered party by the caregivers and the children themselves. There is a strong possibility that other "nonintellective" factors, such as temperaments (e.g., persistence, activity, and distractibility; see Chess & Thomas, 1996; Thomas & Chess, 1977) also contribute to (or retard) the development of cognitive abilities.

If the differential or psychometric perspective of human abilities does not provide adequate explanations for successful learning and rich heuristic values for curriculum and instruction, what are the alternatives? A more promising approach is to see observed or measured abilities of the student from a developmental point of view as developed and developing competencies. Gardner's (1983) theory of multiple intelligences and Sternberg's (1985) triarchic theory of human intelligence have changed the narrow view of intelligence and human ability as unitary and being manifested only in psychometic tests. They point out that each individual is equipped with a unique set of potentialities and strengths. The issue is not who has the ability and who does not, but how to capitalize on and develop these potentialities and strengths. If we accept this view, it follows that the road to success may be different from individual to individual. Naturally, individual learners' characteristic approaches to learning tasks, that is, cognitive and learning styles, rather than their general ability, become a central issue in education. Particularly interesting in the context of individual differences in cognitive abilities is the question of the relation between ability constructs and various style constructs. Lohman (1993) provided an example of how strengths and weaknesses within the person interact with instructional environments to shape one's stylistic approach to learning tasks. He speculated that female deficits in math and science may be the cumulative effects of a relative female strength in phonological-sequential string processing and a relative male strength in analog-image processing. Lohman (1993) explained:

> If young women generally find it easier to remember formulae than to construct mental models, and if instruction is structured in a way that makes it possible to get good grades by doing so, and if knowledge thus assembled becomes increasingly unwieldy over time compared to knowledge represented in mental models (as research suggests), then some part of the cumulative female deficit in math and science and the even larger sex differences in career choice may be more a product of the within-person pattern of specific abilities than their absolute levels. (p.129)

Whether this speculation can stand the test is another issue. It nevertheless provides important clues to the potential causal links of abilities and styles. From this passage, one can infer the following:

1. Within-person patterns of abilities, not absolute between-person differences, may shape one's characteristic modes of learning (i.e., styles) when dealing with a learning task.
2. Styles may be reinforced by instruction and evaluation.
3. There is feedback control in which the learner gauges the effectiveness of certain learning strategies and makes adjustments accordingly (in other words, styles are adaptive). and
4. Given specific learning tasks, certain styles facilitate the development of abilities; others retard the process.

All these conjectures are in line with the person-situation interaction perspective proposed earlier.

One can argue, of course, that the strengths and weaknesses in one's abilities may be the derivative of earlier stylistic predilections (e.g., Wachtel, 1972). We may never resolve this chicken-and-egg problem. However, by looking into these intricate ability–style relationships, we can see that at least some individuals' stylistic approaches are the result of capitalizing on their strengths and compensating for their weaknesses. If this argument holds, individual differences in cognitive and learning styles partly reflect differential responses to environmental demands and different action patterns based on individuals' strengths and weaknesses, consciously or unconsciously. The issue of whether field independence–dependence is an ability or style construct (Davis, 1991; McKenna, 1990; Messick, 1994; Sigel, 1991) may not be that puzzling once we realize that some latent abilities or ability configurations can turn into stylistic dispositions, and some styles have ability ramifications.

Abilities are not the only thing important for successful learning, and surely not the only contributing factor for the development of cognitive and learning styles. From a developmental point of view, a person interacts with the environment as a whole person, with developed and developing competencies as both a precondition and a result of this interaction. Thus, without appropriate consideration of other aspects of this dynamic person–environment interaction, we will never get a whole picture of how styles develop. If ability–style relationships discussed above are mainly cognition based, an affective component should also figure prominently in some aspects of cognitive and thinking styles. In the following section, we discuss an affective construct central to the motivation and functioning of school children: interest.

INDIVIDUAL INTERESTS AND UNDERLYING STYLISTIC DIMENSIONS

Interests may be one of those psychological phenomena that are most familiar to people but least scientifically understood. Because the term is loosely used in daily language, ranging from casual to serious, transient to enduring, a more normative conception is needed. We define interest as an affective leaning toward, or a preference for, certain objects, phenomena, topics, or activities. This definition has three essential features. First, interests are directive or conative; that is, they display a tendency to move or be drawn toward a certain direction (Snow, 1992). Second, all interests have certain degrees of intensity. It could be indicated by behaviors to deeply engage oneself in a purposeful activity or by affective reaction and arousal such as excitement and enjoyment when a specific object or activity is involved. Third, interests are dynamic; that is, they occur or manifest themselves in a flow of events involving person–object interactions and relations, and therefore can be seen as a result of person–situation interaction, as indicated in Fig. 2.2. Thus, the nature of a specific interest can only be understood in dynamic person–object relations (Prenzel, 1992).

Many theories seek to explain what makes an activity or object interesting. Some topics, such as life and death, sex and romance, love and betrayal, are intrinsically interesting (Schank, 1979) because they are fundamental aspects of the human drama that have inspired imagination generation after generation. Some activities, such as playing tennis or chess, are more interesting than others because they provide challenges and immediate feedback (Csikszentmihalyi, 1990). Most pertinent to learning is the question of what makes a learner interested in a domain or a topic to the extent that prompts a desire to learn more about it, and what sustains and develops that interest. Such interests are most relevant, though not necessarily confined, to academic learning settings. Piaget (1977) may be the first psychologist who viewed interests as sine quo non for development. His theory of disequilibration and development of new cognitive structures is predicated on the assumption that there is an inherent, organismic tendency in children toward organizing their experiences and understanding their surroundings. Research on human curiosity has led some researchers to the conclusion that curiosity results from cognitive deprivation when one encounters objects and phenomena that, with their novelty and complexity, are beyond full comprehension (Loewenstein, 1994). This proposition explains possible psychological mechanisms underlying the concept of disequilibration postulated by Piaget.

From a motivational rather than cognitive perspective, several American psychologists postulated that human beings have an innate tendency toward mastery of the environment (effectance motivation; White, 1959), and that experiences of personal causation are intrinsically rewarding (de Charms, 1968), and feelings of personal agency, efficacy, and control are fundamental to human motivation (Bandura, 1977, 1997). The rudimentary form of this competence motivation can be observed in children's play. Manipulating toys is intrinsically pleasurable because it gives the child a sense of control, power, and competence as the child overcomes challenges and experiences successful mastery. Thus, interest is symptomatic of these internal forces of motivation and successful control of important aspects of the environment.

Such an optimistic outlook of human developmental potential only tells one side of the story. After all, why are some children more interested in schoolwork than others, and why do some children display different interest patterns and different degrees of the same interest? The answer is that there are many constraints for interest development. *Social-cultural constraints* refer to what is encouraged and what is discouraged in the society. *Opportunity structure constraints* refer to the limited exposure or access individuals have to certain aspects of civilization, culture, and human endeavor. Related to opportunity structure constraints are *knowledge constraints*. Interest in a domain is always based on some experience and understanding of that domain. *Ability constraints* refer to the way real ability levels or self-perceptions of abilities constrain how interested a person is or will be in a specific task, topic, or domain (Deci, 1992). *Developmental constraints* are constraints due to age-related maturity and experience, cognitive or social-emotional.

Although the preceding constraints are important determinants of individual interests, temperament and personality constraints are more central for understanding how affective experiences with various topics, subjects, or phenomena shape one's interest pattern, and how these affective experiences reflect fundamental preferences for certain content, methods, and modalities of human functioning. Kolb (1971) provided a heuristic model in which individuals differ along two bipolar dimensions: people prefer either *active experimentation* or *reflective observation* (the doing–watching continuum), and at the same time they like either *concrete experience* or *abstract conceptualization* (the feeling–thinking continuum). Thus, a person who prefers doing and concrete experience will find education a particularly enjoyable domain, whereas a person who likes watching and abstract thinking will be more likely to end up in natural science. Such an interest and enjoyment experienced by individuals may reflect an optimal person–environment fit in the sense that task and situational demands and features maximally match the individual's pre-ferred mode of functioning. Although on the surface, interests and styles are unrelated because interests indicate specificity of content (i.e., related to "what") whereas styles refer to manners (i.e., related to "how"), individu-al interests may be symptomatic of deeper personal dispositions that have their stylistic component. Simply put, if ability–style links reflect an intrapersonal dynamic in response to task demands, interest–style links reflect an intrapersonal dynamic in response to task features. Together, they highlight the importance of style constructs as an interface of cognitive ability and personality (Sternberg, 1988).

COGNITIVE-LEARNING STYLES AS EMERGENT CHARACTERISTIC MODES OF INFORMATION PROCESSING

Abilities address the question of whether one is capable of learning or performing specific cognitive tasks, interests address the question of what topic or subject one likes most, and cognitive and learning styles address the question of what are characteristic ways one approaches learning tasks. Defined as such, styles reflect more generalized and pervasive aspects of personal functioning than do abilities and interests. In this sense, cognitive or learning styles should be distinguished from cognitive or learning strategies in that styles, as dispositions, are applied spontaneously across situations, whereas strategies can be conscious or unconscious decision and choice among alternative approaches in response to situational demands. Thus, a spontaneous tendency to draw quick conclusions reflects an impulsive cognitive style (Kagan, 1966), whereas deliberate use of "shallow processing" in a given situation reflects a strategy, for good or ill (Schmeck, 1988). When a strategy is so contrived and overused that it becomes spontaneous and indiscriminate, this is a case of a strategy turning into a style, that is, a stable, self-consistent disposition.

Many style constructs have been proposed as important dimensions of individual differences in how they approach cognitive tasks across situations Of all style constructs, cognitive styles have received the most extensive scientific inquiry. To list but a few major dimensions of cognitive styles, field dependence–independence (Witkin & Goodenough, 1978) refers to individual differences in using external versus internal referents in comprehending the stimulus in question. Conceptual tempo (Kagan, 1966) refers to how reflective or impulsive one is in reaching conclusions under conditions of uncertainty. Cognitive complexity–simplicity (Harvey, Hunt, & Schroder, 1961; Kelly, 1955; Messick, 1994) refers to the extent to which one construes the world in a multidimensional and discriminating way. Although focusing on different stylistic aspects of cognitive functioning, cognitive style theorists assumed, implicitly or explicitly, these styles are general modes and structural properties of cognitive systems, not merely personal preferences that are more or less under volitional control and therefore changeable with conscious decision (Messick, 1984, 1994).

In contrast to cognitive style constructs, learning styles were proposed by more education-minded researchers who emphasize styles as personal preferences based on sensory modality (visual, auditory, etc.; Barbe & Swassing, 1979), content features (abstract vs. concrete; Kolb, 1971), degrees of structure in the learning process (Hunt, 1975), physical and social characteristics of the learning environment (Dunn, Dunn, & Price, 1975), and types of instructional activities and degrees of student involvement (Renzulli & Smith, 1978). Sternberg's (1997, 1998) theory of mental self-government also define styles as personal preferences. Although the psychological foundations of these personal preferences remain to be elucidated by research, they presumably emerge from person–situation interactions, reflecting both the effects of socialization and "natural" predilections, and assuming important adaptation functions under specific circumstances.

Reconciling the objective and subjective, nomothetic and idiographic views of cognitive and learning styles is not easy because of underlying theoretical and methodological differences. Cognitive style researchers employ a more positivist approach, whereas learning style researchers take a more phenomenological perspective, that is, treating styles as subjective. A distinct methodological difference is that cognitive style researchers use almost exclusively performance-based measures, whereas learning style researchers rely primarily on self-report measures. Pask's (1976, 1988) research program on comprehension versus operation learning style is an exception. A dialogue between these two traditions, however, is not only possible but also beneficial to the understanding of origins of cognitive and learning styles. Styles can have both objective and subjective bases. The objective basis resides in the structural properties of cognitive systems or the characteristic modes of cognition that are highly stable and typically operate without conscious awareness (though accessible to metacognitive insights). The ability–style links discussed earlier are partly based on this cognitive makeup. The subjective basis lies in one's direct learning experiences and metacognitive knowledge of what works best for him or her. Affective experiences (including interests) form the second basis. Although style constructs based on measures of subjective preferences may be dispersive and idiosyncratic, they represent an important aspect of self-knowledge and self-understanding that guides the learner's thoughts and actions, hence their legitimacy as part of the self-system. The objective and subjective bases of cognitive and learning styles are not without common grounds. The centrality of both these cognitive and learning styles to learning and instruction can be seen, according to the model presented in Fig. 2.2, in three dimensions: cognitive and affective properties of a school subject or discipline, degrees of structure in instructional activities, and social interaction.

First, certain curricular materials favor the applicability of some styles over others. Thus, learning traditional mathematical concepts may favor abstract, sequential, and analytic styles, particularly when they are presented in a traditional way. Those who prefer more concrete, affectively rich materials find literature or history more congenial (Kolb, 1971). If different disciplines represent different realms of meaning or ways of grasping the essence of the world (Phenix, 1964), there are profound individual differences regarding what become their comfort zones.

Second, with respect to degrees of structure in instructional activities, there is evidence of differential effects of instruction for different learners.

For example, those who are field dependent learn better when structure is provided, because these individuals rely on external frames for information organization. The opposite is true for field-independent learners who impose structures by themselves (Davis, 1991). Similar style by instructional method interaction can be predicted for legislative versus executive style in Sternberg's (1988) theory of mental self-government.

Third, although learning is by nature a social process involving interaction between the child and adults or peers (Vygotsky, 1978) some individuals prefer solitary learning and some prefer social interaction and sharing. In light of the robust findings on the personality dimension of extroversion–introversion (Costa & McCrae, 1992), there is no wonder that several theories of cognitive and learning styles incorporate this aspect (Dunn et al., 1975; Sternberg, 1988; Witkin & Goodenough, 1977).

Having emphasized the cognitive and phenomenological bases of cognitive and learning styles, we should caution not to lose sight of the dynamic and developmental nature of these styles. For styles to have some adaptive values, they should be compatible to important aspects of environmental demands. Otherwise, styles would be completely idiosyncratic without functional significance. If a learning task not only entails a holistic, global approach to comprehend the overall structural features, but also takes a serialistic, analytic strategy to acquire the procedural knowledge, a flexible or versatile style would be superior to either holistic or serialist styles (Pask, 1988; see also Dai & Feldhusen, in press). Sometimes changes in style become crucial make-or-break developmental tasks. For example, Bamberger (1986) identified a "midlife crisis" many musically talented children go through during their adolescent years. To reach a new level of musical competence, these children have to abandon the "natural," intuitive way of mastering musical work they are used to and adopt more analytic and reflective thinking in their approach to music. Failure to make this stylistic change will result in an asymptote of the development of musical talent. Thus, styles, though stable, are also dynamic, interacting with the environment and undergoing adaptive changes. It is not coincidental that clinical psychologists have a more holistic style and experimental psychologists have a more analytic style. Their personal inclinations could be a factor, but so is the professional training they received over years (Kimble, 1984).

Subtle but powerful influences of socialization are also prevalent in school environment. Dominant social reinforcement or reward structure of learning situations influences the development of styles. Teachers who place a premium on order, control, and conformity are likely to promote more conventional and less innovative styles on the part of their malleable learners. School environment can also nurture different motivation-related styles or orientations. Entwistle (1988) identified three orientations among grade school and college students. A *meaning orientation* (or deep approach) is characterized by searching for personal understanding, relating ideas and verifying evidence, and intrinsic motivation. A *reproducing orientation* (or shallow approach), is characterized by memorizing, sticking to what is prescribed in syllabi, and fear of failure. An *achieving orientation* (or strategic approach) is characterized by strategic efforts to win favorable evaluation of teachers, a desire to outperform peers, and an attempt to maximize success with minimum effort. In the same vein, Bereiter (1990) identified similar orientations, what he called contextual modules. A contextual module consists of a set of domain knowledge, goals, attitudes, self–concept, and a code of conduct an individual develops over time relating to a specific context. Thus, a *schoolwork module* is characterized by the mindset that learning tasks are simply "work" that needs to get done, whereas an *intentional learning module* not only incorporates learning as part of one's self-concept but has a model dimension of commitment to pursuing truth and depth of understanding. These modules are stylistic because they show self-consistency and stability over time. Yet they have a salient component of perceptions of the school context, that is, what is expected of them as students in school, whether they perceive the school as an inviting or threatening place, and whether they perceive school learning as only about grades or having a larger purpose. Although we can argue that the development of different contextual modules reflect individual differences among students (including differences in abilities and interests), school practices and climate are also a contributing factor. This scenario of social and personal dynamics of school environment further complicates the nature of cognitive and learning styles. Thus, behaviors identified as stylistic may have different psychological bases (e.g., cognition based, personality based, or motivation based; see Schmeck, 1988; Sternberg & Grigorenko, 1997). What is common about these styles is that they are emergent properties of individual functioning that reflect both the influences of the environment and the person in question.

ABILITIES, INTERESTS, AND STYLES AS APTITUDES: STABILITY AND CHANGE

Constructs of abilities, interests, and styles represent our understanding of various cognitive, affective, and conative aspects of human functioning in general and learning in particular (Snow, 1992). Human beings function as a whole, not as a list of variables, and an overlapping of these constructs becomes almost inevitable. Different aspects of human functioning are so intricately related that it is virtually impossible to get a pure measure of one aspect without being confounded by others (see Messick, 1984, 1994). Also, abilities, interests, and styles are so closely tied to specific situations and contexts that they can best be understood in the contexts in which they manifest themselves.

An emphasis on situations and context naturally begs the question of whether these abilities, interests, and styles are stable personal characteristics or malleable qualities that can be relatively easily changed with proper instructional interventions. To be sure, for aptitudes to have any significant implications and serve any propaedeutic purposes for learning and instruction, they should be relatively stable and salient in individual's cognitive-affective-conative systems. Otherwise, it is pointless to take them into consideration when designing instruction (Snow, 1992). This said, three points need to be kept in mind. First, stability is a matter of degree. One's ability in mathematics, for example, may be relatively stable, particularly compared with his or her peers. However, this ability is undergoing incremental changes over time with more learning experiences and proper instructional facilitation. Second, schoolchildren are in their formative years. The pace of development is not uniform among children. Some abilities, interests, and styles may emerge earlier in some children than in others. Thus, aptitudes should be assessed by their presence, not by their absence. Third, if the person–situation interaction perspective is correct, the emergence and development of abilities, interests, and styles are anchored on optimal situations that facilitate them. We will never know whether a child is interested in astronomy or biology unless he or she is exposed to relevant materials, physically and conceptually. The frequency of exposure and the intensity of experience are not trivial. For instance, think of the nurturing atmosphere of a musical family for a child to develop abilities, interests, and styles relevant to musical competence. It is conceivable that some interests and styles first emerge as situational and transitory, and later become stable and traitlike. As another example, the schoolwork module postulated by Bereiter (1990) is not built overnight but is a result of convergence of numerous experiences across situations within the school context. Many situational encounters eventually lead to dispositional aptitudes, an internalization process that has drawn much research attention from developmental as well as educational researchers (Bereiter, 1990; Ryan, 1993). Paradoxically, instructional design should not only be concerned with what aptitudes children spontaneously display, but also with what aptitudes educators hope to nurture (Bruner, 1969). In short, abilities, interests, and styles should be regarded as both the aptitudes for and outcomes of educational processes. They are stable but undergoing change.

PRACTICAL IMPLICATIONS AND
APPLICATIONS

The person–situation interaction perspective put forward in this chapter has many practical implications for programming and instruction. By tuning into individual differences, particularly each individual's strengths, talents, interests, and styles, we stand to accomplish a major educational goal, that is, to help students find a "niche" for themselves that makes them effective societal members and allows them to make unique contributions to the society. In this sense, we are advocating a growth model rather than a deficit model for education. This model is predicated on two premises. First, there are fundamental developmental and individual differences in abilities, interests, and styles; each child has a unique set of strengths and weaknesses that need to be taken into consideration in instruction. Second, each child has potential for positive growth in terms of self-understanding, self-direction, and self-motivation. The unique configuration of each child's abilities, interests, and styles, coupled with experiences and training, will make them potential candidates as future leaders, professionals, technicians, social workers, artists, entrepreneurs, and businesspersons. If we accept these premises, school becomes a place for talent development rather than mere lesson learning (Renzulli, 1994).

What are some of the educational applications of such a model? How might it work in real classrooms? These are questions no less important than theoretical propositions. After all, such a theoretical model would easily turn into mere rhetoric without careful implementation in educational practices. Based on more than 20 years of field research, we proposed a plan called the Schoolwide Enrichment Model (Renzulli & Reis, 1985, 1997), which was designed to bring about positive changes in students with diverse backgrounds and profiles of abilities, interests, and styles. It is a set of specific strategies for increasing student effort, enjoyment, and performance and for integrating a broad range of advanced learning experiences and high-order thinking skills into any curricular area, course of study, and pattern of school organization. What is central about this plan is its effort to encourage and facilitate the demonstration and development of individual learners' interests and talents.

This goal is achieved by three strategies. First, instructional procedures and programming were developed to provide for all students a broad range of exploratory experiences such as guest speakers, field trips, and interest centers, and to expose students to a variety of exciting topics, ideas, and fields of knowledge not ordinarily covered in the regular curriculum. Students' responses to these experiences were used as stepping stones for more advanced, follow-up activities. For example, pollution may be one of the many topics that attract students. As a result, students who share an interest in pollution problems may form an "enrichment cluster" and may decide later to carry out a research project on the conditions of local rivers. As part of the process, each member's strengths are brought into play and each becomes a specialist within the group. Such activities not only make learning personally meaningful and intrinsically rewarding, they also facilitate critical and creative thinking in a way that cannot be achieved by didactic instruction and textbook learning. Research shows that students who participated in these exploratory activities identified more interests than comparable students who did not (Stednitz, 1985), and that students who were involved in more productive-creative activities had higher self-efficacy with regard to creative productivity (Starko, 1986). It is not unusual that such school experiences develop into an enduring passion and interest, even influencing career choice later (Delcourt, 1993). Here, positive experiences and growth are engendered by affording students opportunities, resources, and guidance usually not available in the regular classroom.

Second, a strength assessment guide called *Total Talent Portfolio* (TTP; Purcell & Renzulli, 1998) was developed to help promote students' self-awareness and forethought as well as to assess their strengths, interests, and cognitive-learning styles on a regular basis. It contains the student's self-ratings; teachers' observations, suggestions, and recommendations; the student's short-term and long-term goals; written products; and documentation of students' activities in and outside of school relevant to the development of interests and talents. Students have autonomy with respect to the folder and its contents. They are also responsible for formulating and refining criteria for the inclusion of products. The TTP changes the way students perceive evaluation, from a focus on who is doing better than whom to a focus on how they can capitalize on their strengths while avoiding or compensating for their weaknesses, and essential ingredient of successful intelligence (Sternberg, 1998). With TTP in hand, students are more mindful of what fascinates them (interests), what is easy or different for them (abilities), what comes naturally for them (styles), what they hope to achieve (goals), and how far they have gone (self-monitoring), a kind of metacognition highly valuable for self-directed and self-regulated learning (see Schunk & Zimmerman, 1994).

Third, assessment becomes an integral part of instruction and learning, and instructional interventions depend on assessment information. Before instruction, information about a student's abilities, interests, and styles—including test scores, grades, and self-ratings—is gathered. This is called *status information*, which permits an initial assessment of a student's propaedeutic conditions. During instruction, further information is obtained by teachers through direct observation in regular classrooms or during enrichment activities. Some new interests or strengths may emerge in the process. This information is called *action information* because it provides up-to-date information about students (the inner environment, if you will). This is typically done through a shared decision making that involves teachers and the student, and sometimes parents. For example, for students who are underchallenged by regular curricular materials, a procedure called *curriculum compacting* (Reis, Burns, & Renzulli, 1992) is used to condense the material so that spared time can be spent on more advanced, "high-end" learning tasks that are commensurate with the student's level of knowledge and skills. It is not surprising, given the current status of many school textbooks and curricula, as much as 50% of regular curricular activities and materials can be eliminated for some advanced students without negatively affecting their achievement across school subjects (Reis et al., 1992). Two principles underlie this instructional sequence or design. One is that assessment is an ongoing, dynamic process, and multidimensional in nature. Traditional standardized tests still serve as one of many indicators of students' strengths. However, no single normative rank score can be a substitute for a sound judgment based on a careful analysis and synthesis of multiple sources and dimensions of information. Also, the purpose of assessment is never to rank order students but to provide appropriate educational service that cultivates the strengths of individual students. The other principle is that instruction should be as differentiated as possible in response to emergent characteristics of the learner, be it a newly found passion for a topic or the difficulty of understanding a mathematical concept. Differentiation of curricula and instructional activities does not mean privileged treatments for high-achieving students and lowering of standards for low-achieving students. Rather, it is designed to address the needs of each student and promote positive experiences (see Fig. 2.2) crucial for successful learning, talent development, and personal growth.

CONCLUSION

In this chapter, we reviewed some major theoretical perspectives on human abilities, interests, and styles, which we believe are critical concepts for understanding human diversity in their approaches to learning tasks, within or outside of school settings. We also believe these concepts are interrelated in many ways and better understood from the context within which they are observed and measured. We therefore propose a person–

situation interaction perspective that sees abilities as outcomes as well as antecedents of human interactions with task demands and opportunities, interests as emergent self-direction and self-differentiation, and cognitive and learning styles as emergent modes of information processing and self-expression in the person–situation interaction. We further postulate the optimal instructional conditions are achieved when both the outer environment of instruction and the inner environment of learning are tuned to and reciprocate with each other. Achievement of such optimal conditions is indicated by students' positive changes in their self-efficacy beliefs, intrinsic interests in academic and other subjects, self-understanding, and self-identity as an intentional learner. We presented some practical applications of this perspective that, when infused into regular school curricula and instruction, have been shown to be effective.

On the threshold of the next century, a call for school reform and improvement has never been so urgent, and justifiably so. The question is how. With the increasing diversity of student populations we are serving in this nation, imposing uniform standards from the top down is a tough sell. We constantly hear the suggestions for more external regulation such as increasing "high-stakes testing." We doubt, however, such measures can achieve the effects of their intended better educational outcomes. They may create the illusion of improved achievement, but the reality is increased pressure on schools to expand the use of compensatory learning models that, so far, have contributed only to the "dumbing down" of curriculum and lowering of standards. We suggest in this chapter a different approach designed to develop each child's talents and strengths, of which cognitive and learning styles are an integral part. We are less concerned with who has the highest test scores and more concerned with what will be the best educational experiences we can provide to a child. We are not as much concerned with raising test scores as we are with increasing student's intrinsic motivation to learn and improving self-direction and self-regulation. Academic achievement is an important part of the overall educational goal. However, we believe that a focus on capitalizing on and developing each child's strengths and talents also places the need for improved academic achievement into a larger perspective about the goal of education. The things that have made our nation great and our society productive are manifestations of talent development at all levels and aspects of human activity. From the creators and inventors of new ideas, products, and art forms to the vast array of people who manufacture, advertise, and market the creations that enrich our lives, there are levels of excellence and quality that contribute to our standard of living and way of live. Our vision of school for talent development grows out of the belief that everyone has an important role to play in the improvement of society and that everyone's role can be enhanced if we provide all students with the opportunities, resources, and encouragement to develop their talents as fully as possible. From this point of view, the diversity of our student population is a strength rather than a weakness. From this diversity come various stylistic differences in adaptation to learning tasks and social environments. Properly developed and used, they can have high functional and adaptive values.

REFERENCES

Anastasi, A. (1980). Abilities and the measurement of achievement. In W. B. Schrader (Ed.), *Measuring achievement: Progress over a decade* (pp. 1–10). San Francisco; Jossey-Bass.

Bamberger, J. (1986). Cognitive issues in the development of musical gifted children. In R. J. Sternberg & J. Davidson (Eds.), *Conceptions of giftedness* (pp. 388–415). New York: Cambridge University Press.

Bandura, A. (1977). Self-efficacy: Toward a unifying theory of behavioral change. *Psychological Review, 84*, 191–215.

Bandura, A. (1977). *Self-efficacy: The exercise of control.* New York: Freeman.

Barbe, W. B., & Swassing, R. H. (1979). *Teaching through modality strengths: Concept and practices.* Columbus, OH: Zaner-Bloser.

Bereiter, C. (1990). Aspects of an educational learning theory. *Review of Educational Research, 60*, 603–624.

Brown, A. (1997). Transforming schools into communities of thinking and learning about serious matters. *American Psychologist, 52*, 399–413.

Bruner, J. (1969). *On knowing: Essays for the left hand.* Cambridge, MA: The Belknap Press of Harvard University Press.

Carroll, J. B. (1993). *Human cognitive abilities: A survey of factor-analytic studies.* New York: Cambridge University Press.

Case, R. (1985). *Intellectual development: Birth to adulthood.* Orlando, FL: Academic Press.

Chess, S., & Thomas, A. (1996). *Temperament: Theory and practice.* New York: Brunner/Mazel.

Costa, P. T., Jr., & McCrae, R. R. (1992). *Revised NEO Personality Inventory (NEO-PI-R) and NEO Five-Factor Inventory (NEO-FFI) professional manual.* Odessa, FL: Psychological Assessment Resources.

Csikszentmihalyi, M. (1990). *Flow: The psychology of optimal experience.* New York: Harper & Row.

Dai, D. Y., & Feldhusen, J. F. (in press). A validation study of the Thinking Style Inventory: Implications for gifted education. *Roeper Review.*

Davis, J. K. (1991). Educational implications of field dependence–independence. In S. Wapner & J. Demick (Eds.), *Field dependence–independence: Cognitive style across the life span* (pp. 149–176). Hillsdale, NJ: Lawrence Erlbaum Associates.

de Charms, R. (1968). *Personal causation: The internal affective determinants of behavior.* New York: Academic Press.

Deci, E. L. (1992). The relation of interest to the motivation of behavior: A self–determination theory perspective. In K. A. Renninger, S. Hidi, & A. Krapp (Eds.), *The role of interest in learning and development* (pp. 43–70). Hillsdale, NJ: Lawrence Erlbaum Associates.

Delcourt, M. A. B. (1993). Creative productivity among secondary school students: Combining energy, interest, and imagination. *Gifted Child Quarterly, 37,* 23–31.

Dunn, R., Dunn, K., & Price, G. E. (1975). *Learning style inventory.* Chappaqua, NY: Rita Dunn & Associates.

Entwistle, N. (1988). Motivational factors in students' approaches to learning. In R. R. Schmeck (Ed.), *Learning strategies and learning styles* (pp. 21–51). New York: Plenum.

Flynn, J. R (1987). Massive IQ gains in 14 nations: What IQ tests really measure. *Psychological Bulletin, 101,* 171–191.

Flynn, J. R. (1994). IQ gains over time. In R. J. Sternberg (Ed.), *Encyclopedia of human intelligence* (pp. 617–623). New York: Macmillan.

Flynn, J. R. (1999). Searching for justice: The discovery of IQ gains over time. *American Psychologist, 54,* 5–20.

Gardner, H. (1983). *Frames of mind: The theory of multiple intelligences.* New York: Basics.

Guilford, J. P. (1959). Three faces of intellect. *American Psychologist, 14,* 469–479.

Harvey, O. J., Hunt, D. E., & Schroder, H. M. (1961). *Conceptual systems and personality organization.* New York: Wiley.

Herrnstein, R. J., & Murray, C. (1994). *The bell curve.* New York: Free Press.

Hunt, D. E. (1975). Person–environment interaction. A challenge found wanting before it was tried. *Review of Educational Psychology, 45,* 209–230.

Kagan, Jr. (1966). Reflection–impulsivity: The generality and dynamics of conceptual tempo. *Journal of Abnormal Psychology, 71,* 17–24.

Kelly, G. A. (1955). *The psychology of personal constructs* (Vol. 1). New York: Norton.

Kimble, G. A. (1984). Psychology's two cultures. *American Psychologist, 39,* 833–839.

Kolb, D. A. (1971). *Individual learning styles and the learning process.* Cambridge, MA: MIT Press.

Lewis, M. D. (1989). Early infant–mother interaction as a predictor of problem–solving in toddlers. *International Journal of Early Childhood, 21,* 13–22.

Loewenstein, G. (1994). The psychology of curiosity: A review and reinterpretation. *Psychological Bulletin, 116,* 75–98.

Lohman, D. F. (1993). Teaching and testing to develop fluid abilities. *Educational Researcher, 22,* 12–23.

McCall, R. B. (1981). Nature–nurture and the two realms of development: A proposed integration with respect to mental development. *Child Development, 52,* 1–12.

McKenna, F. P. (1990). Learning implications of field dependence–independence: Cognitive style versus cognitive ability. *Applied Cognitive Psychology, 4,* 425–437.

Messick, S. (1984). The nature of cognitive styles: Problems and promise in educational practice. *Educational Psychologist, 19,* 59–74.

Messick, S. (1994). The matter of style: Manifestations of personality in cognition, learning, and teaching. *Educational Psychologist, 29,* 121–136.

Newell, A., & Simon, H. A. (1972). *Human problem solving.* Englewood Cliffs, NJ: Prentice-Hall.

Nicholls, J. G. (1989). *The competitive ethos and democrative education.* Cambridge, MA: Harvard University Press.

Pask, G. (1976). Styles and strategies of learning. *British Journal of Educational Psychology, 46,* 128–148.

Pask, G. (1988). Learning strategies, teaching strategies, and conceptual and learning style. In R. R. Schmeck (Ed.), *Learning strategies and learning styles* (pp. 83–100). New York: Plenum.

Phenix, P. H. (1964). *Realms of meaning: A philosophy of the curriculum for general education.* New York: McGraw-Hill.

Phenix, P. H. (1987). *Views on the use, misuse, and abuse of instructional materials.* Paper presented at the annual meeting of the Leadership Training Institute on the Gifted and Talented, Houston, TX.

Piaget, J. (1967). *Six psychological studies.* New York: Random House.

Piaget, J. (1977). The development of thought: Equilibration of cognitive structures. (A. Rosin, Trans.). New York: Viking.

Plomin, R. & Petrill, S. A. (1997). Genetics and intelligence: What's new? *Intelligence, 24,* 53–77.

Prenzel, M. (1992). The selective persistence of interest. In K. A. Renninger, S. Hidi, & A. Krapp (Eds.), *The role of interest in learning and development* (pp. 71–98). Hillsdale, NJ: Lawrence Erlbaum Associates.

Purcell, J. H., & Renzulli, J. S. (1988). *Total talent portfolio: A systematic plan to identify and nurture gifts and talents.* Mansfield Center, CT: Creative Learning Press.

Reis, S. M., Burns, D. E., & Renzulli, J. S. (1992). *Curriculum compacting: The complete guide to modifying the regular curriculum for high-ability students.* Mansfield Center, CT: Creative Learning Press.

Renzulli, J. S. (1988). The Multiple Menu Model for developing differentiated curriculum for the gifted and talented. *Gifted Child Quarterly, 36,* 170–181.

Renzulli, J. S. (1992). A general theory for the development of creative productivity in young people. In F. Monks & W. Peters (Eds.), *Talent for the future: Social and personality development for gifted children* (pp. 51–72). Assen/Maastricht, The Netherlands: Van Gorcum.

Renzulli, J. S. (1994). *Schools for talent development: A practical plan for total school improvement.* Mansfield Center, CT: Creative Learning Press.

Renzulli, J. S., & Reis, S. M. (1985). *The school wide enrichment model: A comprehensive plan for educational excellence.* Mansfield Center, CT: Creative Learning Press.

Renzulli, J. S., & Reis, S. M. (1997). *The schoolwide enrichment model: A how-to guide for educational excellence* (2nd ed.). Mansfield Center, CT: Creative Learning Press.

Renzulli, J. S., & Smith, L. H. (1978). *The learning style inventory: A measure of student preference for instructional techniques.* Mansfield Center, CT: Creative Learning Press.

Ryan, R. M. (1993). Agency and organization: Intrinsic motivation, autonomy, and the self in psychological development. In J. E. Jacobs (Ed.), *Developmental perspectives on motivation* (pp. 1–55). Lincoln: The University of Nebraska Press.

Schank, R. C. (1979). Interestingness: Controlling inferences. *Artificial Intelligence, 12,* 273–297.

Schmeck, R. R. E. (Ed.). (1988). *Learning strategies and learning styles.* New York: Plenum.

Schunk, D. H., & Zimmerman, B. J. (Eds.). (1994). *Self-regulation of learning and performance: Issues and educational applications.* Hillsdale, NJ: Lawrence Erlbaum Associates.

Shulman, L. S. (1986). Knowledge and teaching: Foundations of the new reform. *Harvard Educational Review, 57,* 1–22.

Sigel, I. E. (1991). The cognitive style construct: A conceptual analysis. In S. Wapner & J. Demick (Eds.), *Field dependence–independence: Cognitive style across the life span* (pp. 385–397). Hillsdale, NJ: Lawrence Erlbaum Associates.

Snow, R. E. (1992). Aptitude theory: Yesterday, today, and tomorrow. *Educational Psychologist, 27,* 5–32.

Snow, R. E., Corno, L., & Jackson, D. (1996). Individual differences in affective and conative functions. In D. C. Berliner & R. C. Calfee (Eds.), *Handbook of educational psychology* (pp. 243–310). New York: Simon & Schuster Macmillan.

Snow, R. E. & Lohman, D. F. (1984). Toward a theory of cognitive aptitude for learning from instruction. *Journal of Educational Psychology, 76,* 347–376.

Starko, A. J. (1986). *The effects of the revolving door identification model on creativity and self-efficacy.* Unpublished doctoral dissertation, The University of Connecticut, Storrs.

Stednitz, U. (1985). *The influence of educational enrichment on the self-efficacy in young children.* Unpublished doctoral dissertation. The University of Connecticut, Storrs.

Sternberg, R. J. (1985). Human intelligence: An information–processing approach. New York: Freeman.

Sternberg, R. J. (1988). Mental self-government: A theory of intellectual styles and their development. *Human Development, 31,* 197–221.

Sternberg, R. J. (1997). *Thinking styles.* New York: Cambridge University Press.

Sternberg, R. J. (1998). Abilities are forms of developing expertise. *Educational Researcher, 27,* 11–20.

Sternberg, R. J., & Grigorenko, E. L. (1997). Are cognitive styles still in Style? *American Psychologist, 52,* 700–712.

Sternberg, R. J., & Kaufman, J. C. (1998). Human abilities. *Annual Review of Psychology, 49,* 479–502.

Thomas, A., & Chess, S. (1977). *Temperament and development.* New York: Bruner/Mazel.

Vygotsky, L. C. (1978). *Mind in society: The development of higher psychological processes.* M. Cole, V. John-Steiner, S. Shribner, & E. Souberman (Eds.). Cambridge, MA: Harvard University Press.

Wachtel, P. L. (1972). Field dependence and psychological differentiation: Reexamination. *Perceptual and Motor Skills, 35,* 43–50.

White, R. W. (1959). Motivation reconsidered: The concept of competence. *Psychological Review, 66,* 297–333.

Witkin, H. A., & Goodenough, D. R. (1978). Field dependence and interpersonal behavior. *Psychological Bulletin, 84,* 661–689.

3

The Nature and Effects of Cognitive Style

Richard Riding
Assessment Research Unit, University of Birmingham, UK

INTRODUCTION

This chapter begins with a consideration of the labels used by investigators to describe cognitive style and proposes a categorization of these into two fundamental style dimensions: the wholist–analytic and verbal–imagery. Methods of assessing style are outlined and a simple direct method is described. Style is then examined within the context of other individual difference variables such as intelligence, gender, and personality to establish its independence of these dimensions. The bipolar nature of cognitive style, which distinguishes it from unipolar dimensions of individual difference such as intelligence, is detailed. The evidence for the physiological aspects of style is described. Next, the relation between the style dimensions and a range of behaviors relevant to education is reported and practical implications are explored. Finally, a model of style within the context of other individual difference variables is considered.

COGNITIVE STYLE AND ITS ASSESSMENT

The Style Dimensions

Over the last 60 years, investigators have reported many style dimensions. However, generally, the researchers developed their own instruments for assessment in their own contexts and gave their own labels to the style they were studying with little reference to the work of others. Predictably, this produced a large number of style labels. Taken at face value, this produced a situation that gave the impression there were many style dimensions. If this had been the case, these labels would have been of little practical value for education. Conveniently, several researchers sensed that many labels are only different conceptions of the same dimensions (e.g., Brumby, 1982; Coan, 1974; Fowler, 1980; Miller, 1987; Riding & Buckle, 1990). Riding and Cheema (1991), after reviewing the descriptions, correlations, methods of assessment, and effect on behavior of more than 30 labels, concluded they could be grouped into two fundamental cognitive style dimensions, which they termed wholist–analytic and verbal–imagery. This view was confirmed in a further review by Rayner and Riding (1997). The identification of just two basic dimensions is significant because it makes the practical application of style viable. Cognitive style is seen as an individual's preferred and habitual approach to both organizing and representing information (Riding and Rayner, 1998, p.8). These two dimensions of cognitive style, shown in Fig. 3.1, may be described as follows: the wholist–analytic style dimension of whether an individual tends to organize information in wholes or parts, and the verbal–imagery style dimension of whether an individual tends to represent information during thinking verbally or in mental pictures.

The wholist–analytic dimension is a development of the family of styles that includes field dependence–independence (e.g., Witkin, Oltman, Raskin, & Karp, 1971), leveling–sharpening (Klein, 1954), and impulsivity–refectivity (Kagan, Rosman, Day, Albert, & Philips, 1964). The verbal–imagery dimension is related to the family of abstract–concrete (Harvey, Hunt, & Schroder, 1961) and verbalizer–visualizer (Paivio, 1971). A more extensive consideration of the style families is given in Riding and Rayner (1998, p.20).

It is useful to distinguish between style and strategy. Style probably has a physiological basis and is fairly fixed for the individual. By contrast, strategies are ways that may be learned and developed to cope with situations and tasks, and particularly methods of using styles to make the best of situations for which they are not ideally suited.

Assessment of Cognitive Style

Two approaches have been used to assess style: introspective self-report and tests of information processing based on the assumption that performance is affected by style. The latter is argued to be preferable because introspective self-report measures have inherent weaknesses. These include the subject's possible inability to accurately and objectively report his or her behavior, unwillingness to make the necessary effort to respond accurately, and bias due to the pressure of social desirability in making responses (e.g., Kline, 1995, p. 512).

However, the information-processing approach is not without its problems. In terms of the wholist–analytic dimension, Witkin et al.(1971) used the EFT, which asked subjects to locate simple geometrical figures within more complex figures in a given time. This was intended to assess field dependence–independence, and Witkin et al. assumed field-independent individuals would be able to locate items more quickly than field-dependent individuals. A limitation of this approach was that no subtest was used on which the field-dependent individuals were likely to perform better than the field-independent individuals. It may be objected that the EFT assesses intelligence rather than style, because overall performance is also affected by general ability or "intelligence" (e.g., Flexer & Roberge, 1980; Goldstein & Blackman, 1978, pp. 183–184; Riding, & Pearson, 1994 pp. 419–420 1994,). For the verbal–imagery dimension, Delaney (1978) used tests of both verbal and spatial performance. However the results were used independently of one another and not together, by means of a ratio or a difference.

The method proposed by Riding (1991a) in developing the cognitive styles analysis (CSA) was to assess performance on simple tasks that might then be representative of processing generally, with the intention of measuring an individual's position on both the wholist–analytic and the verbal–imagery dimensions. The background to the development of the CSA was given in Riding and Cheema (1991). The CSA is computer presented, directly assesses both ends of the wholist–analytic and verbal–imagery dimensions, and comprises three subtests. The first assesses the verbal–imagery dimension by presenting 48 statements one at a time to be judged true or false. Half of the statements contain information about conceptual categories (e.g., spring is a season), and half describe the appearance of items (e.g., snow is white). Half of the statements of each type are true. It was assumed imagers would respond more quickly to the appearance statements, because the objects could be readily represented as mental pictures and the information for the comparison could be obtained directly and rapidly from these images. It was assumed verbalizers would respond more quickly to conceptual category items because the semantic conceptual category membership is verbally abstract in nature and cannot be represented in visual form. The computer records the response time to each statement and calculates the verbal–imagery ratio. A low ratio indicates a verbalizer and a high ratio indicates an imager, with the intermediate position described as bimodal. In this approach, individuals have to read both the verbal and the imagery items so that reading ability and reading speed are controlled for.

The second two subtests assess the wholist–analytic dimension. The first of these presents items containing pairs of complex geometrical figures that the individual is required to judge either the same or different. Because this task involves judgments about the overall similarity of the two figures, it was assumed that a relatively fast response to this task would be possible by wholists. The second subtest presents items each comprising a simple geometrical shape (e.g., a square or a triangle) and a complex geometrical figure, and the individual is asked to indicate whether the simple shape is contained in the complex shape by pressing one of two marked response keys. This task requires a degree of disembedding of the simple shape from within the complex geometrical figure to establish that it is the same as the stimulus simple shape displayed. It was assumed analytics would be relatively quicker at this. Again, the computer records the latency of the responses and calculates the wholist–analytic ratio. A low ratio corresponds to a wholist and a high ratio corresponds to an analytic. Ratios between these positions are labeled intermediate. It should be noted that each style dimension is a continuum, and subsequently labels will only be attached to ranges on a dimension for convenience. This is shown in Fig. 3.1.

The CSA provides a simple method of determining a person's position on the two fundamental cognitive style dimensions (Riding, 1991b). The

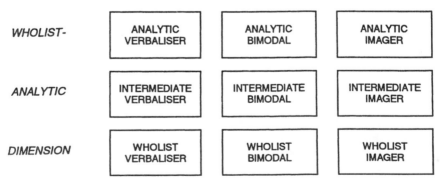

FIG. 3.1.   The groupings of cognitive style.

test has several features in that it is an objective test, as defined by Cattell and Warburton (1967), because it positively assesses both ends of each style dimension and hence measures style rather than ability, it can be used with a wide age range from children to adults, it is context free and can be used in a wide range of situations, and it is probably culture free in nature. The CSA is available in various languages: versions in English for the Australian, North American, South African, and United Kingdom contexts, and versions in Arabic, French, Dutch, German, Malay, and Spanish.

In the following sections on the nature and effects of style the consideration is limited to studies using the CSA approach. Except where stated the studies reviewed were undertaken in the United Kingdom.

THE NATURE OF STYLE

In considering cognitive style as a distinct psychological construct, it is important that the style dimensions should not duplicate other existing constructs that might affect educational performance and should have a physiological basis. Thus, the dimensions should be: (a) unrelated to one another, (b) independent of intelligence, (c) distinct from ability and they fulfill the requirements of a style, (d) separate from personality, and (e) related to physiological measures. A further consideration is the origin of style, whether it is inborn or learned.

The Style Dimensions

The cognitive style dimensions have been found to be separate from one another, such that the position of an individual on one dimension does not affect his or her position on the other. The correlation between the two dimensions has been found to be consistently low and typically $r = \pm 0.1$ (e.g., Riding, Burton, Rees, & Sharratt, 1995; Riding & Douglas, 1993). Furthermore, there do not appear to be overall gender differences with respect to cognitive style. Differences are usually small and nonsignificant on both dimensions ($P < 0.05$; e.g., Riding et al., 1995). Although not usually significant, males frequently have been observed to be slightly more analytic than females. On the verbal–imagery dimension not even a hint of a difference has been found. With respect to age, where samples were from a wide age range, no significant correlation between age and style was observed. For example, with a sample of nurses aged 21 to 61 years, the correlations between age and wholist–analytic style, and verbal–imagery style, were, respectively, $r = 0.00$ and $r = 0.01$ (from the data collected by Riding & Wheeler, 1995).

Intelligence and Style

Cognitive style appears to be unrelated to intelligence. Riding and Pearson (1994) with 12- to 13-year-old pupils found that intelligence as assessed by subtests of the British Abilities Scale was not related to cognitive style. The correlations between the four subtests used and the wholist–analytic and verbal–imagery ratios were all nonsignificant and were, respectively: Digits -0.01, 0.12; Similarities -0.03, 0.01; Matrices -0.10, 0.04; Speed of Information Processing 0.07, 0.02. Riding and Agrell (1997) observed similar findings from a study in Canada of the relationship between style and the Canadian Test of Cognitive Skills (CTCS) with 14- to 16-year-old students. The CTCS contains four subtests comprising intelligence test-type items. These together with the respective correlations with the wholist–analytic and verbal–imagery ratios were: Sequences 0.01, -0.10; Analogies - 0.01, -0.05; Memory -0.03, -0.03; Verbal Reasoning -0.02, -0.10. Again, all the correlations were low.

Style Dimension Positive and Negative Interaction with a Variable

It is important to distinguish between style and ability. Both style and ability affect performance on a given task. The essential difference is that performance on all tasks improves as ability increases, whereas the effect of style on performance for an individual is either positive or negative depending on the nature of the task. Consequently, for an individual at one end of a style dimension, a task of a type they find difficult will be found easier by someone at the opposite end of the dimension, and vice versa. For example, with the verbal–imagery style dimension, verbalizers would find pictorial tasks more difficult than would imagers, but they would find highly verbal tasks easier than would imagers. In summary, for style an individual is both good *and* poor at tasks depending on the nature of the task, whereas for intelligence they are either good or poor.

It is thus a characteristic of a style, as distinct from an ability, that it should interact with a variable such that the relative performance of an individual at one extreme of a dimension should be higher than that of a person at the other end in one condition, but that the situation should be reversed when the condition is changed. Single-dimension interactions have been found. With the wholist–analytic dimension this type of interaction was observed by Douglas and Riding (1993) in the effect of the position, before or after, of a prose passage title on recall. With the verbal–

imagery dimension the interaction was found by Riding and Douglas (1993) on text-plus-text versus text-plus-picture presentation of learning material, and by Riding and Watts (1997) in the preference for verbal or pictorial formats of instructional material. However, in many real-life tasks there is likely to be an interaction between the two dimensions and the condition, rather than an effect of only one of the dimensions without any effect of the other.

Personality and Style

In an investigation of the relation between style and personality measures, Riding and Wigley (1997) gave College of Further Education students aged 17 to 18 years the following: the Eysenck Personality Questionnaire-Revised (EPQ-R) Short Scale (Eysenck & Eysenck, 1991) to assess Extraversion, Neuroticism, and Psychoticism; the Impulsiveness, Venturesomeness, and Empathy (IVE) Questionnaire (Eysenck & Eysenck, 1991) to determine these traits; and the State and Trait Anxiety Inventory (Spielberger, 1977). A factor analysis gave four factors labeled Anxiety, Impulsiveness, Empathy, and Style. No personality measure loaded beyond ±0.33 on Style.

Riding and Wigley also looked at the interactive effect of the wholist–analytic style and verbal–imagery style on personality measures. They noted significant effects such that for Neuroticism, wholist–verbalizers and analytic–imagers were more anxious than analytic–verbalizers and wholist–imagers. For Impulsiveness, wholist–verbalizers and analytic–imagers were more impulsive and decisive than analytic–verbalizers and wholist–imagers. They suggested a model in which physiologically based personality sources are independent of cognitive style but are moderated by style in their effect on behavior.

Style and Physiological Mechanisms

It is important evidence for any psychological construct if it can be shown to have physiological correlates. In reviewing work on electroencephalogram (EEG) relevant to the verbal–imagery dimension, Riding, Glass, and Douglas (1993) suggested that EEG alpha suppression (indicating mental activity) during information processing would probably occur over the left hemisphere for verbalizers and over the right hemisphere for imagers. For the wholist–analytic dimension no clear prediction was made other than it would not be in terms of left–right hemispheric specialization.

Riding, Glass, Butler, and Pleydell-Pearce (1997) reported an investigation of EEG and style. They recorded EEG alpha in subjects while doing computer-presented word-targeting tasks in which words appeared one at a time on the screen. The task required subjects to monitor the displayed words and to press a button whenever a noun from the superordinate categories of "fruit" or "vegetable" was displayed (e.g., *apple* or *carrot*). The study revealed a significant effect for the wholist–analytic dimension along the midline (locations Fz, Cz, and Pz), with alpha suppression being greater for the analytics and fairly uniform along the line and alpha suppression decreasing from anterior to posterior for the wholist. For the verbal–imagery dimension the ratio of the power output at T5 (left) to that at T6 (right) correlated with the verbal–imagery ratio in the expected direction.

An analysis of all the EEG frequency bands (delta, theta, alpha, beta 1, beta 2, and gamma; Glass and Riding, in press), showed for the *midline* (locations Fz, Cz, and Pz) that the wholists had higher output than analytics in theta and alpha, but lower in gamma. In the *paramedial* cluster (Fp_1, C_3, O_1–left and Fp_2, C_4 and O_2–right), verbalizers had greater right power than imagers for all bands except alpha. Furthermore, the overall power was greater on the right for imagers than for verbalisers frontally, and the converse occipitally. In the *lateral* grouping (F_7, T_3, T_5–left and F_8, T_4 and T_6–right), the wholist–verbalizers had greater overall power left anterotemporally than other subgroups.

These results are important because they suggest a physiological evidence for style, although it should be noted that in this study the tasks were likely to favor analytics and verbalizers. Further studies are required using a range of information-processing tasks to establish more clearly the nature of brain activity in different styles.

The Origins of Style

A natural question arises as to the origins of style, particularly whether it is genetically determined or environmentally influenced. If the latter is the case, home background as indicated by parental support, which is a strong environmental influence, might be expected to affect style. Using a sample of 12-year-old pupils, Riding, Rayner, and Banner (2000) explored the relation between style and home background. The teachers of the pupils were asked to rate the home background in terms of the parental support given to each child on a 5-point scale, where 1 was the worst and 5 the best. The ratings were: 1, very poor; 2, poor; 3, moderate; 4, good; 5, very good. The distribution of the home background ratings were: very poor, 7.2%; poor, 9.5%; moderate, 29.4%; good, 30.6%; very good, 23.4%. None of the effects on the style ratios of either gender or background, or the interaction, was significant (smallest $P = 0.33$). There was no consistent style trend with respect to home background for either dimension.

For both style dimensions, comparison of the mean ratios for pupils from the poor homes with those from the very good homes showed little difference. Caution needs to be used in making deductions from the lack of a relation because the rating by the teachers might be an inadequate measure and the lack of a relation could thus be because of poor quality data. On the other hand, the teachers were likely to be aware of very poor home backgrounds, and even if their other ratings were uncertain, the ratings at the lower end were probably more valid. Because the home background is a strong environmental influence, the absence of any relation with such a basic variable suggests style is more likely to be a matter of nature rather than nurture, and this permits the possibility that it is genetic in origin.

To conclude this section, there is evidence that the style dimensions are independent of one another, unrelated to intelligence and personality, and have a physiological basis. The available evidence suggests style dimensions are inborn or learned at an early age.

THE EFFECT OF STYLE

The Action of Style

In considering the effect of style on a range of behaviors relevant to education, the effect will sometimes be that of a single-style dimension, sometimes an interactive effect of the two-style dimension, and at other times an interaction between one or more of the style dimensions and one of the other individual difference variables of intelligence, personality, or gender. It is useful to begin a review of the effects of style with a general model of the ways the two style dimensions may act.

Wholist–Analytic Dimension. This dimension influences the structural way in which individuals think about, view, and respond to information and situations. This affects the manner in which they organize information during learning, perceive their work situation, and relate to other people.

Wholists see a situation as a whole and are able to have an overall perspective, and to appreciate its total context. By contrast, analytics see a situation as a collection of parts and often focus on one or two aspects of the situation at a time to the exclusion of the others. Intermediates are able to

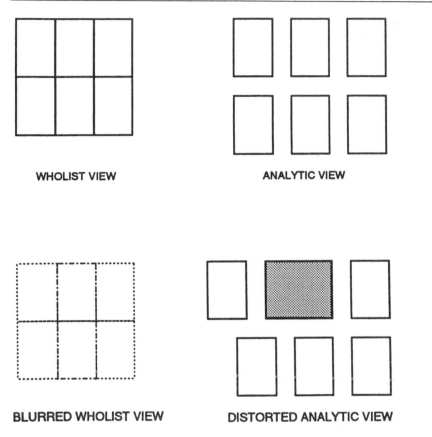

FIG. 3.2.   Wholist and analytic views.

have a view between the extremes, which should allow some of the advantages of both.

Figure 3.2 shows, in a schematic way, how a situation or information might be perceived by wholists and analytics. The former view tends to be unitary, and the latter more separated into parts. Both styles have limitations and advantages. The limitation for wholists is that not only are the parts not separated, but the distinction between them may be blurred (see Fig 3.2) so that it is difficult to distinguish the issues that make up the whole of a situation. By contrast, as also shown in Fig 3.2, analytics focus on just one aspect of the whole at a time. This may distort or exaggerate a part, or make it unduly prominent, with respect to the rest. There is thus the possibility of getting it out of proportion to the total situation.

The positive aspect of the wholists is that when considering information or a situation they see the whole "picture". They are "big picture people".

Consequently, they can have a balanced view and can see situations in their overall context. This makes it less likely that they will have extreme views or attitudes. The negative aspect of the wholists is that they find difficulty in separating a situation into its parts.

The positive aspect of the analytics is that they can analyze a situation into its parts, which allows them to get quickly to the heart of any problem. They are good at seeing similarities and detecting differences. However, the negative aspect is that they may not be able to get a balanced view of the whole, and they may focus on one aspect of a situation to the exclusion of the others and enlarge it out of proportion.

Verbal–Imagery Dimension. This style has two fundamental effects that have implications for behavior: the way information is represented and the external–internal focus of attention.

Representation affects the characteristic mode in which people represent information during thinking, verbally or in images. For instance, when individuals read a novel they can represent the actions, happenings, and scenes in terms of word associations or by constructing a mental picture of what they read. Just as it is possible to set down thoughts on paper in two ways—in words or in sketches—so is it possible to think in those two modes. People can think in words, or they can think in terms of mental pictures or images. On this dimension people may be categorized as being of three types: verbalizers, bimodals, or imagers. *Verbalizers* consider the information they read, see, or listen to, in words or verbal associations. *Bimodals*, in the middle, use either mode of representation. *Imagers* experience fluent, spontaneous, and frequent mental pictures either of representations of the information itself or of associations with it.

The style thus affects the processing of information and the mode of representation and presentation that an individual prefers, and this is likely to affect the types of task they find easy or difficult. However, all groups can use either mode of representation if they make the conscious choice. For example, verbalizers can form images if they try, but it is not their normal, habitual mode.

External–Internal focus, the second effect, influences the focus and type of an individual's activity: externally and stimulating in the case of verbalizers, and internally and more passive in the case of imagers. This has implications for social relationships and for the type of environment people will be content in.

For verbalizers the focus is outward to others and they prefer a stimulating environment. They see the social group as an extension of themselves and are socially aware. For imagers, the focus is more inward, and they are more passive and content with a more static environment. They view the social group as more distant from themselves, and they may be less socially aware.

Complementary–Unitary Styles.   A person's cognitive style is a combination of his or her position on each of the two dimensions. These dimensional characteristics of a person may either complement or duplicate one another, depending on the characteristics. The style characteristics may be put in order according to the degree to which, in combination, they offer complementary facilities. For example, consider an analytic–imager. Because the analytic aspect of his or her style does not provide an overview of a situation, he or she could attempt to use the whole-view aspect of imagery to supply it. If another person was a wholist–verbalizer, then because the wholist facility does not support analysis, he or she might use the "analytic" property of verbalization as a substitute. By contrast, a wholist–imager only has a whole facility available, with no style that may be pressed into service to provide an analytic function. The style groups from complementary to unitary may be ordered as: wholist–verbalizer, analytic–imager, intermediate–verbalizer, intermediate–imager, wholist–bimodal, analytic–bimodal, intermediate–bimodal, analytic–verbalizer, wholist–imager.

Style and Behavior

Style has been found to be related to a range of observed behaviors, including learning, motor skills, social behavior, behavior problems, and stress and aspect of occupation. The relations between cognitive style and these behaviors are reviewed.

Style and Learning

In this section I consider the effect of style on learning in terms of the structure, mode of presentation, and type of content of the material.

The Structure of the Material.   Several studies have shown that an individual's position on the wholist–analytic dimension interacts with the way learning material is structured in its effect on performance. Douglas and Riding (1993) found that when 11-year-old pupils were presented with a prose passage for recall, wholists did best when the title of the passage was given before the passage was presented, rather than at the end, although this had little effect for analytics. This was attributed to the providing to the wholists, who are less able to structure material, a title at the beginning to give some organization to the material.

Riding and Sadler-Smith (1992), with 14- to 19-year-old students, compared performance on three differently structured versions of computer-presented instructional material. The three versions presented that same information about five topics. *Version L* comprised large steps with large chunks of verbal information and line diagrams. *Version O* comprised small steps of verbal information interspersed with pictorial or diagrammatic content, plus overviews at the start, before and after each topic, and at the end. *Version S* was as Version O with small steps but minus the overviews. The four styles were grouped as *complementary* (wholist–verbalizer and analytic–imager) and *unitary* (wholist–imager and analytic–verbalizer). In terms of the recall efficiency, different ways of structuring the material had a large effect on performance for the two complementary style groups, with the small-step format being most effective. For the unitary groups, the structure had relatively little effect, with the groups performing in an "average" manner irrespective of the format. Gender was not included as a variable in this, or the previous, study.

Sadler-Smith and Riding (in press) used a questionnaire approach to study instructional preferences in university business studies students. In terms of locus of control, the analytics preferred to have control themselves rather than to be controlled, whereas the wholists had no preference. There was no significant gender effect.

Riding and Al-Sanabani (1998) with 10- to 15-year-old pupils attending a Yemeni school in the United Kingdom, examined the effect on reading comprehension of dividing a one-page textual narrative into three paragraphs, each with a subheading. This improved comprehension and the degree of the facilitating effect was related to the wholist–analytic style and gender of the student. For male and female wholists there was a similar improvement with the addition of format structure, whereas for analytics the males improved more than the females. A possibility is that female analytics prefer to impose their own structure and find externally imposed structure less helpful than do males. Certainly, the analytic females did well without the external structure. Similar effects were found for conditions where a summary was added.

Riding and Grimley (2000) noted with 11-year-old pupils that, with information in text mode, the patterns of recall for the males and females were similar. With the information available from text and pictures, the males increased in recall from wholist through to analytic, whereas the females declined with the worst performance by the analytics. The requirement to integrate the parts of the pictorial and the textual information is more difficult for the male wholists and the female analytics. This may have been particularly so because the pictures were in the form of cartoons and their content was by way of analogy, from which deductions had to be made, rather than a simple presentation of information in a literal form. This result accords with that of Riding and Read (1996), who found male wholists and female analytics to be more comfortable in situations that are closed and do not require divergent thinking.

There is evidence that the structure of the material to be learned interacts particularly with the wholist–analytic style dimension. Analytics need a large viewing window compared to wholists, when dealing with information (Riding & Grimley, 1999). Individuals of complementary style (wholist–verbalizers and analytic–imagers) are influenced by the step size of the learning material and improve from large to small steps, whereas those of unitary style (analytic–verbalizers and wholist–imagers) are not affected. There is an interaction between gender and wholist–analytic style in the facilitating effect of structure in the form of both headings and overviews, such that these most help male analytics and female wholists. It may be that male wholists and female analytics prefer to form their own structure of materials and find difficulty in copying with externally imposed organizations. More work is needed to clarify the gender and wholist–analytic interactions with structure.

Mode of Presentation.   Two modes of presenting information are available: the verbal and the pictorial. Riding and Ashmore (1980) with 11-year-old pupils gave groups of verbalizers and imagers (as assessed by the earlier Verbal–Imagery Code Test) either a verbal or a pictorial version of the same information. Verbalizers were superior with the verbal mode and imagers with the pictorial mode. Within the instructional situation, although purely verbal presentation is often an option, an alternative purely pictorial version is rarely an option as some words are also required. However, it is usually possible to present information in both modes. Riding and Douglas (1993), along with 15- to 16-year-old students, found that the computer presentation of material in a text-plus-picture format facilitated learning by imagers compared with the same content in a text-plus-text format. A further finding was that at recall in the text-plus-picture condition 50% of the imagers used illustrations as part of their answers compared with only 12% of the verbalizers.

Riding and Read (1996) individually questioned 12-year-old pupils about their preferences for mode of working and social context. For the higher ability pupils, imagers, particularly if they were wholists, said they used less writing and more pictures than verbalizers, especially where the subject allowed. The tendency by imagers to use pictures, and verbalizers to use writing, increased with ability. There was evidence that lower ability pupils were more constrained by the expected format of the subject than were those of higher ability.

Riding and Watts (1997) told female 16-year-old pupils that three versions of a sheet giving information on study skills had been prepared for them, and that each sheet contained the same information but that the formats were different. Pupils were then invited to take one of the versions from the teacher's desk. The versions were unstructured verbal (paragraphs, without headings), structured verbal (paragraphs, each with a clear heading), and structured pictorial (paragraphs, each with a clear heading, and a pictorial icon depicting the activity placed in the left margin). No pupils chose the unstructured-verbal version. For the two structured versions, with the verbal–imagery dimension most verbalizers selected the verbal version and most of the imagers selected the pictorial version. With the wholist–analytic dimension most wholists selected the pictorial version, perhaps because it looked more "lively," whereas most analytics selected the more "neat and tidy" verbal version. Students are attracted to, and prefer to select, materials that suit their own style.

Riding and Grimley (1999) considered the learning from CD-ROM multimedia instructional materials of science topics by 11-year-old pupils. Here three modes of presentation were used: picture plus sound (PS), picture plus text (PT), and picture plus text plus sound (PTS). With PTS the males did the best in the noncomplementary groups (analytic–verbalizers and wholist–imagers), and the females did the best in the analytics (verbalizers and imagers). With PS and PT, there was reversal with gender, which was related to whether the styles were complementary (as with wholist–verbalizers and analytic–imagers) or unitary (as with analytic–verbalizers and wholist–imagers). PS involved "look and listen" (two channels), whereas PT involved "look" only (a single channel). For the wholist–verbalizers and analytic–imagers (the complementary groups), males did better on PS than on PT; this was reversed for females. For the unitary groups, the wholist–imagers and analytic–verbalizers, the tendency was the opposite, where male wholist–imagers were superior on PT, and females wholist–imagers on PS.

Taken overall, imagers generally learn best from pictorial presentations, whereas verbalizers learn best from verbal presentations. However, there is also evidence of an interaction involving gender, and although the precise nature of this is not yet clear, it is likely to be of practical importance. With complementary groups, the males were best on separate channels of pictures and words, whereas the females were best on the single channel of pictures and words. With the unitary groups, the males were best on a single channel, whereas the females were best on separate channels. This hints at a fundamental gender difference in information processing that also involves style.

Type of Content.   With the type of content of learning material, studies of 11- and 12-year-old pupils showed that imagers recall highly visually descriptive text better than acoustically complex and unfamiliar text, whereas the reverse holds for verbalizers (Riding & Calvey, 1981; Riding & Dyer, 1980). Initial reading performance, which is obviously a verbal task, has been found to be superior in verbalizers. Riding and Anstey (1982) with 7-year-old children assessed reading accuracy and comprehension and found that both declined from verbalizer to imager. Riding and Mathias (1991) with 11-year-old children observed that for reading accuracy this effect was still pronounced for wholists, where wholists–verbalizers showed much greater proficiency at reading compared to wholists–imagers. Similarly, with second language learning, which is also verbal in nature, Riding et al. (2000) asked the second-language teachers of 12-year-old pupils to rate the general second-language ability of their pupils on a 5-point scale from very poor to very good. The pupils studied either French or German. Overall, the ability of females was rated higher than that of males, and for the verbal–imagery dimension, verbalizers were superior to imagers. In terms of content type, then, individuals appear to learn best when information can be readily translated into their preferred verbal–imagery mode of representation.

Content and Intelligence.   Riding and Agrell (1997) with 14- to 16-year-old Canadian students found an interaction between style and intelligence in their effect on school achievement, such that style was more critical where pupils were of lower ability and the subject matter did not ideally suit their style. For instance, the difference in performance between high- and low-ability pupils was greater for the analytic–imagers than for the analytic–verbalizers, where in the latter case that style was more naturally suited to learning academic subjects.

Riding and Sharratt (2000) considered performance in English, mathematics, and science in the General Certificate of Secondary Education (GCSE—the British public examination at 16+ years). The samples were also assessed on a test of reasoning ability (National Foundation for Educational Research Non-verbal Test DH). Riding and Sharratt found an interaction between reasoning ability and verbal–imagery style in their effect on overall GCSE performance. For low reasoning ability, verbalizers did less well than imagers, whereas for high reasoning ability, the verbalizers did better than the imagers. The reasons for this shift are not yet clear. By way of speculation, because much schoolwork has a verbal emphasis, verbalizers will find the mode of presentation and the medium used for expression more to their liking than imagers. However, it may be that verbalizers of low reasoning ability, when finding the work difficult, will give up more readily than imagers, because verbalizers are less tolerant of boredom than are imagers. As reasoning ability increases to a moderate level, verbalizers find the work easier and hence more interesting, and so they become more tolerant and they then equal the performance of imagers. When reasoning ability rises to a high level, verbalizers exceed the performance of imagers, because of the match between their style and the mode and type of content of the subject matter taught at GCSE level. If this were so, the low-reasoning-ability verbalizers could be helped by teaching the material more slowly and attractively to ensure understanding and attention. The rationale here is that if the task is easier, those of lower ability will be able to do it. Imagers of all levels of ability will be aided by more use of their preferred mode of representation.

Style and Motor Skills

If cognitive style monitors internal mechanisms that control external actions, it is reasonable to expect that style would be related to motor performance. Riding and Al-Salih (2000), along with 14- to 18-year-old secondary school pupils, explored the relation between style and motor skills and sports performance. The pupils did a battery of motor skills tests. A factor analysis indicated four skills factors: bodily movement, interactive skills, mechanical skills, and aiming. All of these except the mechanical skills showed a significant relation to style. With bodily movement the complementary styles (wholist–verbalizer and analytic–imager) did better than the unitary styles (wholist–imager and analytic–verbalizer). With interactive skills unitary styles were superior for males and complementary styles were superior for females. With aiming, analytic–imagers were best and wholists–verbalizers were worst. Each pupil was rated on a 5-point scale by their teachers on performance in rugby, soccer, and cricket for the boys; and hockey, netball, and tennis for the girls. Here there was a significant style effect for tennis with imagers doing best, but not for the team games.

Style and Social Behavior.

Cognitive style influences the manner in which an individual thinks about and represents social incidents and situations.

Wholist–Analytic Style and Social Behavior.   Riding (1991b) argued the wholist–analytic style is reflected socially in such dimensions as being dependent–self-reliant, flexible–consistent, realistic–idealistic, and vague–organized. Wholists tend to the former and analytics to the latter. Riding and Wright (1995) asked undergraduate students living in university flats with typically five per flat to rate their flatmates in terms of personal characteristics. The wholists were perceived as more assertive, humorous, and helpful, whereas the analytics were rated as more shy. In addition, the degree of unity in each flat was assessed by using statements such as, "Relations in my accommodation have been harmonious." When compared with the majority style in each flat, the order of reported unity from least to highest was: analytic–imager, wholist–imager, analytic–verbalizer, wholist–verbalizer. This order was as expected because analytics are likely to be more separate than wholists and imagers are likely to be more inward and socially isolated than verbalizers.

Verbal–Imagery Style and Social Behavior.   Riding et al. (1995) asked 12-year-old pupils to rate the children in their class in terms of being active (outgoing, lively, humorous), modest (shy, quiet), and responsible (serious, patient). They found verbalizers scored highest on active, bimodals highest on modest, and responsibleness increased from verbalizer to imager.

Style and Behavior Problems

Riding (1991b) suggested that for the Wholist–analytic dimension, wholists are likely to be unstructured, global, and inclusive in their thinking. This may manifest itself as lacking behavioral control. By contrast, analytics are likely to be structured but socially separate, resulting in behaviors that are generally more controlled but that may exhibit frustration and intensity, and they may be socially unaware and exclusive. On the basis of such a consideration of social behavior, it might be anticipated that the school conduct behavior of wholists would be less good than that of analytics because wholists are more outgoing and less well organized with respect to both self-control and learning. Several studies have supported this view.

Riding and Burton (1998) asked the teachers of 14- to 16-year-old secondary school pupils to rate the conduct behavior of their pupils on a 5-point scale from very poor to very good. They found that females were rated higher than males with little variation with the wholist–analytic style. With the males, the wholists were rated poorest in behavior, and the analytics were slightly poorer than the intermediates. Rayner and Riding (1996) considered pupils aged 15 to 17 years attending a truancy unit because of their previous failure to attend school. The percentage of pupils in the wholist–analytic dimension style groupings as defined by a comparison sample of pupils attending mainstream secondary schools was wholists, 41%; intermediates, 53%; and analytics, 6%. Riding and Craig (1998) noted the style characteristics of boys aged 10 to 18 years referred to residential special schools because of behavior problems. They found that their style on the wholist–analytic dimension was skewed to the wholist end of the continuum relative to a comparison sample of male pupils in ordinary secondary schools. The percentages of each style grouping in the special schools were wholist, 46%; intermediate, 34%; and analytics, 20%. In a further study of male 11- to 16-year-old students in special schools, Riding and Craig (1999) found similar results with the majority style group being wholist–verbalizer and the minority analytic–imager. Finally, Riding and Wigley (1997, p. 385) with 17- to 18-year-old College of Further Education students found that males were more psychotic than females, and that for the males wholists were more psychotic than analytics. Cook (1993, p. 87) noted that psychoticism is related to social deviance.

It is interesting to contrast the United Kingdom findings with those of Riding and Al-Hajji (2000) for pupils in the Kuwaiti educational system, which is formal and controlled. The conduct and learning behavior of 15- to 18-year-old Kuwaiti secondary school pupils were assessed by their teachers. Here, conduct behavior did not vary much with style, whereas learning behavior was significantly lower for analytics than for wholists, and for imagers than for verbalizers. The results suggest the interaction among behavior, attainment, and style may depend on the nature of the educational system.

Riding and Baker (2000) considered the school attendance of pupils within socially poor areas over their 5 years of secondary schooling from 11 to 16 years. They found that the worst attendance was by verbalizers for both males and females, with the best attendance by imagers for the males and bimodals for the females.

In summary, problem behavior is more likely in males than in females, and with respect to cognitive style, in wholists and verbalizers.

Style and Occupational Issues

Style studies have shown findings of relevance to career selection and employment. These include decision making, anxiety, optimism, and perceived level of stress.

Style and Decisiveness. Riding and Wigley (1997) assessed the degree of decisiveness for a sample of 16- to 18-year-old College of Further Education students in terms of their position on a dimension of: very indecisive, indecisive, decisive, impulsive. Here, the relevant aspect of style appears to be the wholist to analytic facility, in which the style groups may be ordered from extreme wholist to extreme analytic: wholist–imager, wholist–bimodal, intermediate–imager, wholist–verbalizer, intermediate–bimodal, analytic–imager, intermediate–verbalizer, analytic–bimodal, analytic–verbalizer. Those who are most analytic (i.e. analytic–verbalizers) are less decisive because they are inclined to weigh all the possibilities before making a decision. Those who are very wholist (i.e., wholist–imagers) can see a broad perspective and the relevance of all aspects of the situation in an overall balance, and they are not decisive. People who are more decisive lack the constraint of the high analytic on the one hand, and the overall wholist or balanced perspective, on the other, and this includes those who are wholist–verbalizer, intermediate–bimodal, and analytic–imager. This area needs further examination within practical contexts to see what are the effects on learning performance and problem solving. There could be implications for management.

Style and Neuroticism.   Riding and Wigley (1997) also found that neuroticism, as assessed by the EPQ-R, was highest for wholist–verbalizers and analytic–imagers and lowest for analytic–verbalizers and wholist–imagers. To facilitate the interpretation of the findings for neuroticism, they ordered the styles from complementary to unitary. Neuroticism was found to be highest for the complementary styles (i.e., wholist–verbalizer and analytic–imager) and lowest for those that are not. A possible reason for this is that wholists who lack any analytic facility can see all aspects of a situation in balance and do not focus just on some negative aspects. In reality, nothing is totally bad, only some parts, and this style evens out the bad with the good. Similarly, those who have only an analytic facility have everything ordered and under control and perceive less stress. Those who seem most susceptible to neuroticism are those with the facility to switch between the two modes. The observed level of neuroticism is likely a combination of the level of the physiological source of anxiety, which is then moderated by cognitive style so that for the complementary styles it is increased and for the unitary styles it is decreased.

Optimism Versus Pessimism   Individuals may be described in terms of whether they tend to optimism or pessimism. Whether optimism–pessimism is a separate dimension or related to stability–neuroticism is not clear (Wiebe & Smith, 1997, pp. 903–905). In the present context, optimism is used to describe an inclination to interpret situations positively rather than negatively. In a study of style and optimism (Riding & Rayner, 1998, p. 126), 40 Methodist Church members were asked to rate on a scale from 1 to 5 the threat or comfort they felt when they read each of 25 verses taken from the Bible. Examples of the verses were: comfort, "The Lord is my shepherd, I shall not want" (Psalm 23:1); threat, "The wages of sin is death" (Romans 6:23). The tendency to perceive verses as threatening rather than comforting was found to be related to verbal–imagery style and gender. The male imagers and the female verbalizers were more inclined to see the negative aspects of verses and could be described as more pessimistic than the male verbalizers and the female imagers. As described in the following discussion, a similar pattern has been found for perceived stress.

Perceived Level of Stress   Borg and Riding (1993) gave sample Maltese secondary school teachers a questionnaire where the items were labeled from "no stress" to "extreme stress" and scored from zero to four. Four subscales of sources of stress were derived from the inventory: pupil misbehavior, poor working conditions, poor staff relationships, and time pressures. Borg and Riding found that the male imagers and female verbalizers reported the greater overall stress. These findings were similar to those obtained in the study of the reaction to Bible verses. It may be that those who report the greater stress are more pessimistic. Borg and Riding also observed that the amount of stress was consistent with the expectation of wholists being more open and people orientated and analytics being more structured and organized. The wholists reported more stress from time pressures and staff relations, whereas the analytics reported more stress from pupil misbehavior and working conditions.

Riding and Wheeler (1995) in a study of nurses found that verbalizers had a significantly higher employment grade than imagers. Further, they found evidence that the type of nursing that most suited nurses was related to their style. Using a questionnaire, a suitability index was obtained from (Job Satisfaction − Perceived Stress), and this was compared with style and type of nursing. The styles with the highest satisfaction indices were analytic–verbalizer for general nursing, intermediate–bimodal for orthopaedic nursing, and wholist–imager for psychiatric nursing. The lowest indices were wholist–imager for general nursing, analytic–imager for orthopaedic nursing, and intermediate–verbalizer for psychiatric nursing. General nursing is probably dynamic, requiring conscientious activity; orthopaedic nursing is slower, needing patience: and psychiatric nursing is demanding, benefiting from tolerance. This approach has relevance to other occupations.

In summary, findings of style have implications for employment. These include decision making, level or anxiety, optimism and stress, as well as occupational suitability.

TOWARD A MODEL OF STYLE

Evidence suggests the construct of cognitive style possesses a degree of validity because it is distinctly different from other established constructs such as intelligence, personality, and gender. Furthermore, it has been

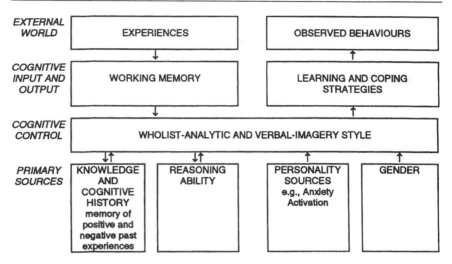

FIG. 3.3.   Cognitive control model.

found to be related to a range of behaviors to a degree that has practical relevance. Cognitive style now needs to be seen in the context of the other variables with a view to developing a model of their operation and interaction.

Riding (1997) proposed a tentative model called the cognitive control model. This model is shown in Fig. 3.3.

At the *inmost level* several underlying primary sources comprise the memory of individuals' past experiences and knowledge, probably their reasoning ability, their underlying personality sources, and their gender. Some of the personality sources have been given tentative names. The *next level is that of cognitive control*, which comprises the fundamental dimensions of style: wholist–analytic and verbal–imagery. It provides the organizational and representational interface between the internal sources and the external environment, and it imposes on the learning and response its own structure and form. The ways the wholist–analytic dimension and the verbal–imagery dimension may affect attitude and behavior have been discussed by Riding (1991b, 1994). The working memory processing system, which gives meaning to the incoming information, operates at the *input level*. The performance of this may be considered a significant contributor to fluid intelligence (cf. Kline, 1991). A computer-presented displacement method for assessing this is the Information Processing Index (Riding, 1999). Learning strategies are at the *output level*. Strategies are ways that may be learned and developed to cope with situations and tasks, and particularly methods of using styles to make the best of situations that are not ideal. These will have been developed, for instance, by the individual sensing that certain modes are easier to use, recognizing a *learning preference*, and deciding to "translate" new incoming information into that representation. At this level there is also the cognitive response "set" that influences social behavior.

The perception of experiences is probably moderated by the cognitive control level in interaction with the cognitive history and the primary personality sources. Some support for the model comes from the finding of interactions between style and other individual difference constructs. For instance: between intelligence and style in affecting academic achievement (Riding & Agrell, 1997; Riding & Sharratt, 2000), between gender and style in affecting learning (Riding & Al-Sanabani, 1998; Riding & Grimley, 1999), and between personality sources and style in affecting social behavior (Riding & Wigley, 1997).

CONCLUSION

The notion of cognitive style, as consisting of two fundamental dimensions, as assessed by the CSA approach, is supported by evidence that the dimensions are independent of one another and gender, they are separate from intelligence, cognitive style fulfills the requirement for the distinction between style and ability, cognitive style is independent of personality, and cognitive style has physiological correlates. Furthermore, the observed relation between the dimensions and behavior are consistent with the view that the wholist–analytic dimension is concerned with organization and the verbal–imagery dimension is concerned with representation. The utility of the construct is further supported by its being shown to be related to a range of practical behaviors, such as learning performance, motor skills, social behavior, problem behavior, stress, and occupational satisfaction. Cognitive style is seen within the context of the other individual difference variables and may represent an interface between them and the external world. The next challenge is to clarify the interactions between style and the other variables in their effects on behavior and educational performance.

Although more work remains to fully understand style, practical application to education is facilitated by the use of the *Learning Enhancement Programme* (Riding & Rayner, 1995, 1999), which raises the awareness of teachers of their own cognitive style and of ways to broaden their teaching styles to suit the needs of a wider range of pupils. Furthermore, details of practical style approaches to helping pupils with behavioral and learning difficulties is given in Riding and Rayner.

REFERENCES

Borg, M. G., & Riding, R. J. (1993), Teacher stress and cognitive style. *British Journal of Educational Psychology*, 63, 271–286.

Brumby, M. N. (1982). Consistent differences in cognitive styles shown for qualitative biological problem-solving. *British Journal of Educational Psychology*, 52, 244–257.

Cattell, R.B., & Warburton, F. W. (1967) *Objective personality and motivational tests*. Urbana, IL: University of Illinois Press.

Coan, R. (1974). *The optimal personality: An empirical and theoretical analysis*. New York: Columbia University Press.

Cook, M. (1993). *Levels of personality*. London: Cassell.

Delaney, H. D. (1978). Interaction of individual differences with visual and verbal elaboration instructions. *Journal of Educational Psychology*, 70, 306–318.

Douglas, G., & Riding, R. J. (1993). The effect of pupil cognitive style and position of prose passage title on recall. *Educational Psychology*, 13, 385–393.

Eysenck, H. J., & Eysenck, S. B. G. (1991). *Eysenck Personality Scales*. London: Hodder and Stoughton.

Flexer, B. K., & Roberge, J. J. (1980). IQ, field-dependence-independence, and the development of formal operational thought. *Journal of General Psychology*, 103, 191–201.

Fowler, W. (1980). Cognitive differentiation and developmental learning. In H. Rees & L. Lipsitt (Eds.), *Advances in child development and behaviour* (pp. 163–206), Vol. 15. New York: Academic Press.

Glass, A., & Riding, R. J. (2000). EEG differences and cognitive style. *Biological Psychology*. (51, 23–4).

Harvey, O. J, Hunt, D. E, and Schroder, H. M. (1961). *Conceptual systems and personality organisation*. New York: Wiley.

Kagan, J., Rosman, B., Day, D., Albert, J., & Philips, W. (1964). Information processing and the child: Significance of analytic and reflective attitudes. *Psychological Monographs*, 78, 578.

Klein, G. S. (1954). Need and regulation. In M. P. Jones, (Ed.), *Nebraska symposium on motivation* (pp.) Lincoln: University of Nebraska Press.

Kline, P. (1991). *Intelligence: The psychometric view*. London: Routledge.

Kline, P. (1995). A critical review of the measurement of personality and intelligence. In D. H. Saklofske & M. Zeidner (Eds.)., *International handbook of personality and intelligence* (pp. 505–524). New York: Plenum Press.

Miller, A. (1987). Cognitive styles: An integrated model. *Educational Psychology*, 7, 251–268.

Paivio, A. (1971). Styles and strategies of learning. *British Journal of Educational Psychology*, 46, 128–148.

Rayner, S., & Riding, R. J. (1996). Cognitive style and school refusal. *Educational Psychology*, 16, 445–451.

Rayner, S., & Riding, R. J. (1997). Towards a categorisation of cognitive styles and learning styles. *Educational Psychology*, 17, 5–28.

Riding, R. J. (1991a). *Cognitive styles analysis*. Birmingham, England: Learning and Training Technology.

Riding, R. J. (1991b). *Cognitive styles analysis user manual*. Birmingham, England: Learning and Training Technology.

Riding, R. J. (1994). *Personal style awareness and personal development*. Birmingham, England: Learning and Training Technology.

Riding, R. J. (1997). On the nature of cognitive style. *Educational Psychology*, 17, 29–50.

Riding, R. J. (1999). *Information processing index.* Birmingham, England: Learning and Training Technology.

Riding, R. J., & Agrell, C. (1997). The effect of cognitive style and cognitive skills on school subject performance. *Educational Studies, 23,* 311–323.

Riding, R. J., & Al-Hajji, J. (2000). Cognitive style and behaviour in secondary school pupils in Kuwait. *Educational Research, 42,* 29–42.

Riding, R. J., & Al-Salih, N. (2000). Cognitive style and motor skill and sports performance. *Educational Studies, 26,* 19–32.

Riding, R. J., & Al-Sanabani, S. (1998). The effect of cognitive style, age, gender and structure on recall of prose passages. *International Journal of Educational Research, 29,* 173–185.

Riding, R. J., & Anstey, L. (1982). Verbal–imagery learning style and reading attainment in eight-year-old children. *Journal of Research in Reading, 5,* 57–66.

Riding, R. J., & Ashmore, J. (1980). Verbaliser–imager learning style and children's recall of information presented in pictorial versus written form. *Educational Studies, 6,* 141–145.

Riding, R. J., & Baker, G.(2000). *Cognitive style and school attendance in secondary school pupils.* Manuscript submitted for publication.

Riding, R. J., & Buckle, C. F. (1990). *Learning styles and training performance.* Sheffield, England: Training Agency.

Riding, R. J., & Burton, D. (1998). Cognitive style, gender and conduct behaviour in secondary school pupils. *Research in Education, 59,* 38–49.

Riding, R. J., Burton, D., Rees, G., & Sharratt, M. (1995). Cognitive style and personality in 12-year-old children. *British Journal of Educational Psychology, 65,* 113–124.

Riding, R. J., & Calvey, I. (1981). The assessment of verbal–imagery learning styles and their effect on the recall of concrete and abstract prose passages by eleven-year-old children. *British Journal of Psychology, 72,* 59–64.

Riding, R. J., & Cheema, I. (1991). Cognitive styles—An overview and integration. *Educational Psychology, 11,* 193–215.

Riding, R. J., & Craig, O. (1998). Cognitive style and problem behaviour in boys referred to residential special schools. *Educational Studies, 24,* 205–222.

Riding, R. J., & Craig, O. (2000). Cognitive style and types of problem behaviour in boys special schools. *British Journal of Educational Psychology, 69,* 307–322.

Riding, R. J., & Douglas, G. (1993). The effect of cognitive style and mode of presentation on learning performance. *British Journal of Educational Psychology, 63,* 297–307.

Riding, R. J., & Dyer, V.A. (1980). The relationship between extraversion and verbal–imagery learning styles in 12 year old children. *Personality and Individual Differences, 1,* 273–279.

Riding, R. J., Glass, A., Butler, S. R., & Pleydell-Pearce, C. W. (1997). Cognitive style and individual differences in EEG alpha during information processing. *Educational Psychology, 17,* 219–234.

Riding, R. J., Glass, A., & Douglas, G. (1993). Individual differences in thinking: Cognitive and neurophysiological perspectives. *Educational Psychology, 13,* 267–279.

Riding, R. J., & Grimley, M. (1999). Cognitive style and learning from multi-media materials in 11-year-old children. *British Journal of Educational Technology, 30,* 43–56.

Riding, R. J., & Grimley, M. (2000). *Cognitive style, gender and learning in 11-year-old children.* Manuscript submitted for publication.

Riding, R. J., & Mathias, D. (1991). Cognitive styles and preferred learning mode, reading attainment and cognitive ability in 11-year-old children. *Educational Psychology, 11,* 383–393.

Riding, R. J., & Pearson, F. (1994). The relationship between cognitive style and intelligence. *Educational Psychology, 14*, 413–425.

Riding, R. J., & Rayner, S. (1998). *Cognitive styles and learning strategies*. London: David Fulton.

Riding, R. J. & Rayner, S. (2000). *A cognitive style preventative intervention for improving behaviour and learning in secondary school pupils*. Manuscript submitted for publication.

Riding, R. J., Rayner, S., & Banner, G. (2000). *The effect of cognitive style and gender on second-language learning performance in 12-year-old pupils*. Manuscript submitted for publication.

Riding, R. J., & Read, G. (1996). Cognitive style and pupil learning preferences. *Educational Psychology, 16*, 81–106.

Riding, R. J., & Sadler-Smith, E. (1992). Type of instructional material, cognitive style and learning performance. *Educational Studies, 18*, 323–340.

Riding, R. J., & Sharratt, M. (2000). *Cognitive style and secondary examination performance*. Manuscript submitted for publication.

Riding, R. J., & Watts, M. (1997). The effect of cognitive style on the preferred format of instructional material. *Educational Psychology, 17*, 179–183.

Riding, R. J., & Wheeler, H. (1995). Occupational stress and cognitive style in nurses: 2. *British Journal of Nursing, 4*, 160–168.

Riding, R. J., & Wigley, S. (1997). The relationship between cognitive style and personality in further education students. *Personality and Individual Differences, 23*, 379–389.

Riding, R. J., & Wright, M. (1995). Cognitive style, personal characteristics and harmony in student flats. *Educational Psychology, 15*, 337–349.

Sadler-Smith, E., & Riding, R. J. (in press). Cognitive style and instructional preferences. *Instructional Science. 27*, 355–371.

Spielberger, C. D. (1977). *State and Trait Anxiety Inventory Form Y-1*. Palo Alto, CA: Consulting Psychologists Press.

Wiebe, D. J., & Smith, T. W. (1997). Personality and health: Progress and problems in psychosomatics. In R. Hogan, J. Johnson & S. Briggs (Eds.), *Handbook of personality psychology* (pp. 891–918). San Diego, CA: Academic Press.

Witkin, H. A., Oltman, P. K., Raskin, E., & Karp, S. A. (1971). *Manual for the Embedded Figures Tests*. Palo Alto, CA: Consulting Psychologists Press.

4

Enhancing Learning: A Matter of Style or Approach?

John Biggs
The University of Hong Kong

INDIVIDUAL DIFFERENCES AND EDUCATIONAL PRACTICE

Today, as in the past, it appears that of all the branches of psychology, differential psychology—the study of individual and group behavioral differences—is the most germane to discussion of the problems of education.

—Jensen (1973, p. 1)

Twenty-five years later, Jensen's view is one that many today would still support, although the nature of the individual differences targeted would be different. Current interest is probably not now so much in powerful earthmovers like general intelligence or in more qualitatively differentiated creators of competence, such as multiple intelligences (Gardner, 1983) or emotional intelligence (Goleman, 1996). The debate between those Gardner mysteriously calls the "hedgehogs," who like Jensen believe in a single function designating mental power, and the "foxes," who like Gardner believe there are several independent ways in which people manifest their competence, is an old one. At the present time, the foxes might seem to be winning, the weight of the evidence suggesting that the full range of intelligent behaviors is not completely captured by any single general ability (Sternberg, 1996).

A different version of the latter argument—possibly by a decorticated fox, but the more stylish and clever racoon comes to mind—would refer not to different abilities, but to *styles*. The fact that individuals go about similar tasks in different ways, or do especially well in some kinds of tasks but poorly in others, may be addressed in terms of their style of operating in the world. Style refers to how you go about a task, ability refers to how well you do a task, and the correlation between style and abilities should be low. In Sternberg's (1997) view, that correlation is often not low enough, so he makes the distinction between styles based on differing patterns of abilities (basically, cognitive styles and learning styles) and styles based on differing preferences for operating one way as opposed to another (thinking styles). Information-processing styles (see the following discussion) also appear to be preference based. The educational implications of the different ability and style models are different, but all could agree with Jensen (1973) that the study of individual differences is psychology's greatest gift to education.

Others however would flatly disagree with the basic individual difference premise, and would argue instead that educators should focus on contextual rather than on within-child factors. In this view, educational theory is to be generated bottom up, not applied top down from psychology (Biggs, 1976a; Burden, 1992; Snow, 1974). As Schon (1987) puts it, "Education is a soft slimy swamp of real-life problems" (p. 3) that makes clean top-down applications hard to make. Educational research deals not with a linear, causal sequence of independent and dependent variables, but with "clouds of correlated events . . . [that] mutually define each other" (Salomon, 1991, p. 13). Certainly, individual differences inhabit the clouds, but their nature and their effects are continually changing. The events involved in teaching and learning form an interactive system, where the outcomes cannot be satisfactorily accounted for by any one set of factors, within or without the learner's skin (Biggs, 1993a). Let us then add badgers to the menagerie, tenacious little animals that stick close to the ground. Badgers take a *systemic* view of the relation between theory and practice.

Two badgers from Sweden derived the concept of *approach to learning*. Marton and Saljo (1976a, 1976b) asked students to read a short passage of text and report back what they had learned. They described two main ways the students learned. Some used a "deep" approach, others a "surface" approach, each approach being reliably associated with a particular kind of learning outcome. This study is described in more detail later. The point is that these differences were not interpreted as individual differences between students, in classic psychological fashion, but as different kinds of relations between learner and task. A "deep" approach describes an adaptive relation, a "surface" approach describes a maladaptive relation. It is thus misleading to describe deep and surface approaches as learning "styles" that inhere in an individual (Schmeck, 1988), because, like a marriage relationship, an approach to learning can exist only in the presence of both parties: the learner and what is being learned, not the learner alone. The conceptual background and the rationale of approaches to learning are different from those typifying the styles literature, and implications for the enhancement of learning are correspondingly different.

Approaches to learning have since become generic concepts in a new genre of educational research, student approaches to learning (SAL), referred to with badger-like territoriality as simply "student learning" research (Entwistle & Waterston, 1988). One stream of this genre is based on the metatheory of constructivism (Biggs, 1996a), the other on phenomenography (Marton & Booth, 1997). Both streams have been influential in the United Kingdom, in Continental Europe, in Australia, and lately in Hong Kong, both as a research paradigm and as the conceptual foundation for instructional design, staff development, and quality enhancement (Biggs, 1999; Marton & Bowden, 1999; Prosser & Trigwell, 1999). Student learning research has so far had little effect in the United States, probably because the study of students learning has already been staked out variously by the hedgehogs, foxes, and racoons in the psychological establishment.

In sum, relations between theory and educational practice are for initial convenience expressed in an extension of Gardner's (1983) bestiary. Hedgehogs and foxes rely on abilities, either general or specific, and racoons rely on style; all operate from an individual differences model, whereby people take their powers and their quirks to the tasks presented to them. Badgers are different. They stick close to the ground and take each task as it comes.

In this chapter I elaborate on these relationships, with particular reference to the implications for enhancing learning. I first consider styles, distinguishing among cognitive, learning, information processing, and thinking styles, each of which has something different to say about my focus question, the improvement of learning. I then consider a different concept, but one that has been confused with that of style: approach to learning.

THE CONCEPT OF STYLE

Cognitive Style

Cognitive styles were described by Gardner, Holzman, Klein, Linton, and Spence (1959) as developmentally stabilized cognitive controls that are relatively invariant over situations. Originally thought to be independent of ability, it soon became clear that many styles were adaptive over a broad range of tasks, especially school tasks. Examples are cognitive complexity (Harvey, Hunt, & Schroder, 1961), reflection–impulsivity (Kagan, 1966), and field dependence–independence (Witkin, Dyk, Faterson, Goodenough, & Karp, 1962).

In cognitive styles research, people are typically classified as *high* or *low* on a style according to their performance in a given criterion task or test, and then the highs are compared with the lows on how they handle other tasks and characteristics. Witkin et al., for instance, used a startling tilting chair test (judging verticality of a stimulus when unknowingly in a tilted environment), a structurally similar task (judging verticality of a rod in a tilted frame), and the familiar (EFT) (the old child's game of "find as many animals as you can in the picture"; a hedgehog would find this test similar to a Wechsler IQ subtest). Thus was field dependence–independence born, a construct that has been widely applied, and the methodology of which led to the reporting of many other such styles—too many in fact. It seemed to have come to the point where anyone who wished to "discover" a new style devised an interestingly different test situation and then compared high and low scorers across a wide front to find in what other ways they might happen to differ from each other (by definition, the literature citations needed to support this statement would occupy more space than they would be worth). Some years ago I was reviewing the styles literature to draw educational implications. I arrived at 18 different styles, then came across Kogan's (1971) review, which added another 8 to my list. I did not finish my review, convinced there had to be better ways of looking at educationally relevant individual differences.

In part as a reaction against this situation, the concept of *learning* style appeared around the 1970s, which, unlike cognitive style, was focused on educational situations where the style concept was seen as most useful (Riding & Cheema, 1991). One model of learning style that was particularly influential was that of Kolb (1976), who based his model on an "experiential" learning theory. He proposed four abilities: to experience, to reflect, to conceptualize, and to experiment. These abilities are based on two bipolar dimensions—concrete–abstract and active–reflective—that intersect to yield four quadrants. Learning styles are said to result from the particular quadrant in which person's cognitive strengths lie: abstract–active yields the "converger"; concrete–reflective, the "diverger"; abstract–reflective, the "assimilator"; and concrete–active, the "accommodator" (the "terminator" was left to Hollywood to invent). Optimal performance in different academic subjects is said to require one style over another.

The styles are measured by the Learning Style Inventory LSI (Kolb, 1976), which Hudak (1985) claimed to be of low reliability and of questionable validity, claiming "the onus is to demonstrate that the construct 'learning style' has reality and relevance" (p. 409). Honey and Mumford (1986) produced the related Learning Style Questionnaire (LSQ), renaming the styles *activist, reflector, theorist* and *pragmatist*. The LSQ is more reliable than Kolb's LSI and appears to measure abilities more directly (Allinson & Hayes, 1990). The usefulness of Kolb's formulations remains to be properly established.

One major difficulty with all such styles is that they are conceived as bipolar (e.g., field dependent versus field independent) and as independent of context. For example, field-independent individuals are said to be able to separate relevant cues from compelling, irrelevant cues, and they are therefore good at finding simple figures embedded in more complex figures, but manifest poor social skills, such as facial recognition. So what would you predict about the relative field dependence–independence of the Chinese or the Japanese? That living in highly collectivist societies they would be field dependent? Or because they use a character writing system relying on fine spatial discriminations that they would be field independent? The answer is both, depending on the context (Hansen-Strain, 1989). This may seem unsurprising, but if a style operates according to the context in which it is applied, it is no longer behaving as a general style, but as something else: in this case, much more like two separate abilities.

In fact, cognitive and learning styles typically address ability-like dimensions, which again is not surprising given that they are derived from good and poor performance on set tasks. Another problem is that they are used as typologies. Thus, whereas a fox like Guilford (1967) refers to convergent and divergent abilities on tests of which people may have high, medium, or low scores, a racoon like Kolb (1976) categorizes people as convergers or divergers. Such labeling is surely likely to increase the chances of misclassification, stereotyping, and reification.

Riding and Cheema (1991) tried to bring some consistency and economy to these formulations by pointing out that both conceptually and empirically cognitive and learning styles may be grouped into two main families:

1. holist–analytic, including inter alia field dependence–independence, reflection–impulsivity, and many others mentioned earlier;
2. verbalizer–imager, which reflects the preferred modality for handling data.

Further elaboration of these styles may be found in Riding, this volume.

Information Processing Styles

Another metaphor for construing the relation between the way students handle tasks and the nature of the outcome is derived from information processing. The information processing model is based on the assumption that "learning style assessed from a behavioral-process orientation is more likely to be useful than one based purely on a personality- or cognitive-style orientation" (Schmeck, Ribich, & Ramanaiah, 1977, p. 413).

Pask's (1976) model of learning styles might be dealt with under this heading. He found that students in classification experiments used two basic strategies: testing one limited hypothesis at a time (*serialist*) and testing more complex hypotheses simultaneously (*holist*). When students habitually adopted a particularly strategy, he said they exhibited a style of learning. Versatile Students who switched strategy as appropriate to the task were considered *versatile*, but those who stuck to one style to the exclusion of the other displayed *improvidence* (excessive use of the serialist strategy, resulting in the student being unable to relate elements to form a whole) or *globetrotting* (excessive use of the holist strategy, resulting in premature conclusions or unjustified overgeneralizations).

More commonly, writers in this tradition draw on levels of processing theories of memory, and research on cognitive and metacognitive strategy use (Moreno & DiVesta, 1991; Schmeck et al., 1977; Weinstein, Schulte, & Palmer, 1987). The emphasis is less on unchanging individual character-istics as on the "on-line" cognitive strategies students use when handling tasks. There is, however, some ambiguity due partly to the method of operationalizing strategy use. Self-report questionnaires, which typically ask how students "usually" adopt this or that strategy or would "prefer" this or that strategy, almost inevitably access the domain of personal traits, not the process domain required by cognitive theory (Biggs, 1993b). Assessing traits rather than processes is also more likely when the instruments' scales are derived from item analyses using methodologies from individual differ-ence psychology, such as maximizing within-scale item correlations. Learn-ing process questionnaires of this kind include the Inventory of Learning Processes (ILP; Schmeck et al., 1977; Schmeck, Geisler-Brenstein, & Cercy 1991) and the Learning and Study Strategies Inventory (LASSI; Weinstein et al., 1987).

Constructs accessed by questionnaires deriving from information proc-essing (IP) theory are meant to be uncontaminated by motivation, affect, and context. Moreno and DiVesta (1991), for example, claim that IP mechanisms are universal and "culture-fair," a state obtained by defining item clusters from first-order factor analysis, a procedure said to exclude motivational and attitudinal aspects and to access directly "information processing control mechanisms" (p. 232). Nevertheless, given the item wording and the methodology, the extent to which the domain addressed is on-line processing, or a personological trait, is an interesting question.

Thinking Styles

Sternberg (1997) approached the problem of accounting for individual differences in handling various tasks in a different way from that underlying the other styles (see also Sternberg, this volume). He thought it important to separate styles from abilities, a conflation that is virtually inevitable when comparing "highs" and "lows" on a performance task. He sees styles more as *preferences* for doing things in a certain way. Preferences are a matter of degree, not of category, so that individuals may have a profile of styles, with one or more dominant. Thus, individuals with a particular style can achieve well if the task allows them to use their dominant style. A person's dominant style might be expected to coincide with his or her dominant abilities, but that may not be the case; when it is, performance is amplified, but when it is not, performance may not be good and the person will be frustrated.

Sternberg is noncommittal about the origins of styles, allowing the possibility of genetic origins, but also saying they appear to be modified by socialization. Here is another important difference from classic learning styles: being modifiable, they are to an extent teachable.

Also unlike previous style theorists, Sternberg derives his styles top down, not from performance on a test. For this, he uses a complex metaphor of mental self-government. Thus, like any civil government, styles have functions: legislative, executive, and judicial; they have forms: monarchic, hierarchic, oligarchic, and anarchic; they may operate on a global or a local level, be internal or external in cope, and liberal or conservative in leaning. Scales and constructs deriving from the government model have good empirical support (Sternberg, 1997).

Nevertheless, it is not clear why he chose this metaphor and not another one. It is possible that a different metaphor would produce a different complex of styles. Each of the metaphors of a business corporation, or of an army, or of a tour operator, or of a theatre company, could no doubt be unpacked to yield its own array of empirically sustainable styles. Be that as it may, Sternberg has departed in several important ways from prevailing formulations of cognitive and learning styles, and in so doing has clarified the concept of style itself and its relation to ability, and the educational implications are richer for that.

STYLES: IMPLICATIONS FOR ENHANCING LEARNING

Cognitive, learning, and thinking styles fit Cronbach and Snow's (1977) definition of an aptitude: a characteristic that promotes a student's performance in one kind of environment as opposed to another. Thus, if individuals high on the aptitude in question are matched with the appropriate context, or "treatment ," and individuals low on the aptitude are given the treatment appropriate to them, it is win-win for everybody. This relation is formalized in the *aptitude-treatment interaction* (ATI). However, significant disordinal interactions of this kind are rare, and providing for them is expensive if not impractical where more than one aptitude is addressed. A major exception to this is the preferred modality dimension mentioned by Riding and Cheema (1991); there is ample evidence that preferred modality interacts strongly with treatment (Moore & Scevak, 1997; see also Riding, this volume).

Sternberg's (1997) model is more flexible than the others because he explicitly allows that styles are teachable. This introduces the possibility of mismatching or matching, student with teaching environment. Matching a teaching environment to the student's dominant style would be done to optimize performance. Such matching might be with the teacher's style, or with the styles optimally required by the task. In this connection, Sternberg (1994) stressed that assessment tasks should be varied, so that learning outcomes can be assessed in ways that are comfortable to most students.

Mismatching a teaching environment would be done where a student's style profile is low on a desirable style that could usefully be strengthened. In this case, the individual's style repertoire is broadened and options for handling future complexity are increased. The aim here is not content learning, but increasing the potential range of a student's competence.

The difficulty with formally matching or mismatching student and environment is largely practical. Which styles do you choose? Does each high and low have its own workable teaching technology?

The above applications refer to the formal matching of instructional or assessment conditions and style. Styles can also be used by teachers in their informal interactions with students. Take the following exchange from Jones (1968):

> *Teacher*: Can anyone tell me what infinity means? (silence). What is infinity?
> *Billy*: Uh. I think it's like a box of Creamed Wheat.
> *Teacher*: Don't be silly! (p. 72)

Creamed Wheat boxes had a picture of a man holding up a box of Creamed Wheat, which had a picture of a man, ... Some knowledge about convergent and divergent abilities would have helped that teacher produce a more constructive and less damaging response. Teachers should know that when some students respond in unexpected ways, they are being genuine, and not just willfully irritating. This example also illustrates why learning outcomes might be assessed in several formats, as Sternberg (1994) suggested.

In sum, then, cognitive and learning styles work on the assumption that individual traits are fixed, or slightly modifiable, and that educational treatments have to work with or around them. Styles are conceived essentially as not sensitive to context, being static "in-built features of the individual" (Riding & Cheema, 1991, p. 196). Sternberg's (1997) thinking styles are less rigid in this respect, and his work has taken styles research ahead in that:

1. he gets away from the tyranny of polarities ("high X vs. low X"), which oversimplified a complex area;
2. he suggests a more fruitful and complex interaction with tasks; and
3. he is more optimistic in suggesting that exposure to other styles and tasks requiring nondominant styles tasks will extend a person's style repertoire.

Information processing styles offer different implications for enhancing learning. Information processing theorists see the strategies as context free and easily modifiable. That is, elaboration, imaging, rehearsal, and the like operate in much the same way whether the material being elaborated or rehearsed is being prepared for an examination or for a laboratory experiment; furthermore, these strategies can be taught. The major implication for enhancing learning is thus more interventionist than that deriving from the others styles, involving training students in the effective use of information processing strategies (Weinstein & Mayer, 1984).

Strategy training has a considerable literature and on the whole has had some success (Hattie, Biggs, & Purdie, 1996), but the extent to which strategy training can transfer across subject content, and across teaching and assessing contexts, is a matter of considerable debate. An interesting counterexample to the usual results of strategy training is a study by Ramsden, Beswick, and Bowden (1986), who trained first-year students from several faculties in a metacognitively oriented course in generic study skills. The only measurable result was an increase in surface or reproductive strategies. Students' perceptions of course demands told them that the reproduction of unintegrated detail was what was required of them (incorrectly, but that was what they perceived), so they projected that perception onto the study skills. Thus, it is not only a matter of teaching the "right" strategies, but making sure the students' perceptions of the teaching–learning context support the appropriate use of the strategies concerned.

The focus of all these styles is on what students bring to the context, rather than on the interaction between student and context. Applications from cognitive psychology suggest that learning takes place in a vacuum, whereas context has profound effects on learning and studying (Entwistle & Waterston, 1988). Others have queried top-down applications from psychology to education on similar grounds, often with a suggestion that they might even be harmful (Biggs, 1976a; Burden, 1992; Snow, 1974; Taylor, 1994). As many psychologists are likely to disagree profoundly with this, I shall for the remainder of this chapter examine the argument using the concepts of styles, and approaches to learning, as representing two positions on this question of using theory to enhance practice.

APPROACHES TO LEARNING

The student learning paradigm is derived directly from students' perceptions of context and on "qualitative analyses of students' reports of their own study processes" (Entwistle & Waterston, 1988, p. 258). Let us return to the original study by Marton and Saljo (1976a, 1976b). Students were asked to read academic articles and to describe what they had learned and how they had gone about learning it. It was found that what students learned depended on what they intended to gain from the article. They generally expressed one of two major intentions: to understand the author's intended meaning or to recall key terms or memorize details as accurately as possible, in anticipation of subsequent questions. Students having the first intention processed the text for meaning, focusing on themes and main ideas; those having the second, focused on words and sentences. These intentions and methods in reading the text were called the deep and surface approaches, respectively. The deep approach was associated with abstract, high-level accounts of the passage, with the details used for illustration and support, whereas the surface approach was associated with simple, factual statements about the details that overlooked the interconnections between them, thereby missing the author's point. As mentioned earlier, these findings were not seen as individual differences but as describing relations between students and task, an interpretation that led Marton to formulate his influential conceptual system he called *phenomenography* (Marton, 1981; Marton & Booth, 1997; see also Marton this volume).

But while phenomenography was gestating in Sweden, Entwistle in England was using individual differences psychology to derive his Approaches to Study Inventory (ASI; Entwistle & Ramsden, 1983), and Biggs in Australia was using information processing theory to derive the Study Process Questionnaire (SPQ; Biggs, 1987). Thus, both Entwistle and Biggs started out from a top-down position but later came to change their perspective. Why Biggs thought that to be necessary becomes apparent in the story of the development of the SPQ.

Work relating to the SPQ commenced in the 1960s with the notion that since a great deal of work had suggested small but consistent positive correlations between personality factors and academic performance, predictions of performance might be boosted through the mediation of students' study behavior (Biggs, 1970a; 1970b). Specifically, it was suggested that factors such as cognitive style, personality, and values would differentially emphasize coding and rehearsal strategies (Biggs, 1969), resulting in different ways of studying, which in turn would determine learning outcomes. The 10-scale Study Behaviour Questionnaire (Biggs, 1976b) was the result of that work.

A problem that dogged that instrument is one already noted in much of the style research; there were too many scales to be useful. Practitioners simply did not know where to start. Which of the 10 ways of studying are most relevant to teaching? Which lead to the most desirable outcomes, and under what conditions? The underlying IP theory did not provide any framework where such questions might be addressed.

A first step was to reduce the number of scales. Second-order factor analysis produced three higher order factors. When items were correlated with each of these higher order factor scores, those correlating highly with each factor score fell into two groups—affective and cognitive—which formed congruent motive–strategy combinations, like "will and skill" theory (Pintrich & deGroot, 1990). This is the situation that Moreno and DiVesta (1991) and IP theorists try to avoid, but out of it arose the motive–strategy congruence theory on which the SPQ was based (Biggs, 1978), with three motive–strategy "packages" (Table 4.1).

Thus, if you want to avoid failure, play it safe and get key facts and principles verbatim; if you want to satisfy your curiosity, try to understand what is going on; if you want to maximize grades, make best use of your time. It seems fairly banal when trimmed to essentials, but it led to many interesting questions and connections.

The first has to do with the stability of what is being discussed here. It was easy to label students as utilizers if they scored high on the utilizing scale, but does that describe a certain sort of person, or a simply a current state of

TABLE 4.1

The Original Study Process Questionnaire: Dimensions, Motives, and Strategies

	Utilizing[a]	Internalizing[b]	Achieving
Motive	Fear of failure	Intrinsic interest	Achievement
Strategy	Narrow target, rote learn	Maximize meaning	Effective use of space and time

[a]Later renamed "surface"; see text.
[b]Later renamed "deep"; see text.

mind? Empirically, it is true that some people go through their university careers with a constant metagoal: to do enough work to avoid failure, for example, and accordingly to develop a stable habit of selectively rote learning academic material, after which it's party time. But it is also true that a good teacher can make the academic earth move, causing fear of failure to give way to burning curiosity. Commonly, a student does the minimum possible in a "fill-in" subject, saving the academic big guns for the important subjects. I am not talking here about a surface style with a low test–retest reliability. It makes more sense to interpret what is happening here as a student who is working consistently and logically in an interpreted context.

Thus, although styles may be modifiable, essentially they act as independent variables, with some intrinsic stability; that is, they determine the events that follow, so that if what follows is a compatible task, performance is good, and if it is an incompatible task, performance is poor. High and low SPQ scorers, on the other hand, are expected to change their motives and strategies as their perceptions of context change, and to affect, and be affected by, the context. The original SPQ, then, was a three-factor instrument, with motive and strategy subscales on each, that were meant to reflect prevailing intentions and perceptions, not personality traits.

The similarity between the natures of the utilizing and internalizing concepts and Marton and Saljo's (1976a, 1976b) surface and deep concepts was apparent. Furthermore, the motive component in the SPQ dimensions paralleled Marton and Saljo's intentional component in surface and deep approaches. Both Marton and Biggs (1987) were saying, as was Entwistle (1998), that the use of strategies per se was not the point; they were deployed in a context the student had appraised and toward which they had intentions, sometimes honorable, sometimes dishonorable.

This coincidence was noted by adopting the "surface–deep" terminology, perhaps too hastily, because there was at least one important difference. Although Marton and Saljo used the term approach to learning to refer to what students actually do while handling the task, the SPQ and ASI questions asked students what they usually do while learning and studying.

The term approach to learning has thus been used to refer to two things: (a) the *processes* adopted during learning, which directly determine the outcome of learning, and (b) the *predispositions* to adopt particular processes. Entwistle (1988) referred to the latter as "orientations" to learning, which are (usually) addressed by questionnaires such as the ASI and SPQ. However, the term orientation did not catch on, which was unfortunate because "approach" was ambiguous, referring to activities performed while learning a specific task, or to preferences for using certain classes of activities, or to both. In the interests of clarity, I resurrect "orientation" here to refer to preferences or predispositions to use a particular approach. The following descriptions apply equally well to approach and orientation.

The *surface approach* is based on a motive or intention that is extrinsic to the real purpose of the task. The task is seen as a hurdle to be cleared as expeditiously as possible, with as little time and effort invested as needed to meet requirements. Thus, low cognitive level activities are used when higher level activities are required to do the task properly. Rote learning content without understanding is one of the most common ways of doing this, but it is not the only way. Rote learning does not in itself mean that the student is adopting a surface approach, because rote learning is quite appropriate when verbatim recall is required; it is "surface" when inappropriate, for example when a student memorizes answers to previous examination questions.

The *deep approach* is based on a perceived need, such as intrinsic interest, to engage the task appropriately and meaningfully. The focus is thus on underlying meaning, not on detail in itself; on main ideas, themes, and principles, rather than on conceptually unsupported specifics. A deep approach, using analogy, metaphor, and the sort of conceptual structure that enables the student to "think high ," requires a sound foundation of relevant prior knowledge. The particular strategies that are optimal for creating meaning depend on the task in question, and the readiness with which these are activated depends on the quality of teaching (discussed later). The essence of the deep approach is that the student is engaging the task with learning processes that are appropriate to completing it satisfactorily.

The *achieving approach* is based on the ego enhancement that comes out of visibly achieving, in particular, by obtaining high grades. The focus is on the recognition gained from top performance. The main strategy is to organize time, working space, and syllabus coverage cost effectively seeking cues, using study skills, planning ahead, and allocating time according to task importance. The achieving motive is related more to personality than to deep or surface motives, although achieving strategies are regularly taught in study skills courses, often to good effect although there can be problems

The three approaches are associated with qualitatively different outcomes (Biggs, 1979; Marton & Saljo, 1976a; Trigwell & Prosser, 1991; Watkins, 1983). The outcomes of surface learning are always inappropriate as far as the task is concerned, as the underlying meaning tends to become lost in lists of unconnected detail. However, from the student's point of view, the surface approach may produce desirable outcomes of a different sort (e.g., the expenditure of less effort in uninteresting or personally irrelevant subjects). The outcomes of deep learning are likely to be high quality and appropriate. The achieving approach, not unexpectedly, is associated with high grades (Biggs, 1987).

The above generalizations are made with approach, not necessarily orientation, in mind. SPQ and ASI orientation scores correlate in these expected ways with outcome if the immediate context is believed to activate the individual's orientations. For example, instructions to read for facts and details are matched with students' surface orientations, and instructions to read for understanding are matched with students' deep orientations (Biggs, 1979). Similarly, a deep orientation correlates with performance in the student's favorite subject (Biggs, 1987). In these cases, orientation and outcome are strongly related.

Orientations are as much dependent variables as they are independent. An orientation is not a stable trait of the individual, as is implied when it is mistakenly identified with learning style, but it is instead a function of individual characteristics and the teaching context. In this, it is like motivation. Motivation is not a substance, something students need to possess before teaching may proceed and without which learning is preempted and teaching impossible. Good teaching creates learner motivation. This is also true for deep learning, which is as much a product of effective teaching as is motivation. Both teacher and student are jointly responsible for the outcome: the teacher for structuring the enabling conditions, the learner for engaging them. Thus, an approach to learning describes the nature of the relation among student, context, and task.

Approaches in the SAL framework, then, are only meaningful in context. They are related to student intentions and the existential teaching–learning context on the one hand, and to the quality of the learning outcome on the other. In this, approaches are in contrast both to learning styles and to the constructs accessed by questionnaires deriving from IP theory.

APPROACHES TO LEARNING: IMPLICATIONS FOR ENHANCING LEARNING

As approaches to learning are part of the teaching–learning system, they need to be considered in conjunction with the system as a whole. The "3P" model of teaching and learning (Biggs, 1993a) is an attempt to represent this system. The 3P model is generalized from Dunkin and Biddle's (1974) original model of teaching, which described three points at which teaching-related factors are placed: presage, before teaching takes place; process, during teaching; and product, the outcome of teaching (hence the 3P model). The thrust here is on learning rather than on teaching, and because

I am dealing with an interactive system, all components affect all others, so the arrows flow in both directions.

Presage factors are of two kinds:

1. *Student based*: the relevant prior knowledge the student has about the topic, interest in the topic, student ability, commitment to university, and so on. In the present context, I distinguish "hard" (not easily changed by teaching) from "soft" (relatively docile) student presage factors.

   Hard: abilities or intelligences, cognitive styles, learning styles, probably thinking styles, but the extent of their docility is unclear as yet.

   Soft: motivation, orientations to learning.
2. *Teaching and context based*: aims and curriculum objectives, teaching and learning activities, assessment tasks and context, the expertise of the teacher, the "climate" or ethos of the classroom and of the institution itself, and so on.

These factors influence each other: the hard presage factors influence the soft, and the soft and the teaching context mutually interact at the process level to determine the student's immediate learning-related activities, that is, their approaches to learning. Many interactions are possible. A student with little prior knowledge of the topic will be unlikely to use a deep approach, even where the teaching is expert. Another student, who already

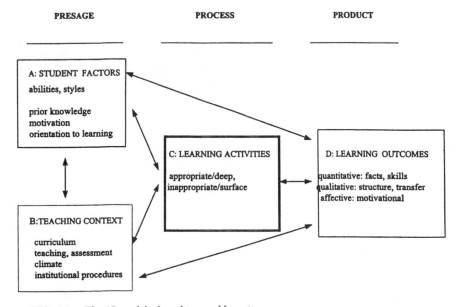

FIG. 4.1.   The 3P model of teaching and learning.

knows a great deal and is interested in the topic, is preset for a deep approach, but will be unlikely to use it if stressed by, for example, time pressure. Yet another student, who typically picks out likely items for assessment and rote learns them, finds that strategy won't work under portfolio assessment and so goes deeper. It is inappropriate to categorize students as surface or deep learners, because their approach depends on context.

As a result of the students' perceptions of the context and of their own goals, feelings of self-efficacy, attributions, and so on, they engage the task using learning activities that may be appropriate (deep) or inappropriate (surface). Appropriateness is defined in terms of curriculum goals and the students own personal goals, both long term and immediate.

The product refers to the outcomes achieved, which may be complex structures, lists of factual information, self-information such as attributions for success and failure, feelings of efficacy, and the like. All such outcomes can provide feedback to the players at the presage level: to the students and the teachers.

Approaches to learning can emerge as quality indicators at all three levels: at the process level, where students engage the task with a deep or surface approach; as a product of a learning episode, when poor teaching induces a surface approach and good teaching a deep approach; and at presage, when students develop orientations appropriate to the context, learning what works and what doesn't for each teaching situation. Approaches to learning thus tell us when the system is working (when orientations, processes, and outcomes are predominantly deep) and when it is not (when orientations, processes, and outcomes are predominantly surface). The key is at the process level, where the learning-related activity produces or does not produce the desired outcomes. As Shuell (1986) puts it:

> If students are to learn desired outcomes in a reasonably effective manner, then the teacher's fundamental task is to get students to engage in learning activities that are likely to result in their achieving those outcomes. It is important to remember that what the student does is more important than what the teacher does. (p. 429)

This statement provides a model for aligned teaching that is powerful (Biggs, 1999), but the relevance here is that it provides a framework for looking at approaches to learning in terms of the learning activities we want students to engage.

I have listed some in Fig. 4.2 generic activities, expressed as verbs, ranging from low cognitive level (memorize, identify), through intermediate level (comprehend main ideas, relate), to high level (apply to far

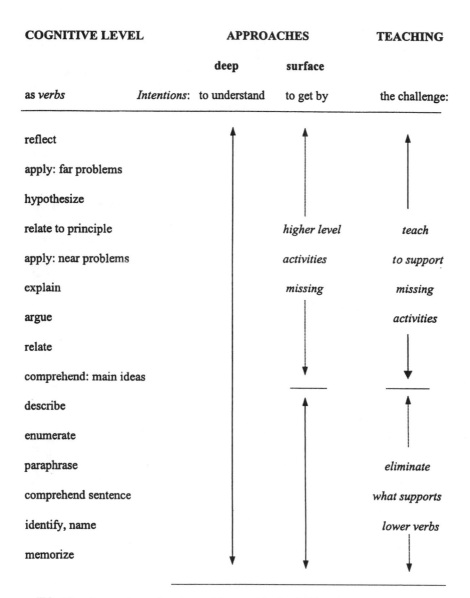

COGNITIVE LEVEL	APPROACHES		TEACHING
	deep	**surface**	
as *verbs*	*Intentions*: to understand	to get by	the challenge:
reflect			
apply: far problems			
hypothesize			
relate to principle		*higher level*	*teach*
apply: near problems		*activities*	*to support*
explain		*missing*	*missing*
argue			*activities*
relate			
comprehend: main ideas			
describe			
enumerate			
paraphrase			*eliminate*
comprehend sentence			*what supports*
identify, name			*lower verbs*
memorize			

FIG. 4.2. Approaches to learning and the cognitive level of learning activities.

domains, reflect). This hierarchy is framed in terms of the structural complexity and abstractness that follows the course of learning as described in the SOLO taxonomy (Biggs & Collis, 1982), where SOLO is an acronym for Structure of the Observed Learning Outcome. The verbs used and the objects they take are determined by the subject content and the level of learning desired, as determined by the teaching objectives.

In an ideal system, all students would be expected to activate the highest level verb, thus handling the task, or solving the problem, appropriately. Such would be a mastery system, where mastery is expressed qualitatively. In fact, we give credit for less than mastery, so that the level reached by a student becomes in effect an assessment, leading to a grading, but that raises different issues. The present concern is with the next two columns of Fig. 4.2. Say the task in question demands reflection as the highest activity used, with many supporting lower verbs (you have to know the terminology, understand principles, and so on to reflect effectively). A student using a deep approach would engage verbs across the entire range, but a student using a surface approach would use lower order verbs in lieu of the higher order. The following statements made by a psychology undergraduate student and quoted in Ramsden (1984) illustrates this:

> I hate to say it, but what you have got to do is to have a list of "facts"; you write down ten important points and memorize those, then you'll do all right in the test. . . . If you can give a bit of factual information—so and so did that, and concluded that—for two sides of writing, then you'll get a good mark. (p. 144)

Now, if the teacher of this student thought that an adequate understanding of psychology could be manifested by selectively memorizing, there would be no problem. But I don't think the teacher did think that. I see this as a case where an inappropriate assessment task allowed the students to get a good mark on the basis of memorizing facts. As it happened, this student wrote brilliant essays and later graduated with First Class Honours. The problem therefore is not that this student is irredeemably cursed with a surface style, but that under current conditions of teaching he made a strategic decision that a surface approach would see him through this task—as indeed it did.

Teaching and assessment methods often encourage a surface approach in this way, because they are not aligned to the aims of teaching the subject. The presence of a surface approach signals that something is out of kilter in our teaching or in our assessment methods, but that it is something we can hope to address. The approaches or orientations that prevail tell us something about the quality of the teaching environment, because students' orientations tend to adapt to the expected requirements. Thus, questionnaires such as the SPQ can be useful for evaluating teaching environments (Biggs 1993b; Kember, Charlesworth, Davies, McKay, & Stott, 1997) and are often more sensitive when reworded for a particular subject (Eley, 1992) or assessment task (Tang, 1991; Thomas & Bain, 1984).

A particularly depressing finding is that most students in most under-graduate courses become increasingly surface and decreasingly deep in their orientation to learning (Biggs, 1987; Gow & Kember, 1990; Watkins & Hattie, 1985). There are exceptions however. Students with aspirations for graduate study do not show this pattern in their chosen area of study (Biggs, 1987) nor do students taught using problem-based learning, who become increasingly deep and less surface in their orientations (Newble & Clark, 1986). For most undergraduate students, however, something is happening as they progress that increasingly supports the use of lower level verbs, which is of course the opposite of what is intended by a university education (Gow & Kember, 1990). One might call it the "institutionalization" of learning, whereby students tend to pick up the tricks that get you by, such as "memorizing the 10 most important points".

The last column in Figure 4.2, deals with the teaching challenge. To maximize optimal engagement by students, teachers need to eliminate what supports the lower verbs and to provide support for the missing high-er verbs.

Minimizing the Surface Approach

What in the teaching environment would support lower level activities than those needed? Individual differences psychology would tell us to look to the students for the source of the problem: they are low Level 2 ability, they are hyperactive, they have the wrong learning style, and so on. Whatever the problem might be, it resides in the students. In the end this might well prove to be true, but externalizing the problem in this way doesn't help teachers engage in reflective practice with a view to teaching better. Most teachers have to take the "hard" presage factors as given, and do their best with that; it is not their role to play psychologists to excuse unsatisfactory teaching and learning outcomes.

Impediments to higher level learning can reside in the instructional context, or in the teacher's personal style of teaching, or in both. A common problem is the obsession with coverage, that "enemy of under-standing" as Gardner (1993, p. 24) put it. In the soul searching following the Third International Math and Science Study (International Associa-tion for the Evaluation of Educational Achievement, 1996), in which the

United States performed worse than many third world southeast Asian countries, the U.S math curriculum was judged to be "a mile wide and an inch deep" (Stedman, 1997, p.10), whereas curricula in other countries were structured for depth. Where topics are brushed past the students and assessed with tests requiring little more than recognition (Porter, 1989), who can be surprised that high-level verbs aren't engaged?

Underlying such curriculum problems is the question of alignment. We might well have decided what topics to teach, but have we anticipated what a satisfactory student understanding of them might look like, and how we might test that to see that they do understand them in the way we want them to? A lesson plan "to cover Newton's Second Law" says what the teacher does, not what the student might have to do, to demonstrate the desired learning has taken place. The design of good instruction demands criterion-referenced assessment of this kind. Ramsden's (1984) psychology student was reacting to a classic case of poor alignment; there were gaps in the assessment system the students could waltz through. How the system can be aligned is dealt with in the next section.

But however well designed the system, teachers sometimes do and say things that communicate low verbs to the students. Questioning is one, which in U.S. classrooms Hess and Azuma (1991) describe in comparison to Japanese classrooms as "quick and snappy". A typical questioning style might be: "You. Tom. Yes, *you*! . . . Too slow. Think, boy, *think*! Sally, you tell him." This teaching style is even regarded by some as admirable, but such short wait time shatters any chances of high-order cognitive engagement; "thinking" is out of the question (Tobin, 1987).

This example also delivers several other teaching pathologies. It communicates to Tom that he is not as quick, not as bright, as Sally. His expectations for future success are to that extent diminished. It also communicates that the answers to the questions are not in themselves important; what is important is saying something, anything, as quickly as possible. This teacher has diminished both Tom's expectancy of success and the value of the task content. Both are necessary conditions of task engagement, as stated in the expectancy-value theory of motivation. Finally, Tom might now be expected to see public questioning as a scene for humiliation, so his future strategies would be directed toward avoiding future humiliation, not toward thinking high.

In short, anything in the teacher's teaching style that distracts from the main game, by engendering cynicism, anxiety, or maladaptive attributions, will focus the student onto lower order or irrelevant cognitive activities. The presence of surface approaches to learning gives the barometer reading.

Maximizing the Deep Approach

It is easy to see why aligned teaching should encourage deep learning. The curriculum is stated in the form of clear objectives, which include the level of understanding required rather than simply a list of topics to be covered. The teaching methods are chosen that are likely to realize those objectives: you get students to do the things the objectives nominate. The clearest example of this is problem-based learning. In a nutshell, the objective is to get the students to solve professional problems, the teaching method is to get them to solve problems, and the assessment is how well they solve the problems. Lecturing students about how to solve problems and giving them a multiple-choice test on problem solving is obviously poor alignment.

In short, assessment should be criterion referenced, so educators can know if the students have learned what the objectives say they should have learned, and how well. Had Ramsden's (1984) psychology teacher included in the objectives expressions such as, "theorize ," "generalize ," or even "comprehend the profundities of the founders of modern psychology ," an assessment task that required only paraphrasing "a bit of factual information for two pages of writing" would obviously be inadequate.

When objectives, teaching, and assessment are aligned, all components in the system address the same agenda and support each other with the same learning verbs. The students are "entrapped" in this web of consistency, optimizing the likelihood they will engage the appropriate learning activities, which is a deep approach by definition.

CONCLUSIONS: ONE SYSTEM, TWO PERSPECTIVES

The constructs of style and approach to learning come from two different schools of thought, and so implications for education are different. Styles derive from mainstream psychology, in particular, the psychology of individual differences. Psychologists are interested in the ways people reliably differ from each other, and a question such as, "How might we use this knowledge in order to enhance the learning of students in school and college?" may certainly be regarded as important, but it is in fact secondary to the main agenda, which is finding out things about children. Given that starting point, with the child as the given, the answer to the educational question becomes a matter of optimally arranging the educational context to suit the child. Do we formally match, or mismatch, teaching environments to student characteristics? How should teachers treat different kinds of children in appropriately different ways in everyday classroom interaction?

Approaches to learning, on the other hand, derive not from research conducted by psychologists to advance psychological theory, but by educators trying to understand what is going on in classrooms. The classroom system is the given, not the child or any other component of the system. The theory that generates teaching-related decisions and actions arises from the context; it is not imposed on it from outside. Of course, psychological constructs and tools are useful, but in service to the game, not in calling the shots. Simply, the psychologist is doing one thing, the student learning theorist another. At times they might overlap, but more frequently they appear to be over-lapping when in fact they are not, as for example when learning approaches are identified as learning styles.

The Case of Educational Assessment: To Educate or to Select?

A case where educational and psychological issues have been confused is that of assessment in education, where two conflicting models of assessment are used (Taylor, 1994). The measurement model was designed by psychologists to measure individual differences. The aim is to see as precisely as possible how individuals differ from each other, or from population norms, and then to make decisions about the individual on that basis. To do this, performances must be reduced to a single, calibrated unidimensional scale along which individuals can be placed. It is also assumed that the trait or characteristic being measured is stable, at least for as long as the decision applies. For example, when selecting students to go to graduate school, academic ability, the trait being measured, is assumed to correlate strongly with the required performances and remain constant, relative to other students, over the 2 or 3 years in question. If these were not so, the selection would be unfair. Similarly, the statistics and procedures used to select items and to establish the reliability of measuring instruments make the assumption that what is being measured is stable, and usually that it is normally distributed. The model does well what it is intended to do.

The trouble is, it has been used in an inappropriate context: attainment testing. Attainments are the results of learning and teaching, and the appropriate model for that is the criterion-referenced standards model. That is, following Shuell (1986), educators decide what are desirable outcomes, teach in such a way as to maximize their likelihood within available resources, and assess to see whether the standards have been met. If not, ideally one should go again until they are, as in mastery learning, or use a grading system that indicates how well they have been met. The target of assessment assumes change (it is called "learning"), so it would seem counterproductive to assess instruments constructed on the assumption of stability. Again, excellent teaching results in skewed distributions; the measurement model is based on normal distributions.

Instead, the most common assessment procedures in education have been based on the norm-referenced measurement model. Following are some examples: the procedure of quantifying ("marking") students' performances, when students don't learn numbers they learn understandings; conducting summative assessment analytically, where a task is broken into parts and arbitrarily quantified, when the desired understandings and performances are meaningful only as whole structures; constructing tests that deliberately produce a wide spread of scores; inserting questions on content that has not been taught to identify the "high fliers"; rank ordering students and grading on the curve; and structurally separating teaching and assessment, as happens in many universities. All such practices destroy alignment and create negative backwash that produces learning pathologies (Biggs, 1996b; Crooks, 1988; Frederiksen & Collins, 1989). The requirements of the measurement model and those of good teaching are juxtaposed in Table 4.2.

It is nothing short of astonishing that such incongruity between teaching and assessment practice could exist. Part of the problem is a genuine if tacit agreement with Jensen (1973) that individual differences between students is what education is about, that education is indeed a selective process. This

TABLE 4.2

The Demands of the Measurement Model and Those of Good Teaching

Measurement Model	Good Teaching
1. Performances need to be quantified, so they are reduced to correct or incorrect units of equivalent value that can be added.	Students learn holistic structures that cannot meaningfully be reduced to units of equal importance.
2. A good test creates "a good spread" between students, preferably normally distributed.	Good teaching produces reduced variance.
3. The characteristic being measured is stable over time.	Good teaching produces change: learning.
4. Students need to be tested under standardized conditions.	Students need to be tested under conditions that best reveal an individual's learning.

is reflected in the language and informal working theories of teachers, administrators, and even parents, despite the rhetoric of the official aims of education in most systems (Shepard, 1991). Thus, in the United States and most Western countries, as opposed to Asian countries, success and failure are attributed primarily to ability, not to effort (Holloway, 1988). It is taken as given in the West that only a few should succeed well, whereas Asian educators expect most children to master what is taught (Stevenson & Stigler, 1991).

The sheer convenience of the measurement model reinforces such beliefs and practices. Teachers need only decide what topics to "cover"; cover them, it is hoped by doing more than talking about them; and give a test, which only needs to produce a numerical and preferably spread-out distribution of scores. The results of assessment can easily be added, averaged, and combined in whatever ways are convenient. But as Table 4.2 suggests, alignment has disappeared. There is no necessary connection between what should have been learned and what has been tested. The substance of learning itself goes unmonitored and unevaluated. What we do know is who is better than whom at test taking, which may be useful information to have, but it is not why most students go to school or college.

How Do We Cater to Individual Differences in Education?

I mention educational assessment simply to illustrate how direct applications from psychology to education can go badly wrong. Of course, this is not the fault of the psychologists who produced the model, which works beautifully in the right context, but that of educators for using it so inappropriately.

To return to the issue of enhancing learning, then, what is it to be: styles or approaches? Perhaps each has it own contribution. It would be easy to suggest that where we are talking about learning focused content, such as mastery of basic skills, or professional education, where prescribed bodies of knowledge must be learned before accreditation, we seem to be talking about a straightforward criterion-referenced system: clear objectives, specifying certain standards, that assessments indicate have or have not been reached.

However, most educational systems also have another kind of aim: the development of individual potential. Thus, through nature and nurture, or both, individuals have a potential repertoire of talents, abilities, and styles. It is education's role to help them realize those strengths and to develop their weaknesses, thereby making them more effective individuals and making society the richer for it. It seems reasonable that through individual differences psychologists cannot only help identify what those strengths and weaknesses might be, but can also develop a technology for optimizing them. But whose formulation of those individual differences, out of the many that have promulgated, do we take? Should it be Guilford's (1967) 120 factors, Gardner's (1983) seven intelligences, or possibly even Jensen's (1973) Level 1 and Level 2? Or should we move away from an abilities model and focus on Sternberg's (1997) thinking styles? Should it be 13 of them, or just a selection? Have we the technology yet for knowing how best to teach to each, either when matching or mismatching the student's styles? I don't think we are nearer any practical resolution of these issues than we were in the 1970s, when the focus was on different aptitudes. But certainly it is a logical way to proceed, and maybe with more research and development we could go down this road.

It is clear that some individual differences catalyze certain kinds of learning and inhibit others, whereas other differences produce their own optimal patterns and kinds of learning. Any formal attempt at a version of ATI as a strategy for doing educational work may be premature at this time. However, it is practical to acquaint teachers with the important dimensions of individual difference, so they are aware of and sensitive to them in their everyday classroom interaction with students.

Now let us look at this another way. The individual differences are some of the hard presage factors in Fig. 4.1, which are just as much part of the system as any other component. The alternative to imposing solutions from top down—hoping the right variables have been nominated—is to open up the system to help it achieve its own equilibrium. I am reminded of Hunt (1971), who did something like this in his handling of the problem of ATI. He presented a smorgasbord of five teaching styles to senior high school students, who were given 3 weeks to sample the styles and choose the style in which they felt most comfortable for the rest of the semester. The styles were differentiated on the basis of low to high structure, which allowed varying degrees of student choice and independence. The problem of identifying and measuring a particular aptitude or thinking style was thus obviated, while still catering to educationally relevant individual differences. There are here some obvious logistic difficulties—five parallel teaching contexts for students to choose from?—but the idea that the "aptitude" should be defined on educational grounds, rather than in terms of a score on a psychological test that measures some hypothetical aptitude, is important. It addresses the problem from within the system, instead of imposing it from without.

It is probably not necessary to set up alternative classroom systems, which in most instances would be unrealistic, but to set up alternative components within the classroom system. There are levels at which there is room for student choice, if desired, without the need to specify which individual differences are important and which are not. For instance, students could negotiate their own objectives, to be attained in ways that suited them, which is virtually what student–teacher contracts do already. This sort of arrangement is likely to be more common at college and university as off-campus flexible learning systems are used. Likewise, the students can begin to take control over their assessment procedures. Usually, the teacher decides what mode of assessment to use. In the interests of fairness, because of students' different thinking styles, teachers could make sure they provide a suitably wide range of alternatives (Sternberg, 1994). If a teacher suggests assessment by a student-selected portfolio of items, students can simply put in the portfolio what they think represents their best relevant performances (Biggs, 1999). If we genuinely do see students as constructing their own learning, it seems bizarre, like choosing to shoot fish in muddy water rather than in clear water, to ask them closed questions that only allow them to respond to our constructions of the content. If some students think they can best display their learning on the basis of multiple-choice test results, so be it. Those of legislative bent might prefer more structurally complex and inclusive ways of displaying their learning. Either way, it is up to them. In doing this, they also have to make the appropriate metacognitive judgments as to the mode and quality of their learning, which is itself a valuable learning experience. The variance, in other words, is in the teaching and assessment processes, not in the outcomes.

However, my aim in this chapter is not to discuss instructional design, but to try to elucidate where psychology and education can most fruitfully interact. The contrast between learning and thinking styles, and approaches to learning, I think has brought out the key issues. Actually, I believe James (1899/1962) made the point 100 years ago:

> I say moreover you make a great, a very great mistake, if you think that psychology, being the science of the mind's laws, is something from which you can deduce definite programs and schemes and methods of instruction for immediate classroom use. . . . Teaching must agree with the psychology, but need not necessarily be the only kind of teaching that would so agree; for many diverse methods of teaching may equally well agree with psychological laws. (p. 3)

The science of the mind's laws has advanced considerably in the intervening 100 years, but James' point is well taken. He thought the design of teaching came from the "art" of the teacher, the product of "an intermediary and inventive mind." And so it is—as indeed is psychology itself the product of such a mind—but education like psychology also needs its own database. The database for education derives from within the system, of which the mind's laws—the hard presage factors if you like—are part, whereas the students' approaches to learning give the barometer readings that tell how well the general system is working.

REFERENCES

Allinson, C., & Hayes J. (1990). Validity of the Learning Styles Questionnaire. *Psychological Reports, 67*, 859–866.

Biggs, J. B. (1969). Coding and cognitive behaviour. *British Journal of Psychology, 60*, 287–305.

Biggs, J. B. (1970a). Faculty patterns in study behaviour. *Australian Journal of Psychology, 22*, 161–174.

Biggs, J. B. (1970b). Personality correlates of some dimensions of study. *Australian Journal of Psychology, 22*, 287–297.

Biggs, J. B. (1976a). Educology: The theory of educational practice. *Contemporary Educational Psychology, 1*, 274–284.

Biggs, J. B. (1976b). Dimensions of study behaviour: Another look at ATI. *British Journal of Educational Psychology, 46*, 68–80.

Biggs, J. B. (1979). Individual differences in study processes and the quality of learning outcomes. *Higher Education, 8*, 381–394.

Biggs, J. B. (1987). *Student approaches to learning and studying.* Camberwell, Australia: Australian Council for Educational Research.

Biggs, J. B. (1993a). From theory to practice: A cognitive systems approach. *Higher Education Research and Development, 12*, 73–86.

Biggs, J. B. (1993b). What do inventories of students' learning processes really measure? A theoretical review and clarification. *British Journal of Educational Psychology, 63*, 1–17.

Biggs, J. B. (1996a). Enhancing teaching through constructive alignment. *Higher Education, 32*, 1–18.

Biggs, J. B. (1996b). Assessing learning quality: Reconciling institutional, staff, and educational demands. *Assessment and Evaluation in Higher Education, 21*, 3–15.

Biggs, J. B. (1999). *Teaching for quality learning at university.* Buckingham, UK: The Open University Press.

Biggs, J. B., & Collis, K. (1982). *Evaluating the quality of learning: The SOLO Taxonomy.* New York: Academic Press.

Burden, B. (1992). Educational psychology: Force that is spent or one that never got going? *The Psychologist, 10*(3), 110–111.

Cronbach, L. J., & Snow, R. E. (1977). *Aptitudes and instructional methods.* New York: Irvington (Wiley).

Crooks, T. J. (1988). The impact of classroom evaluation practices on students. *Review of Educational Research, 58*, 438–481.

Dunkin, M. J., & Biddle, B. J. (1974). *The study of teaching.* New York: Holt, Rinehart & Winston.

Eley, M. G. (1992). Differential adoption of study approaches within individual students. *Higher Education, 23*, 231–254.

Entwistle, N. (1988). Motivational factors in students' approaches to learning. In R. R. Schmeck (Ed.), *Learning strategies and learning styles* (pp. 21–51). New York: Plenum.

Entwistle, N., & Ramsden, P. (1983). *Understanding student learning.* London: Croom Helm.

Entwistle, N. & Waterston, S. (1988). Approaches to studying and levels of processing in university students. *British Journal of Educational Psychology, 58,* 258–265.

Frederiksen, J. R., & Collins, A. (1989). A systems approach to educational testing. *Educational Researcher, 18*(9), 27–32.

Gardner, H. W. (1983). *Frames of mind: The theory of multiple intelligences.* London: Paladin Books.

Gardner, H. W. (1993). Educating for understanding. *The American School Board Journal,* July, 20–24.

Gardner, R., Holzman, P., Klein, G., Linton, H., & Spence, D. (1959). Cognitive control: A study of individual consistencies in cognitive behavior. *Psychological Issues, 1*(4), Monograph 4.

Goleman, D. (1996). *Emotional intelligence.* London: Bloomsbury.

Gow, L., & Kember, D. (1990). Does higher education promote independent learning? *Higher Education, 19,* 307–322.

Guilford, J. P. (1967). *The nature of human intelligence.* New York: McGraw-Hill.

Hansen-Strain, L. (1989). Student and teacher cognitive styles in second language classrooms. In V. Bickley (Ed.), *Language teaching and learning styles within and across cultures* (pp. 218–226). Hong Kong: Institute of Language in Education.

Harvey, O. J., Hunt, D. E., & Schroder, H. M. (1961). *Conceptual systems and personality organization.* New York: Wiley.

Hattie, J., Biggs, J., & Purdie, N. (1996). Effects of learning skills interventions on student learning: A meta-analysis. *Review of Educational Research, 66,* 99–136.

Hess, R. D. & Azuma, H. (1991). Cultural support for schooling: Contrasts between Japan and the United States. *Educational Researcher, 20*(19), 2–8.

Holloway, S. D. (1988). Concepts of ability and effort in Japan and the United States. *Review of Educational Research, 58,* 327–343.

Honey, P., & Mumford, A. (1986). *The manual of learning styles.* Berkshire, UK: Peter Honey

Hudak, M. (1985). Review of "Learning Styles Inventory". In D. Keyser & R. Sweetland (Eds.), *Test critiques,* volume II. Kansas City, KS: Test Corporation of America.

Hunt, D. E. (1971). *Matching models in education.* (Monograph series No. 10) Toronto, Ontario Institute for Studies in Education.

International Association for the Evaluation of Educational Achievement. (1996). *The third international math and science study.* Paris: OECD.

James, W. (1899/1962). *Talks to teachers.* New York: Henry Holt/ Dover Books.

Jensen, A. R. (1973). *Educational differences.* London: Methuen.

Jones, R. M. (1968). *Fantasy and feeling in education.* New York: New York University Press.

Kagan, J. (1966). Reflection–impulsivity: The generality and dynamics of conceptual tempo. *Journal of Abnormal Psychology, 71,* 17–27.

Kember, D., Charlesworth, M., Davies, H., McKay, J., & Stott, V. (1997). Evaluating the effectiveness of educational innovations: Using the Study Process Questionnaire to show that meaningful learning occurs. *Studies in Educational Evaluation, 23*(2), 141–157.

Kogan, N. (1971). Educational implications of cognitive styles. In G. Lesser (Ed.), *Psychology and educational practice.* Glenview, IL: Scott, Foresman.

Kolb, D. (1976) *Learning Style Inventory: Self-scoring test and interpretation booklet.* Boston: McBer and Company.

Marton, F. (1981). Phenomenography—Describing conceptions of the world around us. *Instructional Science, 10,* 177–200.

Marton, F., & Booth, S. (1997). *Learning and awareness.* Mahwah, NJ: Lawrence Erlbaum Associates.

Marton, F., & Bowden, J. (1999). *The university of learning: Beyond quality and competence.* London: Kogan Page.

Marton, F., & Saljo, R. (1976a). On qualitative differences in learning—I: Outcome and process. *British Journal of Educational Psychology, 46*, 4–11.

Marton, F. , & Saljo, R. (1976b). On qualitative differences in learning—II: Outcome as a function of the learner's conception of the task. *British Journal of Educational Psychology, 46*, 115–27.

Moore, P. J., & Scevak, J. (1997). Learning from texts and visual aids: A developmental perspective. *Journal of Research in Reading, 20*, 205–223.

Moreno, V., & DiVesta F. (1991). Cross-cultural comparisons of study habits. *Journal of Educational Psychology, 83*, 231–239.

Newble, D., & Clarke, R. M. (1986). The approaches to learning of students in a traditional and in a problem-based medical school. *Medical Education, 20*, 267–273.

Pask, G. (1976). Styles and strategies of learning. *British Journal of Educational Psychology, 46*, 128–148.

Pintrich, P., & deGroot, E. (1990). Motivational and self-regulated learning components of classroom academic performance. *Journal of Educational Psychology, 82*, 33–40.

Porter, A. (1989). A curriculum out of balance: The case of elementary school mathematics. *Educational Researcher, 18*(5), 9–15

Prosser, M., & Trigwell, K. (1999). *Understanding university learning and teaching.* Buckingham, UK: The Open University Press.

Ramsden, P. (1984). The context of learning. In F. Marton, D. Hounsell & N. Entwistle (Eds.), *The experience of learning* (pp. 144–164). Edinburgh, Scotland: Scottish Universities Press.

Ramsden, P., Beswick, D., & Bowden, J. (1986). Effects of learning skills interventions on first year university students' learning. *Human Learning, 5*, 151–164.

Riding, R., & Cheema, I. (1991). Cognitive styles: An overview and integration. *Educational Psychology, 11*, 193–215.

Salomon, G. (1991). Transcending the qualitative–quantitative debate: The analytic and systemic approaches to educational research. *Educational Researcher, 20* (6), 10–18.

Schmeck, R.R. (Ed.). (1988). *Learning strategies and learning styles.* New York: Plenum.

Schmeck, R., Geisler-Brenstein, E., & Cercy, S. (1991). The Revised Inventory of Learning Processes. *Educational Psychology 11*, 343–362.

Schmeck, R., Ribich, F., & Ramanaiah, N. (1977). Development of a self-report inventory for using individual differences in learning processes. *Applied Psychological Measurement, 1*, 413–431.

Schon, D. A. (1987). *Educating the reflective practitioner.* San Francisco: Jossey-Bass.

Shepard, L. A. (1991). Psychometricians' beliefs about learning. *Educational Researcher, 20*(6), 2–16.

Shuell, T. J. (1986). Cognitive conceptions of learning. *Review of Educational Research, 56*, 411–436.

Snow, R. E. (1974). Representative and quasi-representative designs for research on teaching. *Review of Educational Research 44*, 265–291.

Stedman, L. C. (1997). International achievement differences: An assessment of a new perspective. *Educational Researcher, 26*(3), 4–15.

Sternberg, R. J. (1994). Thinking styles: Theory and assessment at the interface between intelligence and personality. In R. J. Sternberg & P. Ruzgis (Eds.), *Intelligence and personality* (pp. 169–187). New York: Cambridge University Press.

Sternberg, R. J. (1996). Myths, countermyths, and truths about intelligence. *Educational Researcher, 25* (2), 11–16.

Sternberg, R. J. (1997). *Thinking styles*. New York: Cambridge University Press.

Stevenson, H., & Stigler, J. (1992). *The learning gap: Why our schools are failing and what we can learn from Japanese and Chinese education*. New York: Summit Books

Tang, C. (1991). Effects of different assessment methods on tertiary students' approaches to studying. Unpublished doctoral dissertation, University of Hong Kong.

Taylor, C. (1994). Assessment for measurement or standards: The peril and promise of large scale assessment reform. *American Educational Research Journal, 31*, 231–262.

Thomas, P. R., & Bain, J. D. (1984). Contextual dependence of learning approaches: The effects of assessments. *Human Learning, 3*, 227–240.

Tobin, K. (1987). The role of wait time. *Review of Educational Research, 57*, 69–95.

Trigwell, K., & Prosser, M. (1991). Relating approaches to study and quality of learning outcomes at the course level. *British Journal of Educational Psychology, 61*, 265–275.

Watkins, D. A. (1983). Depth of processing and the quality of learning outcomes. *Instructional Science, 12*, 49–58.

Watkins, D. A, & Hattie, J. (1985). A longitudinal study of the appraoch to learning of Australian tertiary students. *Human Learning, 4*(2), 127–142

Weinstein, C., & Mayer, R., (1984). The teaching of learning strategies. In Wittrock, M. (Ed.), *Handbook of research on teaching*. New York: Macmillan.

Weinstein, C., Schulte, A., & Palmer, D. (1987). Learning and Study Strategies Inventory (LASSI). Clearwater, FL: H&H Publications.

Witkin, H., Dyk, R., Faterson, H., Goodenough, D., & Karp, S. (1962). *Psychological differentiation*. New York: Wiley.

5

Conceptions, Styles, and Approaches Within Higher Education: Analytic Abstractions and Everyday Experience

Noel Entwistle
Velda McCune
University of Edinburgh
Paul Walker
University College London

INTRODUCTION

In research on learning and thinking styles, one of the continuing debates concerns the appropriate level of description. Observed behavior and interviews about learning draw attention to the marked differences between individuals and to the complex effects of differing learning environments. In contrast, much of the research effort has been to simplify this complexity and identify underlying constructs that provide a precise language to describe and discuss everyday observations and experiences. Even within the research literature, the theoretical constructs differ in their range and scope: some describe global concepts having wide generality, whereas others relate to a specific situation. These contrasting levels of description have emerged in answer to different research questions and are rooted in differing theoretical perspectives. In deciding which conceptual framework to adopt, both purpose and context have to be considered.

In this area, educational research from a psychological perspective is generally directed toward a deeper understanding of teaching and learning processes in everyday contexts, with the ultimate intention of improving the quality and effectiveness of education. Having an effect on practice depends, in part, on choosing a conceptual framework that simplifies complexity, while providing a description of everyday experience that the participants can recognize. This implies a set of variables or analytic categories that are narrowly focused on the everyday context, yet conveying an overall understanding of how learning takes place often seems to require broader constructs that draw on general psychological theories.

This chapter introduces a set of concepts that have been developed to describe how students learn and study at university and to explain the influences on the quality of learning outcomes. The conceptual framework derives from ideas introduced by Marton and his colleagues in Gothenburg, and since taken up by research groups and staff developers in many countries. The concepts were established through interview studies, with the relations between them being explored through both qualitative analyses of interview transcripts and multivariate analyses of inventory scores. Out of this work came a series of concepts, with differing breadths of focus, but these analytic abstractions are all inevitably distanced from the phenomena they describe. The process of abstraction enables complexity to be handled more easily, but also creates difficulty in identifying with the explanations provided. The chapter thus also suggests ways alternative forms of analysis may retain more of the everyday idiosyncrasy of behavior and thinking, while demonstrating the value of the conceptual framework through which students and staff can reflect critically about their current practices.

CONCEPTS, CONCEPTIONS, AND STYLES

In introducing this research area, a clear initial distinction should be made between the notion of a "concept," as an agreed category, and a "conception," as an individual construction from knowledge and experience. The term concept is generally taken to mean "a mental representation of a class of objects, ideas, or events that share common properties" (Westen, 1996, p. 257). Some everyday concepts, such as "chair," do have recognizable defining features, but abstract concepts are more difficult to classify in this way; their representation depends more on prototypes or instances that convey an image, or even a feeling, of the meaning. In recent years, the central role given to mental representations in conceptualization has been challenged, with thinking being described in terms of both the activation of neural nets (Edelman, 1992) and changing awareness (Marton & Booth, 1997).

In whatever way they are described, individual conceptions of abstract concepts generally differ qualitatively in focus or inclusivity, even within the core meaning of the concept, because of the differing knowledge and life experiences from which they are constructed. These distinctive conceptions, then, influence the ways subsequent events are interpreted. Such differences in conceptualization have been systematically explored through *phenomenography*, the research approach that Marton and his collaborators have developed (Marton, 1994). Studies using this interview methodology have shown that individual conceptions often fall into a relatively small number of recognizably different categories, which phenomenography seeks to identify, describe, and exemplify before analyzing the relationships between them.

Investigating differences in people's *conceptions of learning*, Säljö (1979) asked adults with varying educational experience what "learning" meant to them. His study produced a developmental hierarchy of five distinct conceptions of learning The categories ranged from learning as rote memorization and *reproducing* knowledge, to a recognition that learning rests ultimately on *transforming* the information presented in the light of what is known or has been experienced already. The five categories originally identified can be described as follows:

- building up knowledge;
- memorizing by rote; *Reproducing*
- acquiring facts and methods for future use;
- abstracting meaning for oneself; *Transforming*
- seeking to understanding reality.

Individuals in Säljö's sample who recognized the importance of understanding for themselves were still ready to use rote learning when necessary, but were conscious of the forms of learning available and how they could best be used.

Conceptions of learning are derived from the cumulative effects of previous educational and other experiences, and so tend to be relatively stable and to influence, to some extent, subsequent ways of thinking and acting. Their relative stability also stems from the individual characteristics of the learner—their pattern of abilities; their personality; and, lying between ability and personality, their style of learning. Conceptions do, however, change and evolve as people mature and engage in intellectual activities (Marton, Dall'Alba, & Beaty, 1993).

In research on student learning, the term *style* has been used in two different ways. Vermunt (1998), among others, used it to describe aspects of studying that group together within factor analyses, whereas Pask (1976) preferred the more restricted psychological usage. Sternberg (1997) has

conceptual understanding being an inevitable outcome. In spite of the consistency shown in habits of studying, the early research emphasized the influence of both context and content; subsequently, the general influence of teaching, learning, and the whole learning environment has been well documented (Biggs, 1999; Entwistle, 1998a; Prosser & Trigwell, 1999; Ramsden, 1997; chap. 4, this volume).

Marton's (1976) naturalistic experiment produced just the deep–surface distinction, but interviews about everyday studying brought out the pervasive influence of assessment procedures on learning and studying. It was necessary to introduce an additional category—*strategic approach*—in which the intention was to achieve the highest possible grades by using organized study methods and effective time management (Entwistle & Ramsden, 1983). Biggs (1987, this volume) identified a similar category—*achieving*—although with a different emphasis. The strategic approach also involves an alertness to the assessment process, which can be seen in the following extract from Miller and Parlett (1974):

> I play the examination game. The examiners play it, so we play it too. . . . The technique involves knowing what's going to be in the exam and how it's going to be marked. You can acquire these techniques from sitting in a lecturer's class, getting ideas from his point of view, the form of his notes, and the books he has written—and this is separate to picking up the actual work content. (pp. 59–61)

This extract suggests a student who has two distinct focuses of concern within the lecture: the academic content and the demands of the assessment system. The interest in the content is typical of a deep approach, but the alertness to assessment requirements is essentially strategic.

The intentions to learn in deep or surface ways are mutually exclusive, although the related learning processes may sometimes become mixed in everyday experience. The combination of deep and strategic approaches is commonly found in successful students, but a deep approach on its own may not be carried through with sufficient determination and effort to reach deep levels of understanding.

The defining characteristics of the three approaches to studying (see Table 5.2) have been derived mainly from research on social science students studying texts or writing essays. Although contrast among deep, surface, and strategic intentions seems to apply widely across disciplinary boundaries, the processes and strategies required to carry them through inevitably differ. The processes involved in a deep approach, for example, have to be redefined within each discipline or professional area to ensure they include the learning processes necessary for conceptual understanding in that area of study.

TABLE 5.2

Defining Features of Approaches to Learning and Studying

Deep Approach	*Seeking Meaning*
Intention—to understand ideas for yourself	*By:*
Relating ideas to previous knowledge and experience	
Looking for patterns and underlying principles	
Checking evidence and relating it to conclusions	
Examining logic and argument cautiously and critically	
Being aware of understanding developing while learning	
Becoming actively interested in the course content	
Surface Approach	*Reproducing*
Intention—to cope with course requirements	*By:*
Treating the course as unrelated bits of knowledge	
Memorizing facts and carrying out procedures routinely	
Finding difficulty in making sense of new ideas presented	
Seeing little value or meaning in either courses or tasks set	
Studying without reflecting on either purpose or strategy	
Feeling undue pressure and worry about work	
Strategic Approach	*Reflective Organizing*
Intention—to achieve the highest possible grades	*By:*
Putting consistent effort into studying	
Managing time and effort effectively	
Finding the right conditions and materials for studying	
Monitoring the effectiveness of ways of studying	
Being alert to assessment requirements and criteria	
Gearing work to the perceived preferences of lecturers	

MULTIVARIATE ANALYSES OF INVENTORY RESPONSES

Although the initial work on approaches to studying came from interviews, a substantial body of research has grown out of attempts to measure the relatively consistent elements within studying. Several different inventories have been developed, such as the *Approaches to Studying Inventory* ASI

(Entwistle & Ramsden, 1983), all of which produce similar factors. At the broadest level, deep, surface, and strategic groupings of subscales are commonly found, each constituted from intentions, learning processes, and associated motives (see Biggs, 1993). Other inventories have introduced additional components of motivation (Pintrich & Garcia, 1994) and elaborated elements of metacognition and self-regulation within the general domains of deep and strategic approaches (Pintrich & Garcia, 1994; Vermunt, 1998).

Table 5.3 presents a maximum likelihood factor analysis of 817 first-year university students drawn from 10 contrasting departments in six British universities who completed the most recent version of the ASI. The *Approaches and Study Skills Inventory for Students* (ASSIST; Tait, Entwistle, & McCune, 1998) includes additional scales intended to extend the description of studying and reactions to teaching. The definition of the strategic approach has also been broadened to include an aspect of metacognition and self-regulation—monitoring effectiveness —whereas the surface approach puts more emphasis on ineffective studying through the inclusion of a scale indicating a "lack of purpose." The subscales included in this analysis were those contributing to the three main factors described earlier, supported by items describing students' conceptions of learning and their preferences for different kinds of teaching. Three factors produced eigenvalues above unity, and that solution also provided the best balance between interpretability and the percentage of variance explained.

The original version of the ASI explicitly included Pask's (1976) two styles of learning. In ASSIST, however, these have been subsumed within the definition of the deep approach, which is taken to require both ways of thinking—relating ideas (holist) and using evidence (serialist)—or a versatile style in learning. The factor analysis confirms that these two processes link closely with both the intention to seek meaning and interest in ideas (an attitudinal correlate of intrinsic motivation). Linkages between approach and motive are also clear-cut within the strategic approach, where achievement motivation (Atkinson & Feather, 1966) is strongly associated with both organized studying and time management. Similarly, the "surface apathetic" factor brings together syllabus boundness and lack of understanding with both lack of purpose and fear of failure.

As in previous studies, the deep approach is linked with a conception of learning as "transforming," and with a preference for teaching that encourages and challenges understanding (Entwistle & Tait, 1990). A parallel finding indicates that students adopting a surface apathetic approach prefer teaching that transmits information and directs learning toward assessment requirements. Other research has indicated that students who show a deep strategic approach are also better able to discern and use the aspects of a

TABLE 5.3

Factor Loadings on Approaches and Preferences for Teaching[a]

(N = 817, 54.5% variance)	Factor I Deep	Factor II Strategic	Factor III Surface Apathetic
Conceptions of Learning			
Learning as reproducing			
Learning as transforming	.42		
Approaches to Studying			
Deep approach			
Seeking Meaning	.70		
Relating Ideas	.79		
Use of evidence	.76		
Interest in ideas	.65		
Strategic approach			
Organized studying		.80	
Time management		.92	
Monitoring effectiveness	.39	.45	
Achievement motivation		.76	
Surface apathetic approach			
Lack of understanding			.77
Lack of purpose			.41
Syllabus boundness			.41
Fear of failure			.71
Preferences for teaching that:			
Encourages understanding	.61		
Transmits information			.35

[a]This is a rotated maximum likelihood analysis with delta set a at zero. Loadings less than 0.3 have been omitted.

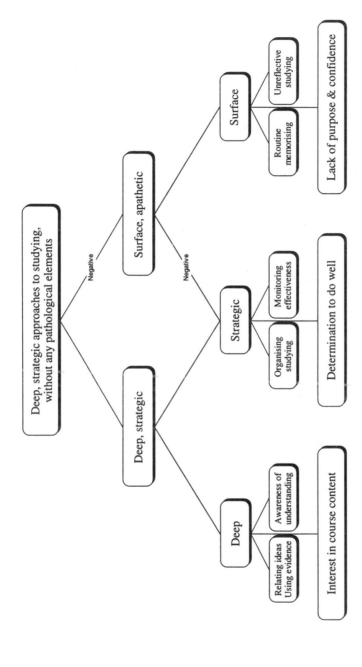

FIG. 5.1. Conceptual map of components of effective studying within ASSIST

learning environment that will support their way of studying (Meyer, 1991; Meyer, Parsons, & Dunne, 1990).

Figure 5.1 presents a conceptual map of the main components included within ASSIST and indicates the ways these dimensions combine to create an idealized description of a deep, strategic approach to studying. The links between concepts indicate the existence of positive relationships, with the exception of the two links shown as negative.

BUILDING MORE HOLISTIC CONSTRUCTS TO DESCRIBE STUDYING

The combination of attributes included in Fig. 5.1 not only summarizes the characteristics of an ideally effective student—what Janssen (1996) has dubbed the *studax*—but also connects with theoretical developments in educational psychology. Bereiter (1990) has argued coherent organizations of cognitive, conative, and affective structures are brought into play within specific learning contexts. These cognitive structures are seen as an "entire complex of knowledge, skills, goals and feelings" that form a mutually interdependent, organic whole (Bereiter, 1990, p. 613). The importance of using these broader, integrated groupings in seeking to understand scholastic or academic performance has also been emphasized by Snow, Corno, and Jackson, (1996) in a review article on affective and conative functions in learning. Perkins, among others, has described such groupings as *dispositions*, which he sees as bringing together abilities, inclinations including motives, and sensitivities to context (Perkins, 1998; Perkins, Jay, & Tishman, 1993). Within this framework, the deep approach could perhaps be seen as a disposition to seek academic understanding within a specific learning context.

Why are these composite constructs being introduced now, when previously the main concern in psychology was to create tightly defined variables? From an educational perspective, one reason is that the broader concepts are readily recognizable to both staff and students in capturing the essence of their experiences. In psychological terms, this coalescence of concepts may imply that certain groups of variables act synergistically to produce learning outcomes, and that this synergy needs to be reflected in the theory, through the use of composite constructs such as dispositions or approaches to studying.

The use of analytic categories to bring out the pattern of relationships between contributory components within effective studying is an essential first step in clarifying how students study. Correlational findings do, however, encourage a view of student learning that implies a consistency and coherence in study behavior rarely found in reality. The apparent conflict between descriptions of stable individual characteristics and the evidence of specific reactions to tasks is well recognized (Entwistle, 1979; Laurillard, 1979). And yet it is still possible for students who have a general tendency to adopt a particular approach or style, nevertheless, to vary it in reaction to specific circumstances (Entwistle & Ramsden, 1983; Ramsden, 1979). A recent study on schoolchildren has identified both stable and less stable patterns in students' reactions to tasks and contexts (Boekaerts, 1999). The stable patterns were found to depend on interest, commitment, and challenge, whereas the less stable patterns reflected students' reactions to specific contexts and developmental changes in the linkages among self-concept, intention, and feelings.

In the research on student learning, the analytic categories provide little or no information about the specific techniques used in tackling academic tasks and take no account of developmental changes. If a more adequate description of how students learn is to be provided, researchers need to draw directly on students' experiences as they carry out specific tasks. Although recent developments have sought to integrate cognitive and conative constructs within specific educational contexts, other studies have sought to describe how students react to those contexts through finer grained descriptions.

Two recent interview studies at Edinburgh go beyond the general conceptual abstractions, bringing to life the actual practice of studying in the words of individual students. The first project looked at how final-year students prepare for examinations, and the second investigated developmental patterns and trends in acquiring skill in learning.

PREPARING FOR FINAL EXAMINATIONS

In traditional British universities such as Edinburgh, final examinations require students to demonstrate a thorough conceptual understanding of topics they have studied. They usually have about 10 weeks to prepare for five, 3-hour examinations, in each of which they are typically asked to answer three general questions in essay form.

A series of small-scale interview studies has focused on how students prepare for their final examinations and the ways they write answers when taking those examinations (Entwistle, 1995; Entwistle, N. J., & Entwistle, A. C., 1991; Entwistle & Marton, 1994;). The interviews followed the style of phenomenographic interviews in being interactive and asking the students to focus on specific instances. They also encouraged reflection on the detail of study activities and reasons for studying in that way. This research was not intended to categorize differing conceptions, but rather to consider the overall experience of preparing for final examinations.

Students who had developed deep, strategic approaches to studying were likely to have worked out in previous years a systematic technique for revising their notes. Their method typically involved writing revision notes that iteratively reduced the detail and brought out, not just the main points, but an outline indicating their own way of thinking about the topic. That process often led to a single page, designed to draw attention to the structure of the student's understanding, sometimes in the form of a patterned note or concept map (Entwistle & Napuk, 1997). The headings or main branches of the note triggered detailed information not displayed in the summary itself. This mnemonic could then be brought to mind during the examination to represent the essence of the student's understanding.

This process can be illustrated through the following composite description, based on the comments of several students who had adopted a deep, strategic approach to preparing for finals:

I made out a timetable and stuck to it very closely. It was really just allocating time for each course and choosing the topics and revising them. I went through the past papers and picked out subjects which I thought might come up, but also that I'd found most interesting, and I'd come to grips with. I revised those, and also any topics that might be linked with them. I would revise whole blocks, so that I felt I had a pretty wide coverage and that I would be covering myself in the exam.

I went through all my notes first and then I took notes on all of them and condensed them into about 17 A4 sheets. Then underline what was important. Then, I'd put them onto another sheet, so they were becoming more and more condensed. Eventually, they went on to index cards, and I would highlight certain key words or phrases. I designed a sort of check-list system to cross off what I knew. As I went through the index cards, I would ask myself if I remembered each bit, and if I could explain it, then that went off the list. Under various headings I would have the important points which showed the understanding, although it was basically names, experiments and important examples, which triggered off the understanding by reading it through.

The structure of the headings in my notes are like clues. I'll write it in a certain way so that it's very structured in paragraphs, so I can envisage how that should be. I realise that using diagrams is just a way that I can retain material, rather than retaining words or descriptions. It's a logical sequence worked out as a 'story' about something. Having imaged a lot of things previously, I got on to this process of constructing kind of mental maps on a sheet of paper based on a series of images. It was a very good and quick way of me putting down the basics. I can see these notes virtually as a picture, which I can review, bringing in more facts about each part. Looking at a particular part of the diagram sort of triggers off other thoughts. It acts as a schematic, a bit like a syllabus; it tells you what you should know, without actually telling you what it is. I think the facts are stored separately, and the schematic is like an index, I suppose.

I had tried to structure my revision so that I could understand what was going on. So, although I had this structure when I went into the exam, I still wanted it to be flexible, so that I could approach the question itself. At the time, as I was writing, I was just using anything that came into my mind and fitted in: as I wrote, it was almost as though I could see it all fitting into an overall picture. Following the logic through, it pulls in pictures and facts as it needs them. Each time I describe a particular topic, it's likely to be different. Well, you start with evolution, say, and suddenly you know where you're going next. Then, you might have a choice to go in that direction or that direction and follow it through various options it's offering. Hopefully, you'll make the right choice, and so this goes to this, goes to this—and you've explained it to the level you've got to.

In an exam, you have to have background knowledge of the subject, and an ability to interpret the information in your own way. You don't sit down and think "How much can I remember about this particular subject"; you try and explain your ideas, using examples which come to mind. You can't use all the information for a particular line of argument, and you don't need to; you only need to use what you think is going to convince the examiner. The more I have done exams, the more I'd liken them to a performance—like being on a stage; having not so much to present the fact that you know a vast amount, but having to perform well with what you do know. Sort of, playing to the gallery. I was very conscious of being outside what I was writing. (Entwistle, 1995; Entwistle, N. J., & Entwistle, A. C., 1991; Entwistle & Marton, 1994)

Several students had mentioned the visual form their revision notes took, or how the notes were remembered as mental images during the examination. When pressed, however, they said that what they could see was not a complete visual image, but was something "like visualising." This intriguing aspect of the students' comments led to a secondary analysis of the data (Entwistle & Marton, 1994). As the comments above indicated, some students could reflect on the structure they had created as a scaffolding for their understanding. In the full transcripts, these frameworks of understanding seemed almost to have an independent existence in their minds that they could review at will. These descriptions of an experience of an entity with perceived structure and shape suggested the concept of a *knowledge object*.

In examinations, a well-established knowledge object provides a generic structure for an explanation that is sufficiently flexible to adapt to the particular requirements of the question set. An explanation in an essay examination needs to be a specific response to the actual question set, to cover a specific context of relevant knowledge, and to keep a particular audience in mind—the examiners who will be reading it. The comments of the deep, strategic students suggested that, as they were writing, their explanations developed a dynamic or a momentum of their own, which partially determined the direction the argument that would follow, drawing in particular examples or evidence as they became relevant. Recent evidence suggests that knowledge objects may be used by staff in presenting talks or lectures and can be recalled after several years if the appropriate triggers are available (Entwistle, 1998b).

The results of these qualitative studies of preparing for examinations have introduced yet another abstraction—the knowledge object—but they have also provided a detailed description of the revision process, going well beyond the broad conceptualization offered by the three approaches to studying. However, the systematic, carefully controlled process of preparing for exams indicated in the composite extract from the interviews is typical of only a small portion of students—those who had developed a deep, strategic, and metacognitive approach to studying.

DEVELOPING SKILL IN LEARNING DURING THE FIRST YEAR AT UNIVERSITY

The other fine-grained qualitative study at Edinburgh has been following up a group of first-year students who were interviewed on three occasions: at the beginning of the year, at or just after the end of the first term when they had submitted their first coursework essay (term paper) and taken their first examination, and around the time of their final assignment. The students also completed the ASSIST inventory and were asked to explain some of their responses. Analyses of the transcripts have focused not only on the developmental trends toward increased sophistication in ways of studying (McCune, 1998; McCune & Entwistle, 1999), but also on the way approaches to studying are influenced by chance events (McCune, 1999). The composite constructs of conception and approach guided thinking in the early stages of analysis, but, increasingly, the voices of individual students focused attention both on the complex interactions needed to explain study behavior and on the need to interpret reactions in terms of the student's history.

Two brief case studies are used to illustrate the interaction between the relatively stable characteristics of the individual and the events met along a developmental track. The examples also indicate how ideas about general relationships between approach and context have to be adjusted to take into account individual reactions to tasks. The first student shows almost no evidence of improvement over the first year, choosing options that allowed her to follow the least strenuous route. In contrast, the second student's attitude to her experiences at university led her to recognize, and capitalize on, opportunities for becoming a more effective learner.

Research on the defining features of approaches to studying point to a coherent set of attributes: the intention to understand, together with an active engagement with the task, linked to interest in the subject matter. There is also a clear indication in several studies that essay assignments tend to encourage a deep approach (Scouller, 1997). Our first case study shows how both these general tendencies need to be qualified when considering a specific instance.

In the first interview, this student expressed a keen interest in becoming an educational psychologist but, in subsequent interviews, she admitted lacking the determination to achieve that goal, as she found it difficult to get down to work. Although recognizing this weakness, she believed it was a facet of her personality she could not change, which advice on study skills thus could not be expected to influence. Given the opportunity to take the easy option, she did so, even though she recognized it would limit her ability to understand the content. This recognition came as she reflected on her responses to the inventory and in commenting on her ways of tackling essay writing. In the inventory, this student showed high scores on "seeking meaning," but these were associated with high scores on "syllabus boundness" and low scores on both "achieving" and "time management," a pattern that comes through in the student's comments.

> I didn't prepare well for the exam at all. . . . When it got to the stage that I maybe had three days to do an essay, then I would miss the lectures on these days. . . . Getting close to the exams, [I realized] I'd obviously missed a load of lectures. . . . But I'm not a worrier . . . [and] nothing really bad has happened yet. . . . I didn't think ahead, and even if I had, it wouldn't really have bothered me at the time, because I'd just think I'll cross that bridge when I come to it. . . . I have to admit the only thing I revised was statistics, and that wasn't really revision because I'd missed it all in the lectures. . . .
>
> I tend to avoid study skills, because I know I don't have them, and . . . I'm a bit cynical about the likelihood that I will adhere to any sort of study skills system,. . . so I haven't bothered with anything like that, although I suppose I should because that's where I'm lacking. . . . I know what my problems are with studying. . . —it's basic laziness, that's all it is really. . . . I suppose I don't really like to mask it in any deeper ideas about why I don't do it, I'm sure it just is laziness.
>
> [In] the questionnaire [we filled in] . . . it was saying, "Do you like books that are straightforward and give you what you need to know, or do you like ones that encourage you to go beyond what the lecturer might have (said)?" I

do like books like that, but for my convenience I prefer the other sort. It's not necessarily that I do prefer them, it's just, knowing the way I work, they suit me better. The essay question was similar, it suits me a lot better to just find out a basic theory;. . . you don't have to think that much. . . .

[In one of the essays we were asked to] "outline Piaget's pre-operational stage." It didn't say "discuss" or "evaluate," that's the point. It was just [to] say, basically, what the theory was, without any of your own thoughts on it, or anyone else's. . . . I thought that was quite strange,. . . [but] that's the sort of essay I like, because you can just get the books you need and it's quite easy, you don't have to struggle over complicated ideas. . . . It's not necessarily what I would enjoy the most, but knowing that I don't tend to put too much work towards my essays, it's the sort of title that I enjoy getting, because I know that there's more chance that I can do it with the minimum of effort.

This student's acceptance of her procrastination was in marked contrast to the second case study, which suggests how chance events can be transformed into learning opportunities by a well-motivated student who is alert to possibilities. And this alertness may well reflect how earlier educational experiences, and the conception of learning formed from them, can shape future reactions to tutors' comments that, in turn, build a more sophisticated view of learning and studying. With this frame of mind, students are more able to capitalize on situations in ways that will strengthen their approaches to learning and studying.

Scores from the inventory suggest that this student had a deep, holistic approach to studying, supported by organized studying and good time management. In the interview, she indicated she had already realized university had changed the way she was thinking, and this recognition seemed to fuel a generally more reflective view of studying.

[My initial reason for coming to university] was the run of the mill thing. . . But now it has turned into, gradually into, just developing how I think. . . . I am finding that the way I am thinking is changing and developing, which is very good, and it wouldn't happen elsewhere.

This change in orientation had parallels in the way she tackled essay writing, although the likelihood that she would respond positively to opportunities to improve her study technique could be seen earlier. She recounted several instances where she had successfully changed her learning at school and where she had sought out, and obtained, helpful advice from teachers. At university, she soon recognized that different demands were being made of her, and her tutor's comments triggered a change in her conception of essay writing. The extent to which this change derived from the advice of the tutor, or from the student's insight into her own experience is, however, not clear.

[Writing essays at university] is different from the ones I wrote in school,. . . For "A" levels, it seems to be more on style to get you through, but by the time you get to university style isn't enough. . . . I used to be a bit of a culprit for a waffley essay, that I didn't actually know that much about what I was writing,. . . and now [it's] actually having to find out what it is you are actually writing an essay on. . . . Before you could get away with being quite airy-fairy about things, as long as it was a nice read for them. So, now it's actually getting into the realms of having to read those big books about it, and having to understand it yourself. . . .

After my first essay I had a bit of a chat with my tutor. . . . What he did, he read it through back to me, and I was the sort of audience to my own essay, and I thought some of it was completely terrible, and I thought "What can he be thinking?" . . . "I just haven't expressed what I thought here." I know I thought it really kind of strongly; I was really excited about it. . . . [When I was given the essay back] I was quite sort of grumpy about the mark I got, I thought I had much better ideas than that. . . . Then you heard it back and, well, I would have given myself exactly the same mark, if not lower, because it was really badly expressed.

From this first essay to her second and final essays the student's grade jumped, as she developed in her approach to essay writing. These developments seemed to stem from reflecting on the feedback on her first essay and her continuing positive attitude to studying. She worked harder to be sure she understood what she read in preparing for her essays, and it is interesting to find that she then saw understanding as difficult, whereas previously she had considered it fairly easy. In commenting on reading for the next essay, she said:

I found it quite frustrating. . . . The first time I read it, I really came away with the feeling I hadn't actually got anything from it. . . . Because it took a lot of grinding through to understand it, I would skim through it and, of course, this is the worst thing you can do with something like psychology, where you have got to understand every little word, and how it fits together. A few of the things, I would just skim through and got completely the wrong meaning, just because I assumed it would be a different meaning. . . . [Then, there was] this one day when I thought I must be doing this a bit wrong; I must be reading it wrong or something. So, I just read through it a second time, very slowly. Sometimes I would read it aloud, that kind of helped. . . . I think actually this time I understood what they were talking about, rather than just made up what they were talking about by making little references back to it. . . .

Having to prepare for a philosophy examination toward the end of the year also caused further reflection on study methods, as this student contemplated the implications of a different way of recording her notes.

I was thinking about this the other day. I had a small breakthrough in my life—I thought of writing stuff down. The way I had always done it before . . . was just, sort of, read through it, and you would note things down on the actual bit of the book. . . . But I [thought], . . . while I am doing that, I might as well note it down. . . . You can only underline so many words, and so you get the sort of seed of the idea, but . . . I kind of forget what it's about when I am going through it again. . . . I found that happened when I did my essays; they'd be quite ambiguous, because I actually wouldn't know what I was talking about, because I hadn't remembered what I had read. So, I find now . . . I actually take the time to write it down, how I think it, and also you find you get little ideas . . . so you spend a bit of time writing them down. . . . You think it takes more time, but I don't think it does actually in the long run, because you actually understand it initially, and you can think about it while it's really fresh in your brain. I don't know what it was (caused this breakthrough); . . . it just happened.

The comments of another student provide a further example of how a tutor can provide an impetus for a change in approaches to studying, as long as the student is alert to the possibilities. The tutor had been asking the group to read articles on nursing before tutorials and helping students see how to criticize them. This student then recognized how that could be used in her other work.

We've been questioning a lot more about . . . whether they [the authors] actually cover the points that they've said they'd cover, and questioning whether the author is biased. That's really made me think a lot more about what I'm actually reading. . . . I think that's helped me with my psychology as well, because I have to keep remembering . . . that they're only ideas and psychologists' views on something, and it's not actually dead set. . . . It makes me less trusting of what I'm reading, but in a way it makes me feel more independent in my work, . . . less like I'm being taken in by what they're writing, if I actually think, "Why are they saying (that)?"

These comments, and those from the previous student, both draw attention to development toward a deep approach stemming from an opportunity, during the process of learning, that the student both recognizes and seizes as a way of improving her ways of studying. This combination of alertness to opportunity and readiness to change suggests important facets of studying not found previously and may parallel the "sensitivity to context" described as a component of "disposition" (see earlier discussion). It was, however, found in only a small proportion of students. Most of the students showed little general improvement in their studying during the first year and yet saw no need for serious reflection on their studying. Indeed, few even recognized their inadequacies (McCune, 1999).

These fine-grained analyses of interview transcripts, particularly where a complete case study is undertaken, seem to offer an important addition to the more abstracted descriptions of studying. We still see the way prior experience, the fairly stable characteristics of the individual, and conceptions of learning, all seem to affect ways of studying, but we also see how specific events can interact with established ways of thinking to produce different outcomes. For example, the student who seemed to accept all too readily her procrastination and lack of sustained effort not only drifted through her first year, but also looked for ways of limiting the effort needed to carry out tasks. The other student seemed to welcome opportunities for improving her ways of studying, and this enabled her to refine her essay preparation and writing techniques.

This alertness to possibilities for change, and the readiness to explore dissonance, may well be an important precondition to development, which we also see when examining an experienced academic's experience of changing his ways of thinking about teaching. This further case study again demonstrates the need to go beyond the abstraction of generalized differences in conceptions to the specific instances in which changes take place, and how that is translated into changes in actions.

CONCEPTIONS AND STYLES OF TEACHING

The concepts identified in describing student learning have parallels in the ways academic staff teach. At the most general level are *conceptions of teaching*. Below that level come *styles of teaching*, which indicate consistency in preferences for particular ways of teaching, rooted in personality. *Approaches to teaching* are more affected by specific purposes and individual teaching contexts, whereas *teaching methods and techniques* cover specific classroom activities.

The most recent phenomenographic research has suggested five conceptions of teaching, similar to the categories describing conceptions of learning. The conceptions are also taken to represent a nested hierarchy in which the more sophisticated conceptions incorporate aspects of the less developed conceptions (Entwistle & Walker, in press). From a review of previous studies, Kember (1997, 1998) suggested the hierarchy can be seen as three conceptions, with the extreme categories each subdivided into two as indicated in Fig 5.2. Looking at the extremes, the least developed conception can be described as teacher focused and content oriented, with an emphasis on the reproduction of correct information. At the other end of this continuum, teaching is seen as student focused, learning oriented,

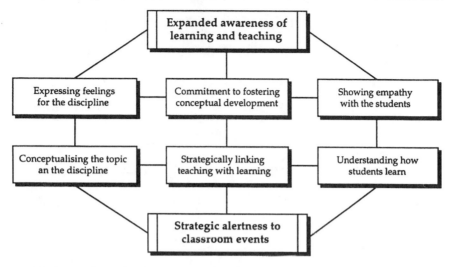

FIG. 5.2.   A hierarchy of conceptions of teaching.

and concerned with conceptual development. These opposite views can be illustrated through the following interview extracts taken, first, from a study by Prosser, Trigwell, and Taylor (1994) (Prosser, personal communication) and, then, from the review by Kember (1998).

Teacher-focused, content-oriented
It is my duty and responsibility to help students develop the specific knowledge and skills which are needed to pass the examinations, although I'm fully aware that this might narrow the kind of education I am giving to the students. . . . I put great emphasis on behavioural objectives and making sure that I cover the syllabus thoroughly. In preparing a lecture,. . . . I know exactly what notes I want the students to get. Students don't have to decide when to take notes: I dictate them.

Student-focused, learning-oriented
I'm aware of how much I used to assume. I now try to take nothing for granted and to question my assumptions about how students learn things. . . . What I want to achieve . . . is confronting students with their preconceived ideas about the subject. . . . [Conceptual understanding is developed] by arguing about things, [confronting preconceptions], and trying to apply ideas. . . . What we're trying to do in learning physics, is . . . to shift [students'] from the layperson's view, to what we would call a scientific . . . view.

Other research has described contrasting styles of lecturing that parallel the styles of learning outlined earlier. Indeed, these styles of teaching may well

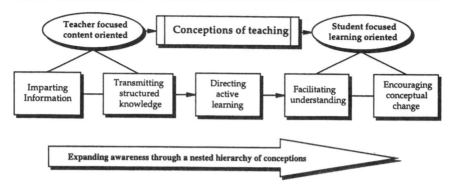

FIG. 5.3. Components of a sophisticated conception of teaching.

stem directly from the ways the teachers themselves prefer to learn (Entwistle, 1988). Brown and Bahktar (1983) identified five styles, based mainly on the way information was organized and presented. Some lectur-ers produced ineffective, disorganized presentations (described in two categories: *amorphous* and *self-doubters*). A stylistic difference could be seen between *oral* lecturers who wove intricate verbal webs, but lacked clear structure or audio-visual support (possibly holists), and *information providers* who followed their notes closely in providing a tedious amount of detail (serialists). Finally, there were the *exemplary* lecturers who had a clear set of objectives, planned and presented clear and well-structured material, avoided too much detail (providing handouts or recommended reading for that purpose), and used audio-visual aids to enliven their presentations.

When students are asked about their experiences of lectures, either in interviews (Hodgson, 1997; Ramsden, 1992, 1997) or through evaluation questionnaires (Marsh, 1987), a clear picture emerges of what constitutes "good lectures" from the student's perspective. They are described in terms of seven main categories: level, pace, structure, clarity, explanation, enthusiasm, and empathy. And of these, the comments of students suggest it is the "three Es"—explanation, enthusiasm, and empathy—that are the most likely to support a deep approach to learning. The quality of the explanation affects the extent to which students are encouraged, and find it easy, to make sense of the topic in their own way. Explanations can also be used to model the forms of argument and use of evidence adopted in the discipline. Brown and Atkins (1988) emphasize the value of evoking intellectual curiosity through the use of problems or paradoxes, and they show how good explanations depend on being apt (both to the topic and to the students' existing knowledge) and on extensively using examples, analogies, metaphors, and personal anecdotes. Combining a supporting framework within the lecture (serialist) with many links to related ideas (holist) is recognizably a versatile style of lecturing.

Although such descriptions of conceptions and styles of teaching have clarified some of the main differences that exist among university teachers' ways of thinking about teaching, they do not do justice to the many aspects that underlie excellent teaching. Research on teaching in school provides much more elaborate descriptions, and drawing on this previous work Entwistle and Walker (in press) have suggested additional components likely to be found within the most developed conceptions. School-based research has identified three main forms of knowledge teachers use: knowledge of subject matter, knowledge of teaching techniques and strategies, and knowledge of how their students learn. But these forms imply teaching is essentially a cognitive activity, although in practice each form of knowledge seems also to have an affective component, as suggested in Fig. 5.3. Moreover, the expanded awareness of learning and teaching found within the most developed conceptions of teaching are exemplified in approaches to teaching that show a strategic alertness to classroom events.

As in the research on student learning, however, these abstractions from university teachers' descriptions of their teaching present an idealized picture, distanced from everyday experiences in the classroom, which are more immediate and not always coherent with underlying conceptions. Murray and Macdonald (1997) found that university teachers were not always able to teach in the ways they believed they should, for various reasons. As Bennett and Dunne (in press) commented:

> Research on teachers' implicit theories . . . [assume] that a teacher's cognitive and pedagogical behaviours are guided by, and make sense in relation to, a personally held system of beliefs, values and principles. . . . [But] what teachers say and do is mediated by contextual . . . [factors which] act either to enable or constrain the enactment of teacher theories in practice. . . . Beliefs and conceptions about teaching and learning gained from interviews may, or may not, be reflected in practices. Contexts, such as those imposed by modularisation or large numbers, mean that teachers may not operate in their preferred way.

THE EXPERIENCE OF TEACHING

The concepts used to present coherent theoretical frameworks thus cannot fully explain everyday classroom practice. Again, we can overcome this limitation through a detailed case study, showing how an approach to teaching developed over time and considering what additional insights may come from teachers' everyday experiences. In a recent study, an experienced university teacher reflected on changes in his conceptions of learning and teaching, and the difficulties involved in translating a sophisticated perspective into practice (Entwistle & Walker, in press).

The seeds of a learning-oriented conception of teaching were traced to a dissatisfaction with this teacher's initial conception of physics, which was also held by most of his colleagues and still underpins teaching and assessment in most undergraduate physics courses. As he began to recognize the problematic nature of knowledge, in general, and considered how his own ways of thinking about physics were changing, he began to experiment with different approaches to teaching. It seems likely that thinking about their own discipline may, generally, be one of the most effective stimuli to changing teaching practice for university teachers, who rarely have had any extensive exposure to pedagogical theory. As this lecturer commented in Entwistle and Walker (in press):

> Over time, I became increasingly intrigued by the discrepancy between my greater command of the concepts, with their wider connections, and the apparent inaccessibility of those concepts and connections to most of my students. I now began to find more interest in epistemological aspects of physics, and this interest spilled over from the realm of private wonderment into the pedagogical imperative to share that knowledge, understanding and interest.

This awareness did not translate immediately into effective practice, rather it led to a series of trial-and-error adaptations of teaching. Initially, the approach was directed wholly to showing students the nature of physical knowledge, but most of the students did not respond. They wanted the knowledge presented to be more obviously related to assessment requirements. Rather than abandon the attempt, a "multiply-inclusive" approach was gradually established. As reported in Entwistle and Walker (in press):

> My initial attempts to focus my teaching on these issues and related learning outcomes met with less success than I would have liked. I experienced indifference, even hostility, to my attempts to broaden the learning inquiry and encourage reflection on learning itself. To the extent that this shift of focus was at the expense of duly delivered information, it created apparent unease and concern about how this might relate to what was on the examination papers. I had to develop a more strategic approach, in which this new agenda ran through my teaching like a thread, rather than featuring somehow as part of the course. Its nature is much more a matter of context than content and this requires a much more considered and multiply inclusive approach to teaching.

Over time, I have developed a teaching approach which begins to satisfy simultaneously a tacit demand for content, for understanding of content, for relevance and applicability of that content, and yet still challenges and attempts to undermine those expectations by only partially fulfilling them. This is a multiply inclusive strategy, wherein different students may have different expectations. I also explain that any sense of frustration among students about incompletely fulfilled expectations may be a function of their own limited view of the nature of learning. I attempt in my teaching to have students develop their view of learning itself, as well as concepts emerging from the subject matter.

Within this multiply inclusive approach, information is provided in logical order for those who want it, but with the oft-repeated rider that relying on my lectures for complete and accurate information is fraught with danger—I might be mistaken (as I have been many times and not realised it until later) or even deliberately misleading (temporarily, to make a point). For students who need to relate to other course content or to the world, there is a thread of conversation making such links, often unexpected ones. This approach is not unusual; physics teachers often highlight examples and provide practical illustrations of the abstract concepts in physics courses. For students who seek to apply the knowledge, there is at least conversational reference to that which, again, is not unusual. But an explicit awareness of inclusively serving the interests and learning approaches of a diversity of students seems to be much less common, as does an agenda for developing students' views of learning, and their ability to learn. . . .

I developed the practice of my teaching on the basis of my more developed view of learning and began, for example, to design and use questions in class to foster engagement, rather than as a token gesture, obtaining the "right answer" from those who already know it. Responding to students' questions (and the "questions behind the questions") in ways which encourage critical thought and dialogue, was equally important. The process requires skilful management—to keep directing attention to issues that are just beyond the current horizon of students' awareness and thus stimulate the expansion of that awareness. . . .

From the point of view of an observer, much of what I am trying to achieve while teaching might not be readily discernible—it might look like a fairly standard lecture, content interspersed with the usual mix of questions, advice, asides and bad jokes. But from my point of view, as the one teaching, it looks very different, and my awareness of what happens in class contrasts markedly with how it used to be. In the early days it was a matter of being prepared, presenting content confidently and accurately, and being in control. Some days it worked well and others it was a struggle, and I never knew quite why—it must have been the students or perhaps the weather that day. Later, as I developed more mastery, I could teach in a more conversational style, maintaining a sense of theatre, creating and taking opportunities to engage students' interest and thinking. Examples, demonstrations and questions can be chosen to maximise such engagement and wherever possible to elucidate and challenge students' preconceptions. The experience of teaching now, from my point of view, is more akin to a masterful jazz musician improvising and interacting with partners, allowing the instrument itself to speak, to express and inspire—rather than having to clumsily pluck or blow to force a predictable outcome.

The metaphor of jazz brings out an important aspect of the teaching experience that rarely comes out in interviews. In Fig. 5.3 it was included as the practical outcome of a sophisticated conception, namely "strategic alertness to classroom events": the ability to build on chance comments or a developing argument in ways that engage the attention and interest of students and challenge them to see aspects of the subject in a different way. A similar conclusion has been reached in other recent studies, where researchers have described "teachable moments" or "learning moments" (Forest, 1998; Trigwell & Prosser, 1997; Woods & Jeffrey, 1996). McAlpine, Weston, Beauchamp, C., Wiseman, and Beauchamp, J. (1999), in a study of exemplary university teachers, found that almost two-thirds of changes to teaching method and content were unplanned, carried out while teaching was taking place rather than in preparation for it. They also noted that about half the changes were not prompted by a strategy having failed or a problem having occurred, but rather by seizing an opportunity arising during the process of teaching—"not the monitoring of student response to their teaching, but monitoring for openings to teach provided by the students" (p. 120).

DISCUSSION

This chapter has focused on concepts used to describe learning and teaching in higher education; on conceptions, styles, and approaches; and on the different focus each of the three has. The limitations of restricting descriptions to these analytic abstractions led to the introduction of fine-grained analyses of everyday studying and the differing reactions to experience. These differing levels of explanation are essentially complementary, contributing in different ways to the purposes of research in this area. What do they seek to describe and how do they relate to each other?

Conceptions, Styles, and Approaches in Learning and Teaching

Conceptions of Learning and Teaching. At the broadest level, we have discussed conceptions of learning and teaching, which seem to represent the integration of a person's knowledge and experience within a general framework of understanding. The categories identified summarize the range of differences found among the comments of students and staff, as they reflect on their views and experiences in higher education. In relation to both learning and teaching, it seems that five broad categories conflate to a single distinction: the contrast between learning as reproducing knowledge presented by a teacher (and ways of transmitting information in a form that can be readily assimilated) and learning as a personal transformation of ideas and evidence leading toward conceptual understanding (with a view of teaching as supporting that endeavour by the students). This difference has proved to be of fundamental importance in making sense of the comments made by both students and staff, and yet the level of explanation does not convey much sense of how learning and teaching are carried out to accord with these conceptions.

Styles of Learning and Teaching. The term styles has been used in various ways in the literature. In the psychological literature it has been widely adopted to convey the marked difference in preference shown by people as they carry out tasks. This preference seems to be sufficiently consistent to suggest that it derives from basic personality characteristics, and yet there is an increasing recognition both that styles can be modified by instruction (Sternberg, 1997) and that the strategies used to carry out specific tasks may show considerable variability (Laurillard, 1979). In other words, there must be an interaction between the style and the nature and perceived demands of the task, such that stability can only be relative. Pask (1988) described his construct with differing emphases that drew attention to learning or conceptual styles (which showed preference and a certain long-term consistency), learning strategies (which could be described within the same dichotomy but were task related), and learning processes (which indicated the thinking processes used to carry out the task). He called the processes *comprehension learning* and *operation learning*, but these categories still carry the meanings of holist and serialist styles.

Approaches to Learning and Studying. In some ways, approaches are similar to styles. Students show some consistency over a range of tasks and situations, reflecting underlying motives and the intentions that stem from them. The processes used by students in adopting an approach to studying can be seen in terms of categories used by Pask (1976). For example, a deep approach depends on the alternation between comprehension learning (relating ideas and looking for patterns) and operation learning (checking and using evidence; see Tables 5.1 and 5.2). Continuing dominance of one preference over another reflects a distinctive style, whereas the appropriateness of the choice of process to task represents versatility.

The deep approach to learning also may also have its own stylistic element. Some people seem to have a strong drive to seek understanding in their own terms, irrespective of the task requirements or the context. As with extremes of Pask's (1976) styles, this can lead to lower levels of performance, where conceptual understanding is not a prime criterion of assessment. In the early years of undergraduate study, the strategic approach, combined with low levels on the "surface apathetic" dimension correlates strongly with grades. In later years, and in forms of assessment that give substantial weight to conceptual understanding, the deep strategic approach proves to be the most adaptive (Biggs, 1999; Prosser & Trigwell, 1999; Ramsden, 1992).

These findings reinforce the conclusion that approaches cannot be simply characteristics of the individual. Although they reflect personal history and elements of personality, they are also strongly influenced by teaching, assessment, and the whole learning environment (as Biggs argued in this volume, chap. 4). It is difficult to accept a concept as being both stable and variable, and as having generality in definition while requiring specificity in indicating the way it will be exhibited in differing situations. These apparent paradoxical combinations of opposites do, nevertheless, accurately represent the complexity of the phenomena the constructs are intended to describe.

Analytic Abstractions and Everyday Experience

In both the fine-grained analyses of study behavior and the reflective retrospective on teaching, the value of sensitivity and alertness to context comes through strongly. The meaning of events and their potential for growth are recognized and the opportunities are built on. These individuals "seize the moment" and use it either to improve their own capacity to learn or to help others to do so. This potentially important insight could only be found through fine-grained analyses of this kind. This research is in the tradition of interpretative research: it is not based on hypotheses, but rather it seeks to describe, and perhaps explain, aspects of experience. On their own, case studies can offer no more than indicative evidence, and yet they may be important in helping students and staff match the meaning of the concepts to their own experience. They may thus play a crucial role in communicating ideas about learning and teaching in ways that influence practice.

Pedagogical Fertility and Recognizable Reality

The main purpose of this area of research on student learning has been to understand the nature of learning and teaching transactions in higher education, with the ultimate goal of improving practice. For this reason, the level of explanation and the choice of constructs and conceptual frameworks cannot be based solely on the views of the theorist. There have to be judgments both of realism (to what extent the explanation is recognized by participants) and of what has been called *pedagogical fertility* (Entwistle, 1994; Entwistle & Hounsell, 1987).

Psychologists put as one hallmark of a good theory its fertility, which means its ability to generate new lines of research. In education there is a need for theories and concepts that are also pedagogically fertile, which generate ideas for innovations or new ways of thinking about learning and teaching.

The constructs and conceptual frameworks emerging from the research on student learning seem to show both forms of fertility. The burgeoning literature on student learning that draws on the distinction between deep and surface approaches is evidence enough in research terms. The readiness with which colleagues accept and use the distinction in staff development is an indication that the terms describe a "recognizable reality" (see Entwistle, 1997). This acceptance may, in part, be due to the origin of the concepts in descriptions of students' experiences of learning, but it may also be due to the accessibility of the terms and the connotative nature of the concepts. Staff and more experienced students, irrespective of subject area, can relate to the core meanings and relationships identified in the literature and create more specific meanings in relation to the nature and demands of their own discipline. When applied to a different subject matter or context, therefore, they act not just as analytic templates but as heuristic tools with which to think about the specific needs and problems presented by each learning context. That is easy to argue, and with some justification, and yet the effect on practice has been neither as strong, nor as widespread, as had been anticipated.

Changing Conceptions and Academic Practice

Attempts at improving the academic practice of both students and staff have, in the past, been largely directed at the level of techniques: study skills training for students and teaching tips and techniques for staff. These methods have generally met with only modest success, sometimes with none at all. They offer immediate applicability, which is initially attractive, and yet they provide no guidance about how or why these techniques should be used in everyday learning or teaching. Only with the type of understanding of the context and the process that comes from a developed conception can the methods come under the control of the individual and make sense to them. This recognition has led to a much greater emphasis on changing the less adaptive conceptions.

The evidence from first-year students presented here suggests only patchy development in the skill of studying, combined with a substantial resistance to study skills advice. Discussions offer one way of engaging students' interest in improving their study methods (Gibbs, 1981; van Overwalle, Segebarth, & Goldchstein, 1989), and yet they may fail to improve conceptions of studying in ways that lead to more effective studying. It may also be necessary to adopt a staged process in which direct advice is given first, and attempts to develop conceptions come later when students have more experience and are more likely to recognize the value of reflecting on their studying (Biggs, 1987). Such differentiated provision in supporting studying is, however, still not well developed, let alone evaluated.

Staff tend to look for specific advice on, say, better ways of presenting information, conducting tutorials, or using learning technology, and yet the techniques in themselves do not guarantee improved effectiveness. Each method depends crucially on the purpose for which it is used and the way in which it is implemented, neither of which can be readily discerned from a description of the approach. They can, however, be deduced within a conceptual framework that interprets how teaching and assessment, generally, influence the quality of student learning.

Reflecting on one's own experience in the light of carefully chosen case studies of teachers within the same general subject area may be a good starting point for bringing about conceptual change. An appropriate conceptual framework can then be offered, once the reality has been established through examples (see, for example, Brockbank & McGill, 1998; Cowan, 1998). A recent study explored various means of prompting conceptual change among lecturers and found that exposure to alternative conceptions was the most successful strategy, in terms of both general appreciation and successful impact (Ho, 1998):

> The participants particularly valued two aspects: that an *in-depth* reflection was facilitated by questions that addressed fundamental issues of teaching and learning, and that an analysis of one's own thought and practices was made possible with the support of a *systematic framework* about issues in teaching and learning. (p.32)

Of course, opportunities to reflect on personal experience against a conceptual framework can be introduced not just in staff development workshops, but also whenever departments or course teams are reviewing their practice as part of normal course development or quality assurance procedures (van Driel, Verloop, Van Werven, & Dekkers, 1997).

The dilemma facing both educational developers and student advisers is how best to bring together experience and conceptual frameworks. Conceptions cannot be changed simply by presenting alternatives, and experience will not lead to change unless it is interpreted against a broader framework of understanding. Such is the paradox at the heart of this situation. Conceptual change seems to depend on engagement with experience in ways that promote reflection, and this is true for both staff and students. How to achieve this is, however, much less clear.

REFERENCES

Atkinson, J. W., & Feather, N. T. (1966). *A theory of achievement motivation.* New York: Wiley.

Bennett, S. N., & Dunne, E. (in press). *The acquisition and development of core skills in higher education and employment.* Buckingham, England: Open University Press/SRHE.

Bereiter, C. (1990). Aspects of an educational learning theory. *Review of Educational Research,60,* 603–624.

Biggs, J. B. (1987). *Student approaches to learning and studying.* Melbourne, Australia: Australian Council for Educational Research.

Biggs, J. B. (1993). What do inventories of students' learning processes really measure? A theoretical review and clarification. *British Journal of Educational Psychology, 63,* 3–19.

Biggs, J. B. (1999). *Teaching for quality learning at university.* Buckingham, England: Open University Press.

Boekaerts, M. (1999). Motivated learning: Studying student*situation transactional units. *European Journal of the Psychology of Education, 14,* 41–55.

Brockbank, A., & McGill, I. (1998). *Facilitating reflective learning in higher education.* Buckingham, England: Open University Press/SRHE.

Brown, G. A., & Atkins, M. (1988). *Effective teaching in higher education.* London: Methuen.

Brown, G. A., & Bahktar, M. (1983). *Styles of lecturing.* Loughborough, England: Loughborough University Press.

Cowan, J. (1998). *On becoming an innovative university teacher.* Buckingham, England: Open University Press/SRHE.

Edelman, G. (1992). *Bright air, brilliant fire: On the matter of mind.* London: Penguin Books.

Entwistle N. J. (1979). Stages, levels, styles or strategies: Dilemmas in the description of thinking. *Educational Review, 31,* 123–132.

Entwistle, N. J. (1988). *Styles of learning and teaching.* London: Fulton.

Entwistle, N. J. (1994, June). Generative concepts and pedagogical fertility: Communicating research findings on student learning. Presidential address to the European Association for Research on Learning and Instruction. *EARLI News, 9–15.*

Entwistle, N. J. (1995). Frameworks for understanding as experienced in essay writing and in preparing for examinations. *Educational Psychologist, 30,* 47–54.

Entwistle, N. J. (1997). Contrasting perspectives on learning. In F. Marton, D. J. Hounsell & N. J. Entwistle (Eds.), *The experience of learning* (2nd ed., pp. 3–22). Edinburgh, Scotland: Scottish Academic Press.

Entwistle, N. J. (1998a). Improving teaching through research on student learning. In J. J. F. Forest (Ed.), *University teaching: International perspectives* (pp. 73–112). New York: Garland.

Entwistle, N. J. (1998b). Approaches to learning and forms of understanding. In B. Dart and G. Boulton-Lewis (Eds.), *Teaching and learning in higher education* (pp. 72–101). Melbourne, Australia: Australian Council for Educational Research.

Entwistle, N. J. (2000). Approaches to studying and levels of understanding: The influences of teaching and assessment. In J. C. Smart (Ed.), *Higher education: Handbook of theory and research (Vol. 15, pp. 156–218)*. New York: Agathon Press.

Entwistle N. J., & Entwistle, A. C. (1991). Contrasting forms of understanding for degree examinations: The student experience and its implications. *Higher Education, 22,* 205–227.

Entwistle N. J., & Hounsell, D. J. (1987, April). *Concepts and communication in student learning and cognitive psychology.* Paper presented at the British Psychological Society, Cognitive Psychology Section Conference, St. John's College, Oxford, England.

Entwistle, N. J., & Marton, F. (1994). Knowledge objects: Understandings constituted through intensive academic study. *British Journal of Educational Psychology, 64,* 161–178.

Entwistle, N. J., & Napuk, S. (1997). *Mind maps and knowledge objects. Organising and explaining understanding in essays and examinations.* Research Report. University of Edinburgh, England, Centre for Research on Learning and Instruction.

Entwistle, N. J., & Ramsden, P. (1983). *Understanding student learning.* London: Croom Helm.

Entwistle, N. J., & Tait, H. (1990). Approaches to learning, evaluations of teaching, and preferences for contrasting academic environments. *Higher Education, 19,* 169–194.

Entwistle N. J. & Walker, P. (in press). Strategic alertness and expanded awareness within sophisticated conceptions of teaching. In N. Hativa & P. Goodyear (Eds.), *Teacher thinking, beliefs and knowledge in higher education.* Dordrecht, The Netherlands: Kluwer.

Forest, J. J. F. (1998). University teachers and instruction: Important themes for a global discussion. In J. J. F. Forest (Ed.), *University teaching: International perspectives* (pp. 35–72). New York: Garland

Gibbs, G. (1981). *Teaching students to learn: A student-centred approach.* Milton Keynes, England: Open University Press.

Ho, A. (1998). A conceptual change staff development programme: Effects as perceived by participants *International Journal of Academic Development, 3,* 24–38.

Hodgson, V. (1997). Lectures and the experience of relevance. In F. Marton, D. J. Hounsell, & N. J. Entwistle (Eds.), *The experience of learning* (2nd ed., pp. 159–171). Edinburgh, Scotland: Scottish Academic Press.

Janssen, P. J. (1996). Studaxology: The expertise students need to be effective in higher education. *Higher Education, 31,* 117–141.

Kember, D. (1997). A reconceptualisation of the research into university academics' conceptions of teaching. *Learning and Instruction, 7,* 255–275.

Kember, D. (1998). Teaching beliefs and their impact on students' approach to learning. In B. Dart & G. Boulton-Lewis (Eds.), *Teaching and learning in higher education* (pp. 1–25). Melbourne, Australia: Australian Council for Educational Research.

Laurillard, D. M. (1979). The processes of student learning. *Higher Education, 8,* 395–409.

Marsh, H. (1987). Students' evaluations of university teaching: Research findings, methodological issues, and directions for future research. [Special issue]. *International Journal of Educational Research, 11* (3).

Marton, F. (1994). Phenomenography. In T. Husen & N. Postlethwaite (Eds.), *International encyclopedia of education* (pp. 4424–4429). Oxford, England: Pergamon.

Marton, F. & Booth, S. (1997). *Learning and awareness.* Mahwah, NJ: Erlbaum.

Marton, F., Dall'Alba, G., & Beaty, E. (1993). Conceptions of learning. *International Journal of Educational Research, 19,* 277–300.

Marton, F., & Säljö, R. (1976). On qualitative differences in learning. I. Outcome and process. *British Journal of Educational Psychology, 46,* 4–11.

Marton, F., & Säljö, R. (1997). Approaches to learning. In F. Marton, D. J. Hounsell, & N. J. Entwistle (Eds.), *The experience of learning* (2nd ed. pp. 39–58). Edinburgh, Scotland: Scottish Academic Press.

McAlpine, L., Weston, C., Beauchamp, C., Wiseman C., & Beauchamp, J. (1999). Building a metacognitive model of reflection. *Higher Education, 37,* 105–131.

McCune, V. (1998). Academic development during the first year at university. In C. Rust (Ed.), *Improving student learning: Improving students as learners* (pp. 354–358). Oxford, England: Oxford Brookes University, Centre for Staff and Learning Development.

McCune, V. & Entwistle, N. J. (1999). First-year students' perceptions of course work outcomes. In C. Rust (Ed.), *Improving student learning: Learning outcomes* (pp. 216–226). Oxford, England: Oxford Brookes University, Centre for Staff and Learning Development.

McCune, V. (1999, August). *Development of first-year students' conceptions of essay writing.* Paper presented at the 8th European Conference for Research on Learning and Instruction, Gothenburg.

Messick, S., & Associates (1976). *Individuality in learning.* San Francisco: Jossey-Bass.

Meyer, J. H. F. (1991). Study orchestration: The manifestation, interpretation and consequences of contextualised approaches to studying. *Higher Education, 22,* 297–316.

Meyer, J. H. F., Parsons, P., & Dunne, T. T. (1990). Individual study orchestrations and their association with learning outcome. *Higher Education, 20,* 67–89.

Miller, C. M. L., & Parlett, M. (1974). *Up to the mark: A study of the examination game.* London: Society for Research in Higher Education.

Murray, K., & Macdonald R. (1997). The disjunction between lecturers' conceptions of teaching and their claimed educational practice. *Higher Education, 33,* 331–349.

Pask, G. (1976). Styles and strategies of learning. *British Journal of Educational Psychology, 46,* 128–148.

Pask, G. (1988). Learning strategies, teaching strategies and conceptual or learning style. In R. R. Schmeck (Ed.), *Learning strategies and learning styles* (pp. 83–100). New York: Plenum Press.

Perkins, D. N. (1998). What is understanding? In M. S. Wiske (Ed.), *Teaching for understanding. Linking research with practice* (pp. 39–57). San Francisco: Jossey-Bass.

Perkins, D. N., Jay, E., & Tishman, S. (1993). Beyond abilities: A dispositional theory of thinking. *Merrill-Palmer Quarterly, 39,* 1–21.

Pintrich, P. R., & Garcia, T. (1994). Self-regulated learning in college students: Knowledge, strategies, and motivation. In P. R. Pintrich, D. R. Brown, & C. E. Weinstein (Eds.), *Student motivation, cogniton, and learning* (pp. 113–133). Hillsdale, NJ: Lawrence Erlbaum Associates.

Prosser, M., & Trigwell, K. (1999). *Understanding learning and teaching.* Buckingham, England: Open University Press.

Prosser, M., Trigwell, K., and Taylor, P. (1994). A phenomenographic study of academics' conceptions of science learning and teaching. *Learning and Instruction, 4,* 217–232.

Ramsden, P. (1979). Student learning and perceptions of the academic environment. *Higher Education, 8,* 411–428.

Ramsden, P. (1992). *Learning to teach in higher education.* London: Kogan Page.

Ramsden, P. (1997). The context of learning in academic departments. In F. Marton, D. J. Hounsell, & N. J. Entwistle (Eds.), *The experience of learning* (2nd ed., pp. 198–216). Edinburgh, Scotland: Scottish Academic Press.

Säljö, R. (1979). *Learning in the learner's perspective. I. Some common-sense conceptions.* (Report 76). Gothenburg, Sweden: University of Gothenburg, Department of Education.

Snow, R. E., Corno, L., & Jackson, D. (1996). Individual differences in affective and cognitive functions. In D. C. Berliner & R. C. Calfree (Eds.), *Handbook of educational psychology* (pp. 243–310). New York: Macmillan.

Sternberg, R. J. (1997). *Thinking styles.* Cambridge, England: Cambridge University Press.

Tait, H., Entwistle, N. J., & McCune, V. (1998). ASSIST: A reconceptualisation of the Approaches to Studying Inventory. In C. Rust (Ed.), *Improving student learning: Improving students as learners* (pp. 262–271). Oxford, England: Oxford Brookes University, Centre for Staff and Learning Development.

Trigwell, K., & Prosser, M. (1997). Towards an understanding of individual acts of teaching and learning. *Higher Education Research and Development, 16,* 241–252.

van Driel, J. H., Verloop, N., Van Werven, H. I., and Dekkers, H. (1997). Teachers' craft knowledge and curriculum innovation in higher engineering education. *Higher Education, 34,* 105–122.

van Overwalle, F., Segebarth, K., & Goldchstein, M. (1989). Improving performance of freshmen through attributional testimonies from fellow students. *British Journal of Educational Psychology, 59,* 75–85.

Vermunt, J. (1998). The regulation of constructive learning processes. *British Journal of Educational Psychology, 68,* 149–171.

Weinstein, C. E., Goetz, E. T., & Alexander, P. A. (1988). *Learning and study strategies.* New York: Academic Press.

Westen, D. (1996). *Psychology: Mind, brain and culture.* New York: Wiley.

Woods, P., & Jeffrey, B. (1996). *Teachable moments.* Buckingham, England: Open University Press.

6

The Lived Space of Learning: An Inquiry Into Indigenous Australian University Students' Experiences of Studying

Gillian Boulton-Lewis
Queensland University of Technology
Ference Marton
The University of Hong Kong, China, and *Gothenburg University, Sweden*
Lynn Wilss
Queensland University of Technology

This chapter is concerned with how to describe learning. This is considered first with regard to other theoretical perspectives presented in this book and then from the perspective of phenomenography. The focus is on learning by Indigenous Australian university students. The main difference between our perspective and those described in other chapters is that in our phenomenographically inspired paradigm we are looking at the world with the learners and trying to describe it as they see it rather than looking at their learning as outsiders.

WAYS OF DESCRIBING LEARNING

Sternberg and Grigorenko (1997) reviewed cognitive styles and defined them as "people's characteristic and typically preferred modes of processing information" p. 700, which are a subset of the general construct of style, that is, a distinctive or characteristic manner of acting. He described *thinking styles* as preferred ways of using abilities and as one manifestation of research on cognitive styles. His approach to styles is based on a theory of mental self-government in the belief that styles of government are a reflection of the way people organize themselves as individuals. He proposes that people have a profile of styles that are as important in what happens to them in life as to the way they think. These thinking styles are variable across tasks; differ in the strength of preference; have some flexibility; are mostly socialized, measurable and teachable; vary across the lifespan; are valued in some contexts and not others; are neither good or bad; and should not be confused with abilities. Sternberg has proposed that styles can serve as an important interface between personality and cognition.

The nature of *cognitive style* has been investigated and described comprehensively by Riding (1997). After reviewing the literature on styles and their descriptions, he and colleagues concluded they could all be grouped into two principle cognitive style dimensions: wholist–analytic and verbal–imagery. The wholist–analytic style dimension is concerned with "whether an individual tends to process information in wholes or parts" (p. 30). The verbal–imagery style dimension is concerned with "whether an individual is inclined to represent information during thinking verbally or in mental pictures" (p. 30).

Riding defined style according to Tennant (1988) as "an individual's characteristic and consistent approach to organizing and processing information" (p. 30). He distinguished between style and strategies on the grounds that style probably has a physiological basis and is fairly fixed for the individual, whereas strategies may be learned to cope with situations and tasks. He explained that the latter may be methods of using styles to make the best of situations and that in the literature the term *learning style* is sometimes used to refer to what he considers a strategy. With regard to learning behavior, it is proposed that wholists benefit from structuring of material whereas analytics should be able to impose their own structure; imagers learn best from pictorial material whereas verbalizers learn best through verbal means. There are some significant interactions between style and educational achievement, but these depend also on variations in teaching: analytics prefer to have control of their own learning whereas wholists have no particular preference. Most learners are attracted to materials that suit their style, underestimate their performance on subjects that do not suit their style, and overestimate their performance on those that do.

Kolb devised a learning style inventory (Smith & Kolb, 1986), which is designed to assess an individual's preferred learning style, that is, in terms of how a person deals with ideas and day-to-day situations. It provides learners with information about strengths and weaknesses in accomplishing tasks, solving problems, relating to and managing others, and realizing natural career choice preferences. The inventory measures an individual's relative position on the abstract–concrete (how we perceive new information) and the active–reflective (how we process what we perceive) dimensions.

People are separated into one of the four quadrants of these dimensions and can be described and labeled in terms of four basic learning styles (accommodator, diverger, assimilator, and converger), which determine how people go about their learning. Learning style is shaped by factors including the following: personality type, academic training (that is, learning how to learn), career experience, current jobs, and tasks. Smith and Kolb (1986) argued that "learning style is not a fixed trait but a current state of mind or of operating" (p. 5).

Biggs and Entwistle (1997a, 1997b) have both been concerned with inventories to measure *approaches to learning*. Biggs identified deep, surface, and achieving approaches, each of which includes motives and strategies and determine how students go about their learning. Generally, if a student adopts a surface approach, the intention is to meet the minimum requirements; a deep approach rests on intrinsic interest and the intention to understand; an achieving approach may be combined with a surface or deep approach and the intention is to enhance ego or self-esteem.

Entwistle has developed a series of inventories to measure students' approaches to learning. Use of the inventories in studies has typically produced three or four factors that represent deep, surface, strategic, and apathetic approaches to studying. Commonly, apathetic and surface approaches are found in students at risk of failure. A deep approach is characterized by behaviors such as seeking meaning, relating ideas, using evidence, and being interested in ideas. A surface or apathetic approach is characterized by lack of understanding, lack of purpose, syllabus boundedness, and fear of failure. A strategic approach is focused on organized studying, time management, monitoring effectiveness, and achievement motivation. Relationships between these approaches and academic performance are fairly consistent, with positive correlations between performance and the strategic approach and negative correlations between performance and the surface or apathetic approach. High scores on the deep approach are more likely to relate to academic success later in a degree course where demonstration of conceptual understanding may be required. The inventories also measure preparation for higher education in terms of knowledge and skills, conceptions of learning, learning and study skills, influences on studying, and preferences for deep and surface features in the learning environment. They provide a description of how students at a particular time go about their study and what other factors influence them.

Styles and Approaches: Differences and Similarities

In the theoretical perspectives considered earlier, we have a range of different descriptions of learning. Sternberg's (1995, 1997) work was concerned with describing and measuring characteristic and preferred modes of using abilities in processing information. These styles are variable and flexible across tasks and are mostly learned. Riding (1991, 1997) described cognitive styles that can be grouped into two dimensions and are concerned with how individuals process and represent information. He believed styles have a physiological base and strategies may be learned to use styles to the best advantage. Kolb (Smith & Kolb, 1986) described individuals' learning styles in terms of how they currently prefer to deal with ideas and day-to-day situations. He conceptualized these in terms of four learning orientations on two dimensions. These three descriptions of styles are concerned with underlying characteristics as well as measurable preferences and ways of processing information. On the other hand, approaches to learning as described and measured by Biggs (1997a & b) and Entwistle (Entwistle, et al., 2000) and colleagues, are more concerned with determining observable motives and strategies for learning.

Traditional and Current Perspectives on Indigenous Australian Learning

Early education policies regarding Indigenous Australians were based on a philosophy of assimilation which meant that Indigenous students were to be educated in more or less the same way as other students (from 1972 at least). As a consequence, no consideration was given to their cultural identity or possible learning style. The environment in which these students learned before their school experience was not considered, and instructional techniques in schools were those that had been established for White children (and probably did not take much account of their learning style either). However, when the background of Aboriginal students is considered, is it is evident they come from a cultural heritage different from that of other Australians. Contrasting heritages such as these have been depicted by Philpot (1990) as a "cultural clash," which is proposed as constituting a barrier to learning, particularly when Aboriginal students endeavor to acquire non-Aboriginal skills that threaten their traditional values and beliefs.

Many differences in learning between Aboriginal and non-Aboriginal people have been noted. For example research into learning by Aboriginal children has suggested they have superior skill in spatial and visual recall (Kearins, 1981) and they are more likely to process information simultaneously rather than successively (Klich & Davidson, 1984). They have the same capacity to process information as other Australian children (Boulton-Lewis, Neill & Halford, 1987), and they are field dependent (Collins, 1993) and have an external locus of control. Aboriginal children in traditionally oriented settings, as opposed to classroom settings, learn by observation and then by trial and error of real-world skills rather than by direct instruction (Christie, 1985).

For Aboriginal people, the family and broader community are central to their existence because it is within these domains that kinship and spiritual bonding, as well as respect for elders and the knowledge they possess, occurs. This has implications for learning. For instance, Aboriginal people regard learning as a process based on unity and not individuality. This means learning often occurs in an activity that involves people working together, usually as a group and for a period of time (Christie, 1994). Involvement from the whole group is important to the process of learning, and the information is important only as it relates to those involved and their unity. Another aspect relevant to Aboriginal learning is that it is not planned in a curriculum. The activities may be planned ahead; however, the learning is a by-product (Christie, 1994). This type of learning is situation specific, not abstract learning such as occurs in a classroom. Situation-specific learning was particularly evident when Aboriginal university students' experiences of informal learning, that is, learning that occurs outside the framework of a curriculum and without designation of student and teacher (Heath, 1991), were ascertained in a recent study by Boulton-Lewis, Marton, Lewis, and Wilss (1999). Informal learning experiences constituted acquiring skills by observation and imitation, acquiring cultural and social knowledge by transmission from family members or elders, independently developing practical skills by active problem solving, and independently seeking information in areas of interest by finding appropriate resources.

Family life may shape learning styles for Aboriginal children in that they are usually brought up with a degree of independence that involves learning to choose when to be involved in activities. They are not always controlled by others and will only learn when they are not pushed or forced to learn. Aboriginal children are often given social equality and are treated as equals by adults, they are not expected to comply immediately with adult requests, and the Aboriginal cultural method of control is indirectness and circumspection (West, 1994). However these aspects of Aboriginal culture may be problematic for students in formal learning situations where the teacher is in control and students are expected to comply immediately. Hughes (1987) also described aspects of Aboriginal cultural influences on learning as they contrasted with expectations of Australian education systems. These included spontaneity, repetition, and preference for the listener role as opposed to many non-Aboriginal learning characteristics that are concerned with structure, inquiry, and verbalization.

Further contrasts in learning style for Aboriginal students are due to their use of language. The language of instruction in Australian schools is often a second or third language for Aboriginal children (Collins, 1993) and many urban Indigenous students practice Aboriginal English in their classroom interactions. Often associated with this is indirectness in asking questions and use of silence, which is regarded as an appropriate response. Additionally, the role of language in learning is reduced as more practical activities that can be observed and imitated take precedence. Clearly, there are differences between Aboriginal cultural backgrounds and that of other Australians, and, as such, differences are faced in learning within an education system that was designed around the needs of the Western society.

Aboriginal Learning in Relation to Styles and Approaches

Although we acknowledge that styles are individual preferred ways of learning, we can consider the research in Aboriginal learning in relation to the range of theoretical descriptions of the ways people engage in thinking and learning, as described earlier, and make some generalized assumptions about Aboriginal learning styles. It is possible to relate assertions about Aboriginal learning to some of the styles Sternberg (1995, 1997) proposed. For example, with regard to the "functions" of thinking styles, it would seem that Aboriginal people may exhibit any one of the three functions—that is, legislative, executive, or judicial—and this may depend on the situation. A legislative style is evident in the sense that traditional learning for Aboriginal children involved trial and error rather than direct instruction; this allowed children to come up with their own way of doing something, within existing parameters, and as such could be considered as legislative. However, Collins (1993) asserted that Aboriginal people are field dependent and have an external locus of control, which is indicative of an executive style of following rules and a preference for participating in prestructured situations. When informal learning experiences were investigated by Boulton-Lewis et al. (1999) it became evident that some Aboriginal university students independently developed practical skills by active problem solving and independently sought information in areas of interest by finding appropriate resources. These activities would require a degree of relational thinking and analysis which fit the judicial function of thinking style. It is also feasible that Aboriginal people may have either a global or local level of thinking style, and that this may vary according to the situation. Most would hold an external scope of thinking style based on a preference for working in groups and being socially sensitive and aware of what is going on with others. Their learning would most likely be conservative because this, in part, gives preference to structured and predictable environments.

With regard to Riding's (1997) dimensions of cognitive style, it could be assumed that Aboriginal people generally possess a cognitive style belonging to the dimensions of wholist and imager. Those who possess a wholist orientation prefer to work with information that is structured as a whole and to process information in wholes. This contention is based on Klich and Davidson's (1984) findings that Aboriginal people process information simultaneously and that they are field dependent (Collins, 1993). Wholist characteristics are also evident in the way Aboriginal people go about their learning in that they prefer to work in groups and for long periods of time. Riding and Read (1996) conducted a study that found group work was particularly liked by wholist–imagers. Aboriginal people prefer learning that is organized around people, with information only important as it relates to them; this too points to the notion that they possess a wholist orientation. However, the university students who stated they experienced informal learning by actively solving problems do not seem to be wholists and may be developing an alternative cognitive style.

People with an imager cognitive style represent information in mental pictures and learn best from concrete and readily visualized information. Because Aboriginal children are believed to have superior skill in spatial and visual recall (Kearins, 1981) and to learn by observation, as do Aboriginal adults in informal situations (Boulton-Lewis et al., 1999), then it is possible that they belong to the imager dimension of cognitive style. An imager orientation is also reinforced by the fact that they are not verbalizers (Hughes, 1987) and they prefer practical activities over learning that is embedded in transmission by language.

According to Kolb's four dimensions of learning styles (Smith & Kolb, 1896), it would be reasonable to suggest that Aboriginal learning generally fits into either an accommodator style (which incorporates concrete experiences and active experimentation) or converger style (abstract conceptualization and active experimentation). The accommodator style is partly based on Hughes' (1987) contention that Aboriginals are spontaneous and repetitive in their learning. They are also known to prefer practical experiences, and, traditionally, Aboriginal children practiced trial-and-error learning, which is similar to an accommodator learning style (Claxton & Murrell, 1987). There is also evidence of a converger learning style for university students whose experiences of informal learning involved independently developing practical skills by problem solving and seeking information in areas of interest by finding appropriate resources.

In terms of approaches to learning, the approach Aboriginal people take may depend on the situation and purpose of the learning activity. According to Entwistle et al. (2000), a surface or apathetic approach is evidenced, in part, by lack of understanding. Aboriginal university students reported informal learning experiences of acquiring skills by observation and imitation. Because these activities can be carried out initially without understanding, this could be construed as constituting a surface approach to learning. However, the informal learning experiences of developing practical skills by problem solving and seeking information in areas of interest by finding appropriate resources would require relational processing of information and, as such, would constitute a deep approach.

Clearly, learning is complex and comprises not only instructional factors but also strategies for learning (Tynjälä, 1997) and the preferred ways individuals have of engaging in learning tasks. The preceding analysis indicates that learning for Aboriginal people is also complex, particularly because it comprises a mix of traditional perspectives and current practices in education that cannot easily be explained with relation to the theoretical styles and approaches described earlier. Additionally, it is clear that informal learning experiences for the Aboriginal university students provided useful means by which they could gain skills and knowledge and differ from their experience of formal learning. Jonassen (1995) recognized the importance of informal learning when he proposed that learners can acquire sophisticated skills and advanced knowledge without support or intervention of formal education. Resnick (1991) and Heath (1991) depicted strategies associated with informal learning as including identifying and solving problems, moving from known to unknown, reasoning analogically, elaborating, and arguing. In fact, the means by which the Aboriginal university students learn in informal settings seemed to extend the type of skills that may be learned in formal situations. Learning for Aboriginal students in formal situations, that is, within the boundaries of curriculum and under the instruction of qualified teachers, is examined in the following section. This is based on phenomenographically inspired research conducted by Boulton-Lewis et al. (2000) over 2 years with Aboriginal and Torres Strait Islander university students. The students' conceptions of formal learning and strategies used to learn in formal situations are presented along with changes noted over the 2 years. On the basis of searching the literature, we believe this is the first study of Aboriginal students' conceptions of learning. What follows is not concerned with styles but with the experience of learning from the learners point of view. This approach describes different models of description that we believe are more illuminating.

CHANGES IN WAYS OF LEARNING

All the previous descriptions refer to differences in what people are like as far as their preferred ways of functioning in various respects are concerned. This does not necessarily imply, of course, that people thus classified were born that way, nor that they will remain so for the rest of their lives. The only assertion made, as a rule, is that some students currently prefer certain ways of thinking and learning whereas others prefer other ways.

Styles do not describe what people are like: they describe what they do when they are trying to learn. An approach, in accordance with what was said in the previous section, denotes not only how students go about their studies, but also what drives them. A complementary perspective on differences in learning amounts to describing how people experience learning or how learning appears to them, instead of describing what people are like or what people do.

The idea is that people can only act in relation to phenomena or situations as they appear to them; they cannot react to things as they are perceived by others. So, to understand people's acts we have to understand what the objects and contexts of acts mean to them. If something is experienced as a promising possibility, people react to that, whereas if the same situation were experienced as a serious threat, they would react differently. In accordance with this, if we want to make sense of people's differing ways of learning, we have to find out the differing meanings learning might have for them.

This was the driving force behind many phenomenographic studies of qualitatively different conceptions of learning. One of the most quoted characterizations of different conceptions of learning was put forward by Säljö (1979). It has been replicated several times (e.g., Giorgi, 1986) and has been shown to be closely related to approaches to learning and to outcomes of learning (see, for example, Van Rossum & Schenk, 1984). Marton, Dall'Alba, and Beaty (1993) extended Säljö's set of categories and argued that adult learners (at least in the European contexts where the studies were carried out) seem to see learning in the following distinctively different ways. Learning can be seen as:

- increasing one's knowledge,
- memorizing and reproducing,
- applying,
- understanding,
- seeing something in a different way, and
- changing as a person.

The learning that is seen in these different ways is academic learning, that is, learning from symbolic representation that mostly constitutes interacting with text. The first three conceptions point to the wording of the text, the last three to the meaning of the text. The second and fourth conceptions refer to what is acquired in learning, the first and the sixth conceptions refer to the effect of learning, and the third and fifth conceptions refer to how use is made of that which is learned (Marton & Booth, 1997, p. 46).

Our research is based on an approach originally developed in Sweden in the 1970s and used more widely later (see Marton, Hounsell, & Entwistle, 1997). The approach is that of phenomenography, which takes the differing ways we experience and understand the world around us as its object of research. The question originally addressed was simply, "Why are some people better at learning than others?" The idea was that, to the extent that people arrive at different learning outcomes, they must have dealt with the learning task differently. They dealt with the learning task differently because they were handling different learning tasks in the sense that "objectively" the same task meant different things to each of them. The fact that the task appeared differently to them meant they were trying to do, and actually doing, different things. What they were trying to do and what they actually did defined their approaches to learning. Differences in their approaches to learning were closely correlated with, and in this sense explained, the observed differences in the outcome of learning.

To the extent that the students participating in the experiments defined them as learning situations, their ways of approaching the tasks were closely related to what learning as a phenomenon meant to them, that is, to their conceptions of learning. Differences in approaches and in conceptions were described in terms of sets of logically related holistic categories. More recently, research has demonstrated that categories depicting different approaches and different conceptions (or, more generally, different ways of experiencing something) are logically related because they reflect partially overlapping sets of critical aspects of the situation (the learning task) or of the phenomenon (learning) that the individual has discerned and focused on simultaneously. These "focused-on" aspects are dimensions of variation in the sense that they are not taken for granted but are alternatively different options attended to by the learner.

The Boulton-Lewis et al. Study

It would seem that, in some respects, learning for Aboriginal students is influenced by cultural factors. It is also known that Aboriginal students have the same capacity to process information as other students, and, as such, one might expect their achievement rates to be similar. However Aboriginal and Torres Strait Islander students have higher attrition rates in Australian schools and universities (Bourke, Burden, & Moore, 1996), and they have lower academic achievement than other students (Partington, Godfrey, & Harrison, 1998). In an effort to contribute to knowledge about learning for Aboriginal and Torres Strait Islander students in higher education, Boulton-Lewis et al. (1999, 2000; Boulton-Lewis, Marton, & Lewis, 1997; Boulton-Lewis, Wilss, & Lewis, 2000) conducted a long-term investigation to find out the conceptions of formal learning these students held. Their experiences of informal learning, reasons for studying, and strategies for learning were also ascertained. The following section details the methods of the research and the findings in regard to conceptions of formal learning for the first 2 years of the study. Changes that were evident in their conceptions of formal learning are also presented.

The investigation was conducted in a phenomenographically inspired manner. By that, we mean various aspects of learning for Aboriginal and Torres Strait Islander university students were ascertained; however, it was only in relation to formal learning that the outcome could be called conceptions of learning. Following is a description of the sample that details demographic as well as background information.

Fifteen Aboriginal and seven Torres Strait Islander students participated. They were enrolled in first-year bachelor degree courses including built environment and engineering, health care, commerce, and science; 14 were male and 8 were female. The students, who were studying in Queensland universities, came from many areas of Australia comprising 8 from capital cities, 11 from regional country towns, and 3 from Torres Strait Islands. Student's ages ranged from 18 to 48 years with most of the students in the 18-to-24 year age bracket. Sixteen students had completed Year 12; the others had completed Year 10 but subsequently completed either a bridging course or a diploma at a technical and further education college before gaining entry to university; one student gained entry through a Cadetship with the local city council. Some had varied work experience, and some had studied in other courses.

The students came from diverse backgrounds and had varied living and cultural experiences. Essentially, it was apparent there were three main areas of influence in the students' formative years: their *transient existence*; their *traditional-cultural heritage*; and, for a smaller number of students, the importance of *family support* in their lives.

Transient Existence.   Twelve of the students experienced several moves in their place of residence during their primary and high school years. One student went to 12 schools, whereas another went to 9 schools.

On average the students had experienced four moves in their place of residence and schools attended. Students explained this as "parents moved around a lot," and most students related their experiences of moving as involving great distances. School experiences were also varied and involved incidents of racism, periods of loneliness, and feelings of inadequacy. Some students countered this by relating almost exclusively to other Indigenous students. Two students stated that in the larger cities they were the only Indigenous students in the school and this, at times, proved to be difficult. However, not all students held negative perceptions of school. One student attended school exclusively in the Torres Strait Islands where he explained there were "lots of cultural influences in my education, everything was done for the community and the curriculum was organized for the Indigenous people of Torres Strait." He stated this fostered a strong link between community and school. He added however, this was not evident at university.

Traditional-Cultural Heritage.   Awareness of traditional-cultural Indigenous heritage varied, with some students stating they had strong ties to their traditional heritage whereas others had only recently become aware of their Indigenous background. Those expressing strong ties were aware of their tribal group. For example, one student was a descendant of the "Wanni Tribe" and another student spoke of the totem system in the tribal community where he grew up. A student from the Torres Strait Islands stated she held many traditional beliefs including those relating to evil spells that make you sick; she also stated she was more practical in her learning because she grew up watching aunties and learned skills in a more practical way. Others experienced cultural dances and feasts either where they grew up or on special occasions when visits were made to traditional family groups. Students expressed pride in their culture and in many instances stated they wished to strengthen ties with their Indigenous community. However, it was also apparent there were inherent dilemmas in being an Indigenous student. For example, a Torres Strait Islander student stated that although his heritage was important to him and he felt relaxed in his cultural environment doing things such as eating turtle and dugong, he also felt that at university he needed to talk and act in a way "respectable to his peers" and that this was "White man's education." This led him to feel "Black in a White man's place." Three students indicated their Indigenous language constituted a part of their cultural heritage.

Family Support.   Seven students indicated they gained "strength" from close family support and they were influenced to study at university by their parents or other family members. Four of these students had parents who had previously undertaken or were currently undertaking university studies. One student was influenced by his auntie who was in her third year of the same course, and another was influenced by her mother who was also studying in the same course. Family support was important to these students.

Methodology

Data were gathered by means of audiotaped semistructured interviews lasting approximately 1 hour. These were conducted by two Aboriginal research assistants in conjunction with the researchers[1]. Predetermined questions, used to stimulate dialogue, were framed to cover the following topics: reasons for studying at university; methods of studying; the meaning of learning, understanding, and knowledge; learning outside university, and memorization and learning. The interviewer followed salient points as they arose and probed to explore phenomena with the interviewee as fully as possible. Interviews were transcribed from the audiotapes, summarized, and analyzed jointly by the researchers using an approach inspired by phenomenography (Marton, 1994). Mutually exclusive conceptions were derived for formal learning and students were allocated to the conception that was most typical for them.

The conceptions of formal learning form a hierarchical system moving from those that are quantitative in nature to those that exhibit qualitative dimensions. For the first year of the study, three main conceptions were evident: (1) *acquiring knowledge,* (2) *understanding,* and (3) *personal growth.* Acquiring knowledge was explained in quantitative terms as accumulation of information or knowledge that may or may not result in its use. As such this conception was defined into two subcategories:

1A. *Increasing one's knowledge* (one student), which was explained as, "Trying to learn things and trying to get it into your head. Just getting more knowledge of things you don't know and what's interesting or in the outside world."
1B. Using knowledge (three students), which was described as "A process of taking in knowledge and outputting it into your words for assignments or tests."

Most students (16) explained formal learning as understanding and this was conceptualized in three ways:

---

[1]We acknowledge the substantial contributions to the research made by Gary Wallace and Barry Malezar in this respect. We also thank Carol Bond for her involvement with some of the interviews.

2A. *Understanding and acquisition* (nine students), which was regarded as acquisition through memorization and then understanding what was remembered. For example, "Learning is information. Remembering things that are important. You are learning and you've got to understand what you are learning."

2B. *Understanding, acquisition, and use* (two students), which was described as being able to move onto the next section of work or use what was understood in a practical sense as follows, "Learning is a series of stepping stones. Unless you've got the basic understanding of an idea, you're not going to be able to take that to the next step which is more information then after that use of that information then expansion of the information is the step after that."

2C. *Understanding, relating, elaborating, and analyzing* (five students), which was described as interacting with information by relating it to relevant experiences that may lead to understanding, "*You are learning because you are relating it to relevant things . . . relearning. Taking it in, knowing what you're knowing, learning what you don't know and building on both so that you've got a good foundation, relate back to reality, to experiences.*"

Learning was also explained as *personal growth* by two students who stated that this was manifested as an improvement in themselves as people. It also concerned relating their learning to life experiences and feeling good about themselves. When asked, "What does learning mean to you?" one student replied, "It's going to benefit you. Trying to gather knowledge that is going to help you within the future . . . learning means probably a better future for me . . . you're going to take something away with you that's going to help you for the rest of life. Like you get somewhere in life, have it within you, make you feel good inside."

The first conception of acquiring knowledge is in two parts, the first of which is similar to increasing one's knowledge found by Marton et al. (1993). The second part, acquiring and using knowledge, is similar to but not the same as Marton et al.'s second conception of memorizing and reproducing. Boulton-Lewis et al.'s next conception of understanding, which comprises three subcategories, is different from Marton et al.'s next two conceptions, which are applying and understanding. Essentially, the Aboriginal and Torres Strait Islander students exhibited a strong emphasis on just making sense of material initially, and then moved to using the materia, followed by developing understanding. In the first year of the study, Boulton-Lewis et al. found no evidence of Marton et al.'s last two conceptions.

Conceptions of formal learning for the second year of the study were ascertained from 17 of the students who had participated during the first year. The second-year conceptions for the pooled data were the same as those found in the first year (although individual students varied) except for personal growth, which became the conception changing as a person. This was due to a realization by three students that university learning had led to a change within themselves. It is exemplified by one student who stated, "Academic pursuit is painful, it's hard because a lot of stuff you hear will conflict with what you believe personally. What I perceived to know before now is minuscule. What I have learned has changed me." Although, for the most part, the conceptions remained constant over the 2 years, not all students evidenced the same conception for both years of the study. In summary, seven students held the same conception of formal learning over the 2 years, five students had a higher level conception, and five students expressed a lower level conception of formal learning during the second year. This is discussed more fully in Boulton-Lewis, Wills, and Lewis (2000).

The Lived Space of Learning

We have applied, to a limited extent, descriptive categories originating from theoretical paradigms (such as thinking styles) to Australian Indigenous students' learning. We also described Australian Indigenous students' ways of experiencing learning in terms of their conceptions of learning. Boulton-Lewis, Wills, and Lewis (2000) described, in addition to the students' conceptions of learning, the differing strategies reported by them from their first to their second year of studying. They concluded that although the conceptions of learning expressed on the two occasions were more or less the same on the group level, the strategies students reported using varied within the levels. So does this mean that although the students carried out their studies in different ways (and used a greater range of strategies) they experienced their studies more or less in the same way (by expressing largely the same conceptions of learning)? To answer this question we take a second look at the data we describe as the "lived space of learning." We call it the lived space because although conceptions of learning remained more or less the same, students were living and experiencing learning in a concretely constructed sense differently. For example, consider the student who expressed the same conception of learning at both occasions, but described his way of actually going about it in different ways:

Year 1

Interviewer: So what actually does study mean to you?

Student: Probably just actually learning the material. Actually sitting there and for an exam . . . if I have to study for an exam I'll be copying out the sheet and rereading it over and over and over.

Interviewer: after you rewrite what you are actually studying, what's the process after that?

Student: I find the easiest way for me to do is probably writing it out again and reading it to myself and then reading it, reading it, reading it.

Year 2

Interviewer: When you read the stuff, how do you get the meaning out of it?

Student: I don't know, you usually try and maybe if you read it and then try and argue a bit.

Interviewer: How do you do that?

Student: Like if you read it and you sort of put yourself like you don't, do you believe it or not and by doing that you sort of put it to more something you know than you don't know.

So would we say that judging from these excerpts from the two interviews this student seemed to experience learning in the same way? Absolutely not! Although the student is talking about what he does, the statements imply different ways of experiencing learning. In the first case, the student is limited to strategies such as reading over and over, writing out and reading, and reading again. He is limited to doing this because it is the only way he knows of learning, as he declares elsewhere. He seems to be looking at the text and reading it again and again. No other options for handling it appear to him. In the second case, he has started "arguing" with the text. He does not take the text as given, but opens it up to different and even contradictory interpretations. He also describes in the interview the different methods he now uses in his studies. Studying has acquired a structure! It is this shift from the experience of learning as something undifferentiated, unstructured, that can only be done in one way, to the experience of learning as a more purposeful and structured activity with different options for acting, thinking and reasoning that is reflected in the changes in the distribution of the students across categories of strategies (Boulton-Lewis, Wilss, & Lewis, 2000). The thing is that our ways of experiencing the world around us are not only expressed through our words (when we are asked to describe how we experience something, for instance) but they are also expressed through our acts or our descriptions of our acts.

So consider again the longitudinal study of Indigenous Australian university students' ways of experiencing learning. Boulton-Lewis et al. arrived at the categories described earlier by analyzing the first- and second-year data separately and described categories for both years that were similar. An alternative way of searching for answers to the question, "How have the students' ways of experiencing learning changed during the second year of studies?" would be to regard all the data obtained as potentially indicative of ways of experiencing learning and, instead of developing categories for both, start with the most striking differences between the data from the two occasions.

The shift is from the experience of a strong focus on getting what is on the pages into one's head without knowing how it can be done, to the experience of a realization that studying has a flexible structure and texts have alternative interpretations, that is, interpretations that are products of certain alternative mental acts. The difference between seeing the text as given or taking it for granted, on the one hand, and seeing it as subject to alternative interpretations by one's own mental acts, on the one hand, can be described as the difference between focusing on the text as such, and focusing on what the text is about.

This distinction is the core of Marton and Säljö's (1976) way of describing differences in approaching learning tasks. The concept of "approaches to learning" originated from Svensson's (1976, 1977) work referring to the learners' differing ways of relating to the learning task. Although Svensson studied how learners differ in delimiting "parts and wholes" and made a distinction between atomistic and holistic approaches, Marton and Säljö distinguished between learners focusing on the text as such, on the one hand, and learners focusing on that which the text was about, on the other hand. Initially, they referred to the distinction as one between surface and deep levels of processing, but later, inspired by Svensson's work, they talked about surface and deep approaches to learning (e.g., Marton & Säljö, 1984). Approaches to learning were described in this Swedish research (both by Svensson 1976, 1977, and by Marton & Säljö, 1976, 1984), by drawing on what the students said about their ways of experiencing learning situations; what they said about their ways of handling those learning situations; and, in Svensson's case, what they did when looking for qualitative differences in the outcome of learning. These approaches to learning were not seen as attributes of the learners, they were seen as functional correlates of the outcome of learning. By describing how the learning task was handled and experienced, one can understand how the outcome came about. Approaches to learning reflect as much the context and conditions of learning as they reflect about the learners. What is important about them is that any attempt to improve the outcomes of learning has to be mediated by the approaches to learning. There is no way of boosting the outcomes of learning without boosting the learners' way of experiencing and handling the learning task.

So, although, approaches to learning are supposed to refer to particular learning experiences in the original Swedish research, conceptions of learning found in analyzing interview data refer to the differing ways in which learners experience, understand, and make sense of learning in general. But is there such a thing as "learning in general"? Säljö (1994) doubted it. He said what are reported as conceptions of learning are differing meanings of learning, constructed and experienced in highly specific and fairly artificial situations, that is, individual interviews about abstract phenomena.

In any case, there is a clear methodological difference in how approaches to and conceptions of learning have been described. When describing approaches to learning, learners are engaged in reflecting on their engage-ment in a learning task. Their focus is on the object of learning and subsequently on themselves focusing on the object of learning. In studies of conceptions of learning, the learners' focus is supposed to be on learning itself (in a general sense). This is also how questionnaire studies of approaches to learning differ from the original studies of approaches to learning. Whereas the latter refer to specific learning tasks and specific objects of learning, the former usually lack an identifiable object of learning unless respondents are specifically directed to consider a nominated learning context.

Expanding the Lived Space of Learning

We have described above the difference between the first and second years of study, but we can take another perspective from which we do not have to make the distinctions among strategies, approaches, and conceptions. What is revealed with the Aboriginal and Torres Strait Islander students over the 2 years of the study are dimensions of variation, based on a greater awareness of their own learning, that are explained and exemplified with second-year interview extracts as follows:

> Interviewer: Now (at university) you seem to have a set goal?
> Student: Yes, you know what you are working towards, whereas in school well I didn't even know what I wanted to do. I didn't do anything . . . whereas now I want to know more. I'm asking more questions, questioning other students. Like if they say something and you know there is something else to it so you go deeper. Like you gotta do this test, but WHY are you doing that test and HOW is that test done, so it's more those sort of questions. At school it was more memorizing, whereas now I'm reading and sitting back and thinking about it and Oh OK light bulbs on in there. I'll make my own notes not write it out from the text book.

The way I study is read over things, try and think how I can use these, depends on what I read trying to think how that relates to life and individual events and basically take into consideration what other people say too. I'm finding that's something that has changed from my first year that I listen more to what other people say in the class. I've learnt to think more broadly . . . to take other peoples issues aboard like think about what they are going through. Like lean more towards other people's views.

These interview extracts indicate there was a shift from being restricted to a taken-for-granted way of handling studies (basically writing out notes, reading books, and reading again and again) to becoming aware of possible alternative ways of studying. During the second year of studies, 12 students evidenced alternative ways of studying that were not apparent during their first year. For some, the alternate ways included arguing the point about what they were learning, questioning themselves, making connections in their learning, engaging in a deeper way with topics, and incorporating other ideas. However, for 3 of the 12 students, the greater awareness of what was required in their learning in second year resulted in alternate ways of studying that meant being less organized or not as structured as they were in first year. This is exemplified in the following students' statements:

> Student: Study for me at present is disorganized, last year was a lot more organized. I don't have any structure to what I do, I just grab whatever is on top of the pile. I'm not making drafts or plans any more. That's very reflective in the marks I'm getting but the marks haven't dropped enough for me yet to be forced to restructure my study. First year . . . I spent a lot more time studying notes and handouts. I don't even read class handouts any more. It's a major change in study pattern. I only write information that is new, that way stuff that I understand isn't getting cluttered up with something that is slightly different to what I already know. If I'm reading my lecture notes and I understand a paragraph I dump it and I won't put that into point form. I'll only read what I do understand to the point I do understand it.
>
> What I've tried to do is cut down on the time so I really try and focus, really try and concentrate so it goes in one time and where you don't have to go back . . . What I'm trying to do is just focus and concentrate on it just once or twice so it really does just cement in to my learning, in to my memory. Trying to get a system where it is more time efficient. It's not as elaborate but it is elaborate because it's a better way to learn for myself instead of spending hour and hours on something whereas it could just take you one hour to knock it on the head.

Second, there was a shift from being constrained to formal studies at university to connecting formal and informal learning. This was evidenced by students being able to think of the content of the formal studies, and of everyday experience, and of what was learned previously in informal settings, at the same time, thus connecting the two. Whereas 5 students made connections between their formal and informal learning during the first year of study, this had increased to 11 students during second year. The following extracts exemplify this change:

> Student: An arbiter dicta in legal terms is basically a principle adviser to a crown prosecution. He is the person who organizes researchers. He finds correct acts. Legislation and laws that fit into a particular case. The arbiter in that case is the person, he is the principle finder, he's the one that will get you off. He's the one that'll fry you. So it is one or the other. The traditional term, the arbiter dicta in my family would be like elders of course. They're the ones that'll determine whether you can stay within the community or you're pushed out of the community. When you look at it from a traditional point of view and you try and relate to that, there are a lot of similarities, but similarities from a distance. It's something more of a Europeanistic view of it in a cultural sense. You can understand it, you can explain it really simple. But when you got to try and talk the White man's way, you got to use words like this to say, "Oh look, he's the arbiter dicta and he'll be helping you in the case."
>
> I write key points, relate to personal experiences, look up the Internet, surveys, look at one side like your experiences and your personal way you learn in the classroom then what you look at in the library or the Internet and then combining both of them to have a knowledge that's formal and informal but yet it's formal. When you write it down it's like making yourself become aware of the topic, specify keys about that topic then develop a procedure whether it's informal or formal about engaging into that topic for the information that you need.

Third, there was a shift from taking the claims made by the teachers, the texts, and other authorities for granted to realizing that things could actually be otherwise and, hence, challenging the assertions. Boulton-Lewis et al. described this as challenging teachers, texts and others. During first year, one student actively challenged the authority of the lecturers, stating they were too rigid in their approach as they focused on course content without any consideration given to the development of knowledge. However, during second year, five students asserted that they no longer simply accepted everything that was presented to them; rather, they started to question and challenge information and beliefs of others. This change is exemplified as follows:

> Student: Well learning at uni is more theoretical, I think than the home place. Because you know, in home you know, what you see you do and what you hear you say you know. I find anyway has been the case with me and that

can even be applied here in uni as well I suppose. But what you hear here, like you can debate more things you know. Like at home I think like with Dad and that sort of thing, like he sort of always, he's the father figure and he's right. What he says is right, you don't go against your parents or your relatives. But here, in uni you can say what you want, so long as you can back it up. But even at home, if you say something back you may not be standing up, you'd be flat on your back. I realize his [Father's] opinion is only based on what he's seen. You know there's generational ideas that are handed from his parents to him and so on and I can see defects in some of his views. Yes, I suppose yeah there's a little differences.

Fourth, there was a shift from taking ways of viewing the world for granted to becoming aware of alternative ways of seeing the world. During first year, three students indicated that learning had broadened their outlook and that this resulted in their viewing phenomena from a different perspective; this number had increased to five during second year. The following interview extracts exemplify this change:

Interviewer: Has the meaning of learning changed for you?

Student: Learning now is painful.

Interviewer: Is painful?

Student: Academic pursuit is painful. I don't care what anyone says a marriage of the academic pursuit is painful. Learning is hard simply because a lot of stuff you hear will conflict with what you believe personally and what you hold dear. Like I said my academic base was insignificant compared to what it is now. What I perceived to have know before now is minuscule to what I know how but in that what I have learnt now has changed me personally as well so learning is very painful because it's always conflict with what I believe and what I think I believe. For example I used to think that HIV AIDS was a cure for homosexuality. I no longer believe that simply because I was brought up being told that homosexuality was wrong. Now it's a choice or how they're born. It's not wrong in their eyes and I've come to learn and understand or understand before I learnt the difference between a choice and a way of life.

These changes in awareness are summarized in Table 6.1 for each student under the four major shifts identified in Boulton-Lewis et al.: alternative ways of studying, connecting formal and informal learning, challenging teachers texts and others, and alternative ways of seeing the world.

What do all these shifts have in common? In every case there is a change from the taken for granted and not being aware of options to the opening up of different possibilities. This is a shift from little variation between alternatives (because few alternatives were seen) to variation between different options that one is aware of. Hence, variation is the awareness of different possibilities. The different respects in which an opening up of

TABLE 6.1

Changes in Awareness for Each Student Over the 2 Years of the Study

Student	Alternate Ways of Studying		Connecting Formal and Informal Learning		Challenging Teachers, Text and Others		Alternative Ways of Seeing the World	
	1997	1998	1997	1998	1997	1998	1997	1998
1	.	x	.	x	.	x	.	x
2	.	x	.	x	.	.	.	.
3	.	x	.	.	.	.	.	.
4	.	.	.	x	.	x	.	.
5	.	x	.	.	x	.	x	x
6	.	x	.	.	.	x	.	x
7	.	.	x	.	.	.	.	.
8	.	x	.	.	.	x	.	.
9	.	x	.	x	.	.	x	x
10	.	x	.	x	.	.	.	x
11	.	.	x	x	.	.	.	.
13	.	x	x	x	.	.	.	.
14	.	x	x	x	.	.	.	.
15	.	x	x	x	.	.	.	.
16	.	x	.	.	.	.	x	.
18	.	.	.	x	.	.	.	.
22	.	.	.	x	.	x	.	.

Note.   x denotes students who evidenced a change in awareness.

variation occurred belong to a set of dimensions in which the students are aware of alternative possibilities, constituting a space of variation. Adopting such a perspective enables Boulton-Lewis et al. to assert that one year of studying at university brought about a widening of the *space of variation* in the students participating in their investigation.

The concepts of dimensions of variation and the space of variation originate from the following line of reasoning more fully developed in Marton and Booth (1997) and Bowden and Marton (1998). The most important form of learning implies the development of the capability of seeing something differently from before. To see something in a certain way amounts to discerning some critical features of the phenomena and focusing on them simultaneously. But discerning a particular feature requires the experience of variation in the dimension corresponding to that feature. For example "color" can only be experienced because there are different colors (that is, variation); "happiness" can be experienced because there are variations in happiness; the "threeness" of three can be experienced because numerosity varies. Furthermore, this variation may be explicit and experienced (that is, something varies and this variation is experienced by the learner) or implicit (that is, the learner is aware of alternative possibilities of potential variation). Experiencing variation in a certain respect is the opposite of taking that respect for granted. For example, frame of reference is usually taken for granted but you may be aware that the same movement appears differently if you see it from different frames of reference. In that case you experience variation in the frame of reference.

There have been some recent studies of teaching as described from this perspective (Runesson, 1999). Questions raised in these studies are: In what respects does the teacher introduce variation in his or her teaching, and in what respects do the students and the teacher together constitute variation? What dimensions vary simultaneously? The complex of different dimensions of variation is referred to as the space of variation or the space of learning, that, is the space in which learning is taking place. It may or may not be experienced by the students. But the space of variation discussed in Boulton-Lewis et al. is brought about (and hence experienced) by the learners themselves (there is actually one such space for each learner). Therefore, it is called "the lived space of learning." The most important change the first year of university studies gave rise to was the opening up of what was previously taken for granted, the awareness of alternatives, options, and possibilities where there was only one thing to begin with. This is what is called "expanding the lived space of learning," as epitomized in the following second-year extract:

> Interviewer: OK, we've just put a bit of a timing piece between Western learning and other learnings. So how do you see the difference in those two?
>
> Student: Well they're something that you've got to go through before you can be the other. Like to be an Aboriginal boy, until you've been through a certain learning where you're taken with your elders and you learn things and then you, certain things happen to you, and then you're classed as a man. And like even in this context you come here, you learn things and certain things do happen to you here as well that qualify you to be highly credible yeah. And that's like your trophy like you know I think. Something you've got to show, well look I have done this and people respect you for that you know. They respect you that you've been able to do that and if they want to know certain things and you've been trained, they can go to you and ask questions about that and hopefully get good answers.

DIFFERENT PERSPECTIVES ON LEARNING

It is reasonable to assume that better understanding of what constitutes learning may lead to educators improving educational experiences and to learners participating more fully to achieve more productive learning outcomes. This type of assumption has inspired many studies learning, and, as a consequence, learning has been viewed and explained from different perspectives. For example, as explained at the beginning of this chapter, Sternberg proposed the construct of styles of learning as thinking styles, Riding described cognitive styles, and Kolb explored and delineated learning styles. From yet another perspective, approaches to learning have been proposed by Biggs and Entwistle and in phenomenographic studies. Each of these aspects of learning have illuminated the ways people engage in thinking and learning, and they may even help explain outcomes of learning. However, it is our contention that we can only truly begin to understand the functional correlates of learning by exploring the situated experience of learning as practiced. We believe this to be the case because this can explain people's awareness of their own learning based on how they experience it. By exploring students' views of learning through interview and discussion, we gain an understanding of the phenomena and situations of learning as they appear to the learner. This perspective is also useful because it can capture changes that may occur in learning that might otherwise be lost.

In the first part of this chapter we presented the statements, from research, that have been made about Aboriginal learning and an explanation of these results based on research in learning styles. The second part of the chapter is a phenomenographically inspired empirical study of the views and practices of learning held by Aboriginal and Torres Strait Islander university students in Australia. The difference between the descriptions in the first and second parts of this chapter is that in the first part we deal with what others have said about Aboriginal learning and in the second part we deal with what the Aboriginal students themselves said.

Initially to contextualize this study we described traditional and current perspectives on learning by Indigenous students. We noted that, because of variances in cultural backgrounds, there were some differences in their learning as compared with learning for mainstream students. Learning for Aboriginal children was depicted as being grounded in visual activities, as occurring largely through participation and trial and error, and as an activity in which the learning was secondary to the actual participation and people involved. Child-rearing practices for Aboriginal children were also depicted as being different from those experienced by mainstream Australian children, and one result of this was possible difficulties for Aboriginal children in classroom situations. Aspects of learning that traditional Indigenous Australians practiced were evident in the informal learning experiences for the Indigenous university students in the study conducted by Boulton-Lewis et al. (1999). For example some of the students stated they learned outside university by observing, and in some instances imitating, what they had observed. However, it was also apparent that, in many respects, learning for these students was similar to that of any other student. This was based on the general assumptions about learning as experienced by Indigenous people in relation to thinking styles, cognitive styles, and learning styles that were explained earlier. It was also clear that these students held conceptions of formal learning that were similar to those of other university students. However, small changes in learning for some of the students emerged from the second-year interviews when they responded to questions about their conceptions of learning, experiences of informal learning, and strategies used to learn.

It was evident that these students, in second year, had developed an awareness of their learning that made their practices more purposeful and structured. A direct consequence of this was that some of the students developed an awareness that alternatives existed in the way they could go about learning; in the way they thought about connecting formal and informal learning, in that they could question sources of authority; and, for some students in how they thought about the world generally. We believe these shifts in awareness illustrate a lived space of learning and that this was a result of participation in first-year studies at university. Thus, although the students in second year, as a group, held almost the same conceptions of learning, the way some of them went about their learning changed; that is, they lived and experienced learning in a concretely situated sense different-ly. What seemed to be the case with these students was that because the learning strategies used during the first year were not congruent with the demands of formal learning, they developed an awareness that resulted in alternative ways of learning. It is also possible that, in part, these changes were brought about by a supportive learning environment where students had access to tutors, or may have occurred in response to their reasons for undertaking university study, or they may have been influenced by their prior life experiences. However, we believe the greatest influence that contributed to widening the lived space of learning was the experience of being a university student and taking part in day-to-day activities and learning at university, where there is some need to understand and explain phenomena in relation to theory.

Essentially, the second-year Indigenous students began to evidence the most important form of learning, that is, being able to see something differently from the way it was seen before. This means that, as a consequence of their first year of study at university, the students developed an awareness of learning that made it possible for them to discern critical features. These students then selectively applied these to their own learning as evidenced in the four dimensions of change as described earlier.

Thus, investigating, in a phenomenographically inspired way, the views of learning held by these students, revealed valuable information that we believe would not otherwise have become apparent. It is from such information about views of learning held by different groups of students that we can continue to explore and refine what we understand about the phenomenon of learning.

We did not really find defining differences in terms of learning for this group of Indigenous students as compared with other groups of students in other studies. However, they have several characteristics in common with other students who do not have extensive experience of academic studies. Nevertheless, there was considerable variation within the group, which is consistent with the possible range of learning styles postulated on the basis of other research in Aboriginal learning from other theoretical perspectives. Instead of trying to characterize these students as individuals or as a group, it is more fruitful, we believe, to capture their ways of making sense of studying. When we do this, we find some remarkable changes in the second-year students in their ways of experiencing learning in a concretely situated sense and in their ways of going about it. These changes have been referred to as the widening of the lived space of learning, that is, the opening up of previously taken-for-granted aspects of studying. As these students experienced, in their studies, ways of thinking that were different from their own, we could claim that by experiencing variation, their thinking opened up to variation and ensuing alternative options.

ACKNOWLEDGMENT

The research upon which the study was based was funded during 1997 to 1999 by an Australian Research Council Large Grant. We also acknowledge the financial support of the Swedish Council for Research in the Humanities and Social Sciences.

REFERENCES

Biggs, J. (1997a). *Study process questionnaire manual: Student approaches to learning and studying.* Hawthorn, Australia: Australian Council for Educational Research.

Biggs, J. (1997b). *Student approaches to learning and studying.* Hawthorn, Australia: Australian Council for Educational Research.

Boulton-Lewis, G. M., Marton, F., & Lewis, D. (1997). Conceptions of learning held by Aboriginal students in a tertiary program in indigenous primary health care. In R. Murray-Harve & H. C. Silins (Eds.), *Learning and teaching in higher education: Advancing International perspectives*, Proceedings of the Higher Education Research & Development Society of Australasia conference (pp. 21–36). Adelaide, South Australia: Flinders Press.

Boulton-Lewis, G. M., Marton, F., Lewis, D. C., & Wilss, L. A. (1999). *Learning in formal and informal contexts: Conceptions and strategies of Aboriginal and Torres Strait Islander university students.* Manuscript submitted for publication.

Boulton-Lewis, G. M., Marton, F., Lewis D., & Wilss, L. A. (2000). Aboriginal and Torres Strait Islander university students conceptions of formal learning and experiences of informal learning. *Higher Education, 00,* 1–20.

Boulton-Lewis, G. M., Neill, H., & Halford, G. S. (1987). Information processing and scholastic achievement in Aboriginal Australian children in south east Queensland. *The Aboriginal Child at School, 14*(5), 42–55.

Boulton-Lewis, G. M., Wilss, L. A., & Lewis, D. (2000). Indigenous Australian university students' changing conceptions of learning and strategies. In H. P. Langfeldt (Ed.), *Implicit theories of learning—products and processes. Learning and Instruction Special Issue.* Manuscript submitted for publication.

Bourke, C. J., Burden, J., & Moore, S. (1996). *Factors affecting performance of Aboriginal and Torres Strait Islander Students at Australian universities: A case study.* Canberra, Australia: ACPS.

Bowden, J., & Marton, F. (1998). *The university of learning: Beyond quality and competence in higher education.* London: Kogan Page.

Christie, M. J. (1985). *Aboriginal perspectives on experience and learning: The role of language in Aboriginal education.* Victoria, Australia: Deakin University Press.

Christie, M. J. (1994). Aboriginalizing post primary curriculum. *The Aboriginal Child at School, 22*(2), 86–94.

Claxton, C. S., & Murrell, P. H. (1987). *Learning styles: Implications for improving educational practices.* Washington, D C: Association for the Study of Higher Education.

Collins, G. (1993). Meeting the needs of the Aboriginal students. *The Aboriginal Child at School, 21*(2), 3–16.

Entwistle, N. J., Tait, H., & McCune, V. (2000). Patterns of response to an approaches to studying inventory across contrasting groups and contexts. *European Journal of Psychology of Education, XV (1),* 33–48.

Giorgi, A. (1986). A phenomenological analysis of descriptions of concepts of learning obtained from a phenomenographic perspective. *Publikationer fran institutionen för pedagogik. Göteborgs universitet, 18.*

Heath, S. B. (1991). It's about winning! The language of knowledge in baseball. In L. B. Resnick, J. M. Levine, & S. Teasley (Eds.), *Perspectives on socially shared cognition* (pp. 101–124). Washington, DC: American Psychological Association.

Hughes, P. (1987). *Aboriginal culture and learning styles: A challenge for academics in higher education institutions.* Publications Office, University of New England, NSW, Australia.

Jonassen, D. H. (1995). Supporting communities of learners with technology: A vision for integrating technology with learning in schools. *Educational Technology, July/August,* 60–63.

Kearins, J. (1981). Visual spatial memory in Australian Aboriginal children of desert regions. *Cognitive Psychology, 13,* 436–460.

Klich, L. Z., & Davidson, G. R. (1984). Toward a recognition of Australian Aboriginal competence in cognitive functions. In J. R. Kirby (Ed.), *Cognitive strategies and educational performance* (pp. 155–202). Orlando, FL: Academic Press.

Marton, F. (1994). Phenomenography. In T. Huson & T. N. Postlethwaite (Eds.), *The international encyclopedia of education* (2nd ed., Vol. 8, pp. 4424–4429). Oxford, England: Pergamon Press.

Marton, F., & Booth, S. (1997). *Learning and awareness.* Mahwah, NJ: Lawrence Erlbaum Associates.

Marton, F., Dall'Alba, G., & Beaty, E. (1993). Conceptions of learning. *International Journal of Educational Research, 19*, 277–300.

Marton, F., Hounsell, D. J., & Entwistle, N. J. (Eds.) (1997). *The experience of learning* (2nd. Ed.). Edinburgh, Scotland: Scottish Academic Press.

Marton, F., & Säljö, R. (1976) On qualitative differences in learning: 1—Outcome and process. *British Journal of Educational Psychology, 46*, 4–11.

Marton, F., & Säljö, R. (1984). Approaches to learning. In F. Marton, D. Hounsell, & N. J. Entwistle (Eds.), *The experience of learning* (pp. 36–55). Edinburgh, Scotland: Scottish Academic Press.

Marton, F., Watkins, D., & Tang, C. (1997). Discontinuities and continuities in the experience of learning: An interview study of high-school students in Hong Kong. *Learning and Instruction, 7*(1), 21–48.

Partington, G., Godfrey, J., & Harrison, B. (1998, November/December). *Perspectives on retention of Aboriginal students*. Paper presented at the *annual conference of the Australian Association for Research in Education*, Brisbane, Australia.

Philpot, S. (1990). *Training needs analysis of community government councils in the Northern Territory*. NT, The Northern Territory Local Government Industry Training Committee Incorporated, Darwin, Australia.

Resnick, L. (1991). Shared cognition: Thinking as social practice. In L. B. Resnick, J. M. Levine, & S. Teasely (Eds.), *Perspectives on socially shared cognition* (pp. 1–10). Washington DC: American Psychological Association.

Riding, R. J. (1991). *Cognitive styles analysis*. Birmingham, England: Learning and Training Technology.

Riding, R. J. (1997). On the nature of cognitive style. *Educational Psychology, 17*(1, 2), 29–49.

Riding, R.J., & Read, G. (1996). Cognitive styles and pupil learning preferences. *Educational Psychology, 16*(1), 81–105.

Runesson, U. (1999). *Variations pedagogik* [The pedagogy of variation]. Göteborg, Sweden: Acta Universitatis Gothoburgensis.

Säljö, R. (1979). *Learning in the learner's perspective. I. Some common-sense conceptions* (Report No. 76). Göteborg, Sweden: University of Göteborg.

Säljö, R. (1994). Minding action. Conceiving of the world versus participating in cultural practices. *Nordisk Pedagogik, 14*, 71–80.

Smith, D. M., & Kolb, D. A. (1986). *User's guide for learning style inventory*. Boston: McBer.

Sternberg, R. J. (1995). Styles of thinking and learning. *Language Testing, 12*(3), 265–291.

Sternberg, R. J. (1997). *Thinking styles*. New York: Cambridge University Press.

Sternberg, R. J., & Grigorenko, E. (1997). Are cognitive styles still in style? *American Psychologist 52*(7), 700–712.

Svensson, L. (1976). *Study skill and learning*. Göteborg, Sweden Acta Universitatis Gothoburgensis.

Svensson, L. (1977). On qualitative differences in learning III. Study skill and learning. *British Journal of Educational Psychology, 47*, 233–243.

Tennant, M. (1988). *Psychology and adult learning*. London: Routledge.

Tynjälä, P. (1997). Developing education students' conceptions of the learning process in different learning environments. *Learning and Instruciton, 7*(3), 277–292.

Van Rossum, E. J., & Schenk, S. M. (1984). The relationship between learning conception, study strategy and learning outcome. *British Journal of Educational Psychology, 54*, 73–83.

West, L. (1994). Cultural behaviour, conflict and resolution. In S. Harris & M. Malin (Eds.), *Aboriginal kids in urban classrooms* (pp. 7–19). Wentworth Falls, Australia: Social Science Press.

7

Correlates of Approaches to Learning: A Cross-Cultural Meta-Analysis

David Watkins
University of Hong Kong

Developing countries around the world typically see education as a route to economic progress (Altbach & Selvaratnam, 1989). Surveys such as those in the well-known IEA series have told us much about what is being learned in different countries. Much less information is known about why international differences in such outcomes are achieved except in relatively macro-terms such as the percent of gross national product spent on education, class sizes, teacher training, and so on. To achieve such insights requires intensive research into the range of factors that influence how students learn and the outcomes they achieve.

Such research has been carried out in Western countries using both quantitative and qualitative methods and much more is known now about the teaching–learning complex and how high-quality learning outcomes can be achieved (see, for instance, Fraser, Walberg, Welch, & Hattie, 1987; Marton, Hounsell, & Entwistle, 1984; Ramsden, 1988, 1992; Schmeck, 1988; Wittrock, 1986). A common cry even from developing countries such as India and the Philippines, which have been relatively successful in their educational progress in quantitative terms, is that the quality is lacking (Gonzalez, 1989). So there is an urgent need for research to be conducted in non-Western countries to investigate the generalizability of

Western findings. Depending on the findings of such investigations, it may prove necessary to conduct subsequent research to find out the factors affecting quality of learning in particular non-Western countries.

Although qualitative research using either phenomenographic or ethnographic perspectives would be valuable to achieve full understanding, it is also a long, expensive process requiring a highly trained indigenous research team capable of conducting in-depth interviews and detailed field observations, or both. On the other hand, questionnaires are available that can rapidly and accurately assess at little cost how students learn, and requiring few if any local specialists, so speedy progress may be possible. However, researchers from Third World countries have long warned about the "imposition" of Western social science theories and measuring instruments on subjects from non-Western cultures (Enriquez, 1982). The main purpose of this chapter is to quantitatively summarize research based on such instruments to provide a better understanding of student learning in different cultures. A second purpose is to provide evidence of the relationships between approaches to learning and personality and contextual variables. Such relationships are salient to the person-situation debate, which is involved in the distinction between learning strategies and styles addressed at greater depth in other chapters.

THE STUDENT APPROACHES TO LEARNING POSITION

Most of the learning questionnaires used in this research are based on what has become known as the SAL position, which arose out of dissatisfaction with the information-processing approach. SAL theory is derived bottom up from the perspective of the student, not the researcher. As most students recognize that affect and context influence their learning methods, this is reflected in SAL theory (Biggs, 1993). The SAL approach is thus consistent with the current advocacy of the notion of situated cognition (Brown, Collins, & Duguid, 1989). The impetus for the SAL approach was a paper by Marton and Säljö (1976), one of the most widely cited sources in the literature of educational psychology (Walberg & Haertel, 1992). That paper described a study where Swedish university students were asked to read an academic article and explain what they had learned and how they had achieved that learning. These students generally expressed two major ways of tackling this task. Some tried to memorize details or key terms to be able to answer subsequent questions. They focused on the reading at word or sentence level. Most of the other subjects tried to understand the message the passage was trying to impart. They focused on the themes and main ideas and generally tried to process the reading for meaning. These intentions and their associated reading strategies were called *surface* and *deep* approaches, respectively. The researchers reported qualitative differences in learning outcomes depending on the approach to reading that had been used. Students adopting a surface approach typically could not explain the authors' message and could only recall isolated factual fragments of the passage. Those adopting a deep approach provided a more sophisticated overview of the authors' intentions and frequently used extracts from the reading to support their reasoning.

At this point the SAL literature proceeded in two contrasting but not incompatible directions. The Swedish researchers developed a qualitative approach to research, which they called *phenomenography* (Marton, 1981). The aim of this approach was to understand how students perceived the content and process (the "what" and "how") of learning. The underlying rationale was the phenomenological notion that people act according to their interpretation of a situation rather than to "objective reality."

The basic principle behind the phenomenographic view of learning is that "learning should be seen as a qualitative change in a person's way of seeing, experiencing, understanding, conceptualizing something in the real world" (Marton & Ramsden, 1988, p. 271). From this perspective there is no point trying to derive general principles of learning independently of the context and content of learning. The ways students learn are a function of how they perceive the learning task and the learning environment. Although phenomenography itself is seen as descriptive, rather than prescriptive, principles based on this approach have been shown to lead to a higher quality of teaching and learning. In particular, researchers emphasized that the focus of learning is conceptual change and that teachers need to understand their students' conceptions of learning and how they can facilitate conceptual change (Bowden, 1988; Ramsden, 1992).

The quantitative SAL approach was founded by Biggs in Australia and Entwistle in the United Kingdom. Both researchers developed, relatively independently, learning process inventories that owe a debt to Marton and Säljö (1976) and later phenomenographic studies by adopting the "surface and deep" and "approaches to learning" terminology.

Biggs (1987) in developing his Learning Process Questionnaire (LPQ) and its tertiary counterpart, the Study Process Questionnaire (SPQ), and, Entwistle and Ramsden (1983) in developing their ASI added a third approach: *achieving*. Students adopting this approach tried to achieve the highest possible grades by strategies such as working hard and efficiently and being cue conscious. They would use any strategy, be it rote memorizing lots of facts or understanding basic principles, that they perceived would maximize their chances of academic success.

Biggs' instruments are based on a neat motive-strategy model of learning. He operationalized the constructs of approach to learning in terms of this motive-strategy combination. Factor analysis of responses to the SPQ, LPQ, and ASI has generally supported the underlying structure of surface, deep, and achieving approaches to learning for Western students (Biggs, 1993). Biggs emphasized that the motive-strategy model is related to the students' intentions and their perceptions of the learning context, and is therefore only meaningful in context. He has adapted a model of teaching proposed by Dunkin and Biddle (1974) to capture the relationships between characteristics of the learner and the learning context (presage), student approaches to a particular learning task (process), and outcomes of learning (product) in his 3P model of learning. He emphasized the systemic nature of this model. The variables involved in the 3P model do not form a simple linear path from presage to process to product. Rather, each component interacts with all other components until equilibrium is reached. Inspection of this model indicates why simple, general laws of learning have not been possible to validate, and why attempts to improve learning outcomes based on the deficit model are ineffective. To explain student learning requires an appreciation of the interactive, multidimensional nature of "the swamp" of real-life learning. General laws that focus on just one aspect of the learning situation, such as reinforcement, cannot achieve this.

STRATEGIES VERSUS STYLES: THE STATE–TRAIT DEBATE

One of the longest running wars of words in the psychological literature has been over what is known as the state-trait debate: the degree to which our constructs are stable properties of an individual or can vary according to the situation. This debate was brought to a head in the area of personality by Mischel (1968), who challenged one of the core assumptions of personality theory. Rather than interpreting personality research as supporting global, stable individual differences, Mischel argued for predicting specific behaviors across different situations.

In the learning area the related debate is over the strategy–style distinction discussed elsewhere in this volume. The basic issue is whether learners are relatively consistent in their way of learning or whether they vary their approach according to the learning task and content. The phenomenographic approach emphasises that an approach to learning is context specific and that a conception of learning is the relation between the learner and the task (Marton et al., 1984). However, subsequent research showed much evidence of individual consistency, at least in conceptions of learning (Marton, Dall'Alba, & Beaty, 1993).

Questionnaires such as the SPQ and LPQ are used to assess how a student would usually go about their learning tasks in general (although instructions can be changed to ask respondents to focus on a particular course rather than on their learning in general). The elements of the state–trait issue are portrayed in the 3P model of learning (Biggs, 1987), where the presage stage, which includes both personality and situational ele-ments, in turn affects the process and product of learning.

A secondary aim of this research is to provide empirical evidence relevant to the person–situation issue by assessing the strength of the relationships between approaches to learning and the personality variables of self-esteem and locus of control and the students' perceptions of their learning environment in different cultures.

CROSS-CULTURAL EQUIVALENCE

Before using any instrument in cross-cultural research, its cross-cultural validity needs to be demonstrated. The central notion that needs to be understood is that of equivalent usage. There is a hierarchy of possible uses to which an instrument can be put, each level of which requires the demonstration of a corresponding hierarchy of assumptions (Hui & Triandis, 1985). The lowest level involves conceptual equivalence and the highest involves metric (or scalar) equivalence. In this section I first ask whether the constructs of conceptions of and approaches to learning at the heart of the SAL position, which is the theoretical basis for instruments such as the SPQ (and ASI), are relevant to non-Western cultures. If so, are responses to such instruments reliable and do they have the hypothesized underlying factor structure in such cultures? Because I am not concerned with comparing scores of students in different cultures, I do not need to demonstrate metric equivalence, that is, the equivalence of raw scores.

CONCEPTUAL EQUIVALENCE

The notions of conceptual equivalence and *etic* and *emic* approaches to research are closely associated (Berry, 1989). The former approach seeks to compare cultures on what are thought to be universal categories. By way of contrast, the latter aproach uses only concepts that emerge from within a particular culture and is associated with the traditions of anthropology but also more recently those of indigenous psychology (Kim & Berry, 1993). Triandis (1972) has pointed to the dangers of "pseudoetic" research, which involves the imposition of the concepts of one culture upon another as if they were universal without any prior research into the veracity of this assumption.

To assess the conceptual equivalence of the constructs underlying the SAL position and learning instruments such as the SPQ requires qualitative analysis. To my knowledge such studies in non-Western cultures have been conducted with students in China, Hong Kong, Nepal, and Nigeria.

To illustrate, several studies support the proposition that the concepts underlying the SAL position are relevant to Nigerian students. An ethnographic study based on 120 hours of observations in Lagos primary schools claimed that Nigerian pupils are trained to believe that getting the right answer by any means, even cheating, is the essence of learning (Omokhodion, 1989). Neither the teachers nor the pupils considered the processes of understanding the problem and of obtaining the solution to be of any importance. Thus, it was concluded that a superficial, surface approach to learning was being encouraged. Further evidence comes from a study where 250 Nigerian university students responded to the question, "What strategies do you use to study?" (Ehindero, 1990). Content analysis indicated three main themes in the students' responses: dilligence, building up understanding, and memorizing content material without understanding. These themes seem to correspond to the notions of achieving, deep, and surface approaches to learning, respectively.

More recent evidence comes from a study by Watkins and Akande (1994), who content analyzed the answers of 150 typical Nigerian 14- to 16-year-old secondary school pupils to the question, "What do you mean by learning?" Using a phenomenographic-type approach, the analysis looked not only for the uniqueness of a subject's responses but also for similarities across subjects. Eventually four categories emerged: *learning as an increase in knowledge, learning as memorizing and reproducing, learning as applying,* and *learning as understanding.* The first three categories were congruent with the three quantitative conceptions of learning identified by Marton et al. (1993) with United Kingdom Open University students. The fourth conception was also similar to the lowest order qualitative conception reported in Marton et al., where the focus is now on the meaning of what is being learned. However, there was no evidence in this Nigerian study of the higher order qualitative conceptions involving insight and changing as a person as was found in the Open University research. Considering the findings of these Nigerian studies together, it appears the approaches to learning and quantitative and qualitative conceptions of learning identified in Western studies and forming the theoretical basis for the SAL position are relevant to Nigerian students, but the present studies question whether higher level qualitative conceptions are reached by Nigerian students. However, this can only be determined by further in-depth phenomenographic studies with more mature and select Nigerian university students and graduates such as used in the Open University studies.

Several recent qualitative investigations have focused on the learning approaches and conceptions of Chinese learners in Hong Kong and China (Hong, 1998; Kember, 1996; Kember & Gow, 1991; Watkins & Biggs, 1996). These studies have partially supported the conceptual validity of the constructs of deep and surface approach underlying the SAL position for Chinese students. However, they all have concluded that Chinese students tend to view memorization as relevant to both approaches, whereas Western students and education are more likely to view memorization as characteristic of a surface approach. Research in Nepal (Watkins & Regmi, 1992, 1995) concluded that although deep and surface approaches were relevant for these students, the concept of learning as character development emerged at a lower cognitive level than in Western studies. It may be fair to conclude that although the constructs of deep and surface approaches to learning are relevant to non-Western cultures, culturally specific aspects of these constructs are also likely.

RELIABILITY

The responses to any measuring instrument need to be assessed for reliability in any culture where the questionnaire is used. Watkins (1998) reported the alpha internal consistency reliability estimates for responses to the SPQ scales by 14 independent samples of 6,500 university students from 10 countries. The alphas ranged as follows: surface motivation, .37 to .67 (median .55); surface strategy, .25 to .66 (median .55); deep motivation, .44 to .70 (median .64); deep strategy, .47 to .76 (median .69); achieving motivation, .48 to .77 (median .68); and achieving strategy, .56 to .77 (median .72). All but 13 of the 84 alpha coefficients exceeded .50: a magnitude considered acceptable for a research instrument used for group comparisons but well below the level required for important academic decisions about an individual student (Nunnally, 1978). Not surprising, the reliability estimates were slightly higher for the Australian students for whom it was developed and particularly low for the Nepalese for whom the concepts may not have been as relevant (see the previous discussion) and whose level of English competence is relatively low. Also, the internal consistencies of the two surface approach scales were generally lower than those of the other scales. Again, this was not unexpected because these scales are less conceptually pure than the others, because there are several motives (extrinsic or fear of failure) and strategies (from doing little to rote learning everything) that may be involved (see Biggs, 1993). Research has supported, often even more clearly, the internal consistency of responses to the other instruments used in this meta-analysis for the participants whose data are reported.

WITHIN-CONSTRUCT VALIDITY

The within-construct validity of the LPQ and SPQ have been examined by comparing the results of internal factor analysis of responses to the LPQ and SPQ scales for different cultures, both with each other and with the theoretical model. Moreover, correlations between scales of inventories supposed to be tapping the same constructs should be statistically significant and of a magnitude indicative of convergent validity.

Watkins (1998) reported the factor loadings of the SPQ scales based on two factor solutions (which typically explained 65% of the variance) obtained after principal axis factor analysis followed by rotation to oblique simple structure using the Oblimin procedure for samples of university students from eight countries. In all eight samples the results were clear cut with distinct surface and deep approach factors. The achieving scales as explained earlier were not expected to load consistently on one or the other factors but rather be associated with the approach that was more likely to succeed in that context; thus, the United Arab Emirates and Hong Kong students sampled associated both the achieving approach scales with a deep approach to learning. There was a tendency in the remaining countries for achieving strategies to be strongly associated with a deep approach, but this trend was weaker for the corresponding motivation scale whose loadings tended to be divided between the two factors. Confirmatory factor analysis of responses to the LPQ, which shares the same underlying motive-strategy model as the SPQ, by 10 samples of school students from six countries also confirmed the two basic factors of deep and surface approaches (Wong, Lin, N. Y., & Watkins, 1996). A review of the factor analytic studies of the ASI by Richardson (1994) also supported the cross-cultural validity of underlying deep and surface approaches.

CORRELATIONS BETWEEN LEARNING QUESTIONNAIRES

Several questionnaires tap scales parallel to those of the SPQ and LPQ. These include the ASI (Entwistle, Hanley, & Hounsell, 1979), the Cognitive Styles Inventory (CSI; Moreno & DiVesta, 1991), the How I Study Inventory (HIS; Hattie & Watkins, 1998), and the ILP (Schmeck, Ribich, & Ramanaiah, 1977). There appear to be few studies that have used the SPQ and one or more of these other inventories, but those few studies are encouraging. For example, Wilson, Smart, and Watson (1996) found correlations for two samples of Australian psychology students between the SPQ and ASI to be .45 and .61 for Deep Approach, .44 and .62 for Surface Approach, and .46 and .46 for Achieving Approach (all $p < .001$). In an unpublished South African study (Watkins & Akande, 1994) referred to earlier, correlations between these same approach scales were .41, .40, and .34 for Black students and .26, .18, and .31 for White students (all $p < .01$). Moreover, as would be predicted, the CSI's Integrating Strategy and the SPQ's Deep Strategy scales correlated .28 and .42 for the White and Black South African students, respectively (both $p < .01$). In this research, it is tentatively assumed the questionnaires are all basically tapping the same approaches to learning, but more evidence is needed in this regard. Other scales such as the Inventory of Learning Styles (ILS; Vermunt, 1992) and Motivated Strategies for Learning Questionnaire (MSLQ; Pintrich, Smith, Garcia, & McKeachie, 1993) have several scales that seem to be conceptually consistent with the constructs of surface, deep, and achieving approaches and are also included in this analysis.

AIMS OF RESEARCH

The purpose of this research was to use quantitative synthesis in the meta-analytic tradition (Glass, McGaw, & Smith, 1981), to test the cross-cultural relevance of variables proposed in SAL theory to be significantly correlated with surface, deep, and achieving approaches to learning. According to Biggs (1987), how a student learns depends on presage factors related both to the person and the learning environment. In particular, the following relationships are examined from a cross-cultural perspective:

Correlates with self-concept and locus of control. Students who are more self-confident, particularly with their academic abilities, and who accept greater responsibility for their learning outcomes are more likely to adopt deeper, more achieving approaches to learning, which require them to rely more on their understanding of the course materials rather than on the teacher or textbook (Biggs, 1987; Schmeck, 1988).

Correlates with learning environment. Hundreds of studies, albeit mainly from either the United States or Australia, have shown that the classroom environment as perceived by pupils influences their learning outcomes (Fraser, 1986). Classrooms perceived as orderly, organized, cohesive, and goal directed were found to be consistently associated with better achievement. Deeper level approaches to learning are likely to be encouraged by a warm classroom climate, an appropriate workload, interaction with others, and a well-planned and well-resourced learning environment (Biggs & Watkins, 1995).

Correlates with academic grades. The students' approaches to learning are expected to influence their academic performance. In particular, it is predicted that in any culture a surface approach will be significantly negatively correlated with academic achievement. It is further predicted that deep and achieving approaches will be positively associated with grades (Biggs, 1987; Schmeck, 1988). However, it is also recognized that these relationships assume that higher quality learning outcomes are rewarded by the assessment system.

METHOD

The first stage of any meta-analysis is to select the studies to be quantitatively synthesized. A decision that has to be made at this stage is whether only studies satisfying some predetermined quality criteria should be included and what such criteria should be (for example, see Slavin, 1987, for a discussion of this issue).

In this chapter all studies that reported correlates of at least one approach to learning and measures of self-esteem, locus of control, learning environment, and academic achievement (or where it was possible to statistically estimate such correlations from the data provided) were included, provided responses to the scales showed a reasonable level of internal consistency (alphas of at least .50) for the culture being studied. This led to dropping four studies. The studies were obtained both by formal searches of established CD-ROM databases and by more informal means such as a hands-on search of the journal collection in the Hong Kong University library, requests for relevant published and unpublished material at international conferences, and letter and e-mail appeals to established researchers in the area.

Another issue in this type of meta-analysis is whether scales from different instruments really measure the same variables so that they can be combined. In this chapter several learning process instruments are each assumed to assess a student's approach to learning (see earlier discussion). In addition, different measures of self-esteem (such as the Self Description Questionnaire; Marsh, 1990), locus of control (such as the Causal Dimension Scale, Russell, 1982), and academic achievement (measured by school tests, grade-point average, standardized achievement tests, and so on) were assumed to measure the same variable. With the learning environment instruments it was more difficult to identify scales in common, and all scales from the few relevant instruments are reported here.

Once all the studies to be included were identified and the relevant correlations obtained, average correlations were then calculated (in this chapter, for simplicity, the size of the sample is not considered and each correlation is given equal weight; see Hedges & Olkin, 1985, for a discussion of weighting in meta-analysis). One of the main aims of meta-analysis is not just to obtain an overall estimate of the strength of a relationship, but, more important, to find if the relationship varies according to the characteristics of the sample. It is hoped this may provide insights into the nature of a relationship only possible through such a synthesis. In this chapter I hope to find out whether the relationships between approaches to learning and the other variables vary between Western and non-Western samples and at school and university levels. The correlations obtained may also be an artifact of characteristics of the research, such as the questionnaire used. In this chapter correlations with the Biggs LPQ and SPQ are compared with those obtained from other learning questionnaires.

RESULTS

The correlations found and the characteristics of the studies from which they are taken are shown in Tables 7.1, 7.3, and 7.5, and the relevant average correlations are in Tables 7.2, 7.4, and 7.6 for the relationships between approaches to learning and academic achievement, self-esteem, and internal locus of control, respectively.

Approaches to Learning and Academic Achievement.

The 60 correlations shown in Table 7.1, based on data from 28,053 respondents (from 55 independent samples with 27,078 respondents from 15 countries), provided average correlations of -.11, .16, and .18 for surface, deep, and achieving approaches, respectively. The average correlations

TABLE 7.1

Summary of Research Reporting Correlations Between Learning Approach Scales and Academic Achievement

Country	Learning Questionnaire	Participants	Surface Approach	Deep Approach	Achieving Approach
(1) Australia[a] (a)	SPQ	815 university students	-.18*	.22*	.23*
(2) Australia[a] (b)	SPQ	1550 university students	-.10*	.22*	.21*
(3) Australia (c)	SPQ	278 university students	-.03	.12*	.25*
(4) Australia (d)	SPQ	249 university students	-.25*	.24*	.18*
(5) Australia (e)	ILP	249 university students	-.19*	.31*	.35*
(6) Australia (f)	ASI (S)	175 university students	-.14	.16*	–
(7) Australia (g)	ASI (S)	503 mature age university students	-.19*	.01	.03
(8) Australia[a] (h)	LPQ	1,352 secondary school students	-.13*	.18*	.22*
(9) Australia (i)	HIS	1,274 secondary school students	-.14*	.23*	.25*
(10) Australia (j)	SPQ	152 university students	-.23*	.22*	.35*
(11) Australia (k)	ASI	74 university students	-.07	.14	–
(12) Australia (l)	ASI	143 university students	-.07	.15	–
(13) Australia (m)	SPQ	105 university students	-.07	-.02	.00
(14) China (a)	LPQ	130 university students	-.08*	.10*	.08
(15) China (b)	SPQ	215 university students	-.20*	.13	.13
(16) China (c)	LPQ	915 secondary school students	-.08*	.10*	.08
(17) China (d)	LPQ	5400 secondary school students	-.18*	.28*	.33*
(18) Fiji	ASI (S)	918 secondary school students	-.20*	-.11	-.08
(19) Hong Kong (a)	SPQ	162 university students	-.23*	.20*	.23*
(20) Hong Kong[a] (b)	LPQ	3,770 secondary school students	-.09*	.11*	.16*
(21) Hong Kong (c)	LPQ	127 secondary school students	-.12	.13	.25*
(22) Hong Kong (d)	LPQ	314 secondary school students	-.10	.14*	.06
(23) Hong Kong (e)	SPQ	326 university students	.09	.13*	.12
(24) Hong Kong (f)	SPQ	34 university students	.15	.23	.18
(25) Hong Kong (g)	SPQ	417 university students	-.06	.10	.16*

TABLE 7.1 (continued)

Summary of Research Reporting Correlations Between Learning Approach Scales and Academic Achievement

Country	Learning Questionnaire	Participants	Surface Approach	Deep Approach	Achieving Approach
(26) Hong Kong (h)	ASI (R)	183 university students	-.02	.07	.08
(27) Hong Kong (i)	LPQ (S)	115 secondary school students	--	--	.24*
(28) Hong Kong (j)	LPQ	237 secondary school students	-.20*	.18*	.42*
(29) India	LPQ	250 secondary school students	-.23*	.08	.07
(30) Japan (a)	SPQ	182 university students	-.15*	-.07	-.05
(31) Japan (b)	LPQ	41 secondary school students	-.19	-.14	.09
(32) Nepal (a)	SPQ	342 university students	-.10*	.06	.06
(33) Nepal (b)	LPQ	509 secondary school students	-.14*	.09	.09
(34) Nepal (c)	HIS	202 secondary school students	-.11	.21*	.29*
(35) Netherlands (a)	LPQ	557 secondary school students	-.27*	.08	--
(36) Netherlands (b)	LSI	451 university students	-.03	.19*	.31*
(37) Nigeria	LPQ	265 secondary school students	.01	.20*	.28*
(38) Philippines (a)	LPQ	147 secondary school students	-.14*	.29*	.27*
(39) Philippines (b)	ASI (S)	445 secondary school students	-.14*	.28*	.13*
(40) Philippines (c)	ILP	123 university students	.16	.30*	.10
(41) South Africa (a)	SPQ	179 White university students	-.23*	.10	.08
(42) South Africa (b)	ASI	179 White university students	-.18	.19*	.30*
(43) South Africa (c)	CSI	179 White university students	-.02	.21*	--
(44) South Africa (d)	SPQ	184 Black university students	.00	.12	.10
(45) South Africa (e)	ASI	184 Black university students	-.18*	.33*	--
(46) South Africa (f)	CSI	184 Black university students	.08	.18*	--
(47) South Africa (g)	LPQ	234 Black secondary school students	-.05	.24*	.27*
(48) Spain (a)	SPQ	347 university students	-.10	.41*	.37*
(49) Spain (b)	LPQ	175 secondary school students	-.30*	.24*	.34*
(50) United Arab Emirates	SPQ	246 university students	-.27*	.25*	.36*

TABLE 7.1 (continued)

Summary of Research Reporting Correlations Between Learning Approach Scales and Academic Achievement

Country	Learning Questionnaire	Participants	Surface Approach	Deep Approach	Achieving Approach
(51) United Kingdom (a)	ASI (S)	188 university students	-.07	.22*	.19*
(52) United Kingdom (b)	ASI (R)	245 university students	-.11	.26*	.14
(53) United Kingdom (c)	ASI (R)	225 university students	-.09	.20*	.07
(54) United States (a)	SPQ	524 university students	-.11*	.16*	.14*
(55) United States (b)	SPQ	202 university students	.02	.11	.27*
(56) United States (c)	SPQ	67 university students	-.14	.31*	.24*
(57) United States (d)	MSLQ	173 secondary school students	--	.36*	--
(58) United States (e)	MSLQ	283 secondary school students	--	-.02	.31*
(59) Zimbabwe (a)	LPQ	153 Black secondary school students	--	.11	.22*
(60) Zimbabwe (b)	LPQ	206 White secondary school students	--	.02	.14*

Note. Australia (a) and (b) (Biggs, 1987); Australia (c) (Murray-Harvey & Keeves, 1994); Australia (d) (Watkins, 1982); Australia (e) (Watkins & Hattie, 1981); Australia (f) (Provost & Bond, 1997); Australia (g) (Fogarty & Taylor, 1997); Australia (h) (Biggs, 1987); Australia (i) (Watkins & Hattie, 1990); Australia (j); Australia (k) and (l) (Trigwell & Prosser, 1991); Australia (m) (Beckwith, 1991); (Eley, 1992); Fiji (Richardson, Landbeck, & Mugler, 1995); China (a) and (c) (Gao, 1998); China (b), Hong Kong (e), and United States (c) (Zhang, 1999, personal communication); China (d) (Gao, 1999, personal communication); Hong Kong (a) (Drew & Watkins, 1998); Hong Kong (b) (Biggs, 1992); Hong Kong (c) and (d) (Wong, N. Y. 1995); Hong Kong (f) (Kember et al., 1995); Hong Kong (g) (Drew, 1998); Hong Kong (h) and (i) (Ma, 1994); Hong Kong (j) (Ho, I. T., 1992); India (Watkins & Dhawan, 1999 unpublished data); Japan (a) and (b) (Stribling, 1998, personal communication); Nepal (a) (Watkins & Regmi, 1990); Netherlands (a) (Struyf, Waeytens, Lens, & Vandenberghe, 1997); Netherlands (b) (Busato, Prins, Elshout, & Hamaker, 1998); Nigeria (Watkins & Akande, 1994); Nepal (b) and (c) and Philippines (a) (Watkins, Regmi, & Astilla, 1991; Philippines (b) (Watkins, Hattie, & Astilla, 1986); Philippines (b) (Watkins & Hattie, 1981); South Africa (a) to (f) and Kenya (Watkins & Akande, 1996 unpublished data); South Africa (g) (Watkins & Mboya, unpublished data); Spain (a) (Torre Puente, 1997, personal communication); Spain (b) (Torre Puente & Muñoz, San Roque, 1997); United Arab Emirates (Albaili, 1995); United States (a) and (b) (Rose, Hall, Bollen, & Webster, 1996; Bollen, 1996, personal communication; United Kingdom (a) (Newstead, 1992); United Kingdom (b) (Sadler-Smith, 1997); and Zimbabwe (a) and (b) (Mpofu & Oakland, 1998).

Learning Questionnaires were ASI = Approaches to Studying Inventory; ASI (S) = Short version of ASI; ASI (R) = revised ASI; CSI = Cognitive Skills Inventory; HIS = How I Study Inventory; ILP = Inventory of Learning Processes; LPQ = Learning Process Questionnaire; SPQ = Study Process Questionnaire; LSI = Learning Styles Inventory; MSLQ = Motivated Strategies for Learning Questionnaire.

[a]These correlations are based on self-estimates of academic achievement.

*p < .05

TABLE 7.2

Average Correlations Between Learning Approach Scales and Academic Achievement

Groups	Sample Size	Surface Approach	Deep Approach	Achieving Approach
Total	28,053	-.11	.16	.18
Western	11,023	-.13	.18	.21
Non-Western	17,030	-.10	.14	.16
University	9,991	-.09	.17	.18
School	18,062	-.15	.14	.20
School (Western)	3,814	-.21	.18	.28
University (Western)	7,209	-.12	.18	.20
School (non-Western)	14,248	-.13	.12	.18
University (non-Western)	2,782	-.06	.16	.13
LPQ or SPQ	21,473	-.12	.15	.19
Other Learning Questionnaires	6,580	-.09	.18	.18

appeared to be higher at school level for Western samples. Whether learning approaches were measured by the LPQ or SPQ or some other questionnaire did not seem to make much difference to the average correlations.

Approaches to Learning and Self-esteem.

The 30 correlations shown in Table 7.3, based on data from 8,710 respondents (involving 28 independent samples from 15 countries with 8,352 respondents), provided average correlations of -.05, .30, and .28 with surface, deep, and achieving approaches, respectively. The average correlations with deep and achieving approaches exceeded .20 for all subsamples but was particularly strong (.39) for Western university students with deep approach.

Approaches to Learning and Internal Locus of Control.

The 28 correlations shown in Table 7.5, based on data from 13,012 respondents (involving 27 independent samples with 12,711 respondents

TABLE 7.3
Summary of Research Reporting Correlations Between Learning Approach Scales and Self-Esteem

Country	Learning Questionnaire	Participants	Surface Approach	Deep Approach	Achieving Approach
(1) Australia (a)	SPQ	386 university students	.01	.20*	.32*
(2) Australia (b)	HIS	1274 secondary school students	.18	.33*	.34*
(3) Australia (c)	LPQ	130 secondary school students	-.10	.35*	.52*
(4) Australia (d)	SPQ	65 university students	.09	.36*	.29*
(5) Germany	MSLQ	451 university students	--	.47*	--
(6) Hong Kong (a)	SPQ	162 university students	-.13	.25*	.22*
(7) Hong Kong (b)	LPQ	240 secondary school students	-.09	.26*	.32*
(8) Hong Kong (c)	SPQ	417 university students	-.16*	.14*	.14*
(9) India	LPQ	250 secondary school students	-.10	.32*	.34*
(10) Kenya	LPQ	88 university students	-.14	.20	.30*
(11) Lithuania	LPQ	222 secondary school students	-.12	.29	.37*
(12) Malaysia	LPQ	301 secondary school students	-.03	.26*	.38*
(13) Nepal (a)	ASI	302 university students	-.15*	.29*	--
(14) Nepal (b)	LPQ	398 university students	-.02	.54*	.30*
(15) Philippines (a)	LPQ	261 secondary school students	-.11	.22*	.18*
(16) Philippines (b)	ASI(S)	445 secondary school students	-.12*	.12*	.16*
(17) Philippines (c)	HIS	184 secondary school students	.16	.42*	.31*
(18) South Africa (a)	LPQ	179 White university students	-.03	.17*	.10
(19) South Africa (b)	ASI	179 White university students	.11	.50*	.38*
(20) South Africa (c)	CSI	179 White university students	.10*	.38*	.34*
(21) South Africa (d)	LPQ	184 Black university students	-.07	.18*	.09

TABLE 7.3 (continued)

Summary of Research Reporting Correlations Between Learning Approach Scales and Self-Esteem

Country	Learning Questionnaire	Participants	Surface Approach	Deep Approach	Achieving Approach
(22) Spain (a)	LPQ	175 secondary school students	-.19*	.37*	.28*
(23) Spain (b)	SPQ	347 university students	-.10	.41*	.37*
(24) Sweden	LPQ	149 university students	-.04	.43*	.32*
(25) United Kingdom	ILP	135 university students	-.32*	.41*	--
(26) United States (a)	LPQ	221 Hispanic secondary students	.09	.08	.21*
(27) United States (b)	LPQ	473 Anglo secondary students	-.08	.18*	.18*
(28) United States (c)	MSLQ	173 secondary school students	--	.44*	--
(29) United States (d)	MSLQ	283 secondary school students	--	-.01	.24*
(30) Vietnam	MSLQ	457 university students	--	.56*	--

Note. Australia (a) (Murray-Harvey, personal communication); Australia (b) (Watkins & Hattie 1990); Australia (c) (Thomas, T. A., 1984); Australia (d) (Gordon, Lim, McKinnon, & Nkala, 1996); Hong Kong (a) (Drew & Watkins, 1998); Hong Kong (b) (Wong, 1998); Hong Kong (c) (Drew, 1998); Kenya and South Africa (a) to (d) (Watkins & Akande, 1996, unpublished research); Lithuania (Watkins & Juhasz, 1994 unpublished data); Malaysia (Watkins & Ismail, 1994); Spain (a) (Torre Puente & Muñoz, San Roque, 1997); Spain (b) (Torre Puente, 1997, personal communication); Nepal (a) and (b) (Watkins & Regmi, 1990, unpublished research); Sweden (Dahlin & Watkins, 1997); Philippines (a) and (c) (Watkins et al., 1991); Philippines (b) (Watkins et al., 1986); United Kingdom (Abouserie, 1995); United States (a) and (b) (Watkins & Sethi, in press); United States (c) (Pintrich & DeGroot, 1990); United States (d) (Pokay & Blumenfeld, 1990); and Vietnam and Germany (Helmke & Vo, 1998 unpublished data)

Learning Questionnaires were ASI = Approaches to Studying Inventory; ASI (S) = Short version of ASI; ASI (R) = revised ASI; CSI = Cognitive Skills Inventory; HIS = How I Study Inventory; ILP = Inventory of Learning Processes; LPQ = Learning Process Questionnaire; SPQ = Study Process Questionnaire; LSI = Learning Styles Inventory: MSLQ = Motivated Strategies for Learning Questionnaire.

*p < .05

TABLE 7.4

Average Correlations Between Learning Approach Scales and Self-Esteem

Groups	Sample Size	Surface Approach	Deep Approach	Achieving Approach
Total	8,710	-.05	.30	.28
Western	5,478	-.03	.33	.30
Non-Western	3,232	-.08	.27	.25
University	4,078	-.06	.34	.26
School	4,632	-.04	.26	.29
School (Western)	2,951	-.04	.25	.31
University (Western)	2,527	-.02	.39	.30
School (non-Western)	1,681	-.05	.27	.28
University (non-Western)	1,551	-.11	.27	.21
LPQ or SPQ	4,648	-.07	.27	.28
Other Learning Questionnaires	4,062	-.01	.36	.30

from 11 countries), provided average correlations of -.20, .09, and .12 with surface, deep, and achieving approaches, respectively. It appears that the negative correlation with the surface approach may be higher at school level in both non-Western and especially Western samples. For the latter, the correlations with both deep and achieving approaches were much higher at university level.

Approaches to Learning and Student Perceptions of Their Learning Environment

Correlations reported in relevant studies are shown in Tables 7.7 and 7.8 for school and university levels, respectively. Although in most studies either versions of the CES or CEQ were used, these versions varied considerably in the actual scales used. This made it difficult to summarize the results in a form similar to the previous tables. The school data involved about 4,000 student respondents from seven studies conducted in four countries. It appears across all samples that a deep approach to learning is encouraged by a classroom where the students feel involved and believe the teachers are supportive and likeable. The university data also involved more than 4,000 student respondents from five studies in three countries. Studies 1–3 are consistent in finding that a surface approach is associated

TABLE 7.5

Summary of Research Reporting Correlations Between Measures of Learning Approach Scales and Internal Locus of Control

Country	Learning Questionnaire	Participants	Surface Approach	Deep Approach	Achieving Approach
(1) Australia (a)	SPQ	65 university students	.23	.33*	.39*
(2) Australia (b)	SPQ	83 university students	-.18	.22*	.18
(3) Australia (c)	ASI	741 university students	-.21*	.11*	.23*
(4) Australia (d)	LPQ	1353 secondary school students	-.18*	.12*	.17*
(5) Australia (e)	LPQ	979 secondary school students	-.22*	.13*	.22*
(6) Hong Kong (a)	SPQ	162 university students	-.34*	.00	.24*
(7) Hong Kong (b)	LPQ	244 secondary school students	.06	.23*	.27*
(8) Hong Kong (c)	LPQ	314 secondary school students	-.24*	.09	.08
(9) Hong Kong (d)	SPQ	417 university students	-.11	.05	-.03
(10) Hong Kong (e)	LPQ	3770 secondary school students	-.28*	.09*	.12*
(11) Hong Kong (f)	LPQ	237 secondary school students	-.27*	.22*	.33*
(12) India	LPQ	250 secondary school students	-.46*	.05	.10
(13) Indonesia	SPQ	90 university students	-.18	.16	.15
(14) Lithuania	LPQ	222 secondary school students	-.33*	-.22	-.15
(15) Malaysia (a)	LPQ	301 secondary students	-.19*	.02	.17*
(16) Malaysia (b)	LPQ	301 secondary students	-.49*	-.16	-.18
(17) Nepal (a)	SPQ	128 university students	-.18*	.10	.20*
(18) Nepal (b)	SPQ	342 university students	-.10*	.24*	.21*
(19) Nepal (c)	LPQ	509 secondary school students	-.32*	.19*	.17*

TABLE 7.5 (continued)

Summary of Research Reporting Correlations Between Measures of Learning Approach Scales and Internal Locus of Control

Country	Learning Questionnaire	Participants	Surface Approach	Deep Approach	Achieving Approach
(20) Nigeria (a)	LPQ	150 secondary school students	-.29*	.02	.09
(21) Nigeria (b)	LPQ	195 secondary school students	-.24*	-.14	-.16
(22) Nigeria (c)	LPQ	323 secondary school students	-.32*	.11	.08
(23) Philippines (a)	LPQ	261 secondary school students	-.07	.21*	.16*
(24) Philippines (b)	ASI(S)	445 secondary school students	-.08	.21*	.10
(25) South Africa	LPQ	234 Black secondary school students	-.15	.01	.02
(26) United States (a)	SPQ	202 university students	.04	.06	.20*
(27) United States (b)	LPQ	221 Hispanic secondary sch. students	-.28*	-.05	.02
(28) United States (c)	LPQ	473 Anglo secondary school students	-.25*	.23*	.07

Note. Australia (a) (Gordon et al., 1996); Australia (b) (Murray-Harvey, 1996, personal communication); Australia (c) (Watkins, 1987); Australia (d) and (e) (Biggs, 1987); Hong Kong (a) (Drew & Watkins, 1998); Hong Kong (b) (Chan, I., 1990); Hong Kong (c) (Wong, N. Y., 1995); Hong Kong (d) (Drew, 1998); Hong Kong (e) (Biggs, 1992); Hong Kong (f) (Ho, I. T., Salili, Biggs, & Hau, 1999); India (Watkins & Dhawan, unpublished data); Indonesia (Hotma Ria, 1993, personal communication); Lithuania (Watkins & Juhasz, 1994 unpublished data); Malaysia (a) and (b) (Watkins & Ismail, 1994); Nepal (a) and (b) (Watkins & Regmi, 1990, and 1994 unpublished data); Nepal (c) (Watkins et al., 1991); Nigeria (a) to (c) (Watkins & Akande, 1994); Philippines (a) (Watkins et al., 1991); Philippines (b) (Watkins et al., 1986); South Africa (Watkins & Mboya, 1999 unpublished data); United States (a) (Rose et al., 1996); United States (b) and (c) (Watkins & Sethi, in press).

Learning Questionnaires were ASI = Approaches to Studying Inventory; ASI (S) = Short version of ASI; ASI (R) = revised ASI; CSI = Cognitive Skills Inventory; HIS = How I Study Inventory; ILP = Inventory of Learning Processes; LPQ = Learning Process Questionnaire; SPQ = Study Process Questionnaire; LSI = Learning Styles Inventory: MSLQ = Motivated Strategies for Learning Questionnaire.

*p < .05

TABLE 7.6

Average Correlations Between Learning Approach Scales and Internal Locus of Control

Groups	Sample Size	Surface Approach	Deep Approach	Achieving Approach
Total	13,012	-.20	.09	.12
Western	4,339	-.15	.10	.15
Non-Western	8,673	-.22	.09	.11
University	2,230	-.11	.14	.20
School	10,782	-.24	.07	.09
School (Western)	3,248	-.25	.04	.07
University (Western)	1,091	-.03	.18	.25
School (non-Western)	7,534	-.24	.08	.10
University (non-Western)	1,139	-.18	.11	.15
LPQ or SPQ	11,826	-.21	.09	.12
Other Learning Questionnaires	1,186	-.15	.16	.17

with students' perceptions of inappropriate workload and assessment. Good and supportive teaching is also typically associated with a deep approach.

CONCLUSIONS

Like any meta-analysis, these results must be treated with caution because of the danger of combining statistics based on non comparable measures. In this study those dangers are exacerbated because of the different cultures involved. As discussed earlier, although the constructs of deep, surface, and achieving approaches to learning are generally comparable in non-Western cultures, there may also be culturally specific aspects that render the constructs of Western theories and instruments only partially appropriate. Moreover, such instruments are likely to be of less reliability and validity when used in other cultures. In this research, samples where responses to the scales did not achieve an acceptable reliability level were omitted. Nevertheless, it is likely that correlations at least in some of the non-Western samples may underestimate the actual size of the relationship because of the attenuation effect.

However, meta-analyses, if treated with caution, have the power to provide insights not possible from single studies or narrative reviews. In this research, for the first time on such a scale, evidence is provided about the

TABLE 7.7

Correlations Between Approaches to Learning and Actual and Preferred Classroom Environment (School Level)[a]

	Actual Environment			Preferred Environment		
	Surface Approach	Deep Approach	Achieving Approach	Surface Approach	Deep Approach	Achieving Approach
Study 1: Ma, 1994 (109 Hong Kong students)						
Enjoyable	-.16	.08	-.06	-.10	.10	.02
Order	.03	-.01	.08	.01	.05	.10
Student involvement	-.05	.23*	.06	.03	.07	.07
Achievement orientation	-.05	.31*	.23*	.06	.05	.10
Teacher led	.04	.26*	.22*	-.01	.03	.11
Teacher support	-.07	.18	.10	.01	.12	.08
Teacher involvement	-.04	.10	.03	-.04	.06	.09
Collaborativeness	-.04	.30*	.12	-.05	.18	.09
Study 2: Chan & Watkins, 1994 (180 Hong Kong students)						
Order	.00	.04	.13	-.21*	.41*	.31*
Student involvement	.12	.23*	.13	-.10	.48*	.27*
Achievement orientation	.17*	.08	.13	.06	.29*	.22*
Teacher led	.11	.22*	.25*	.06	.40*	.28*
Teacher support	.02	.20*	.10	-.17*	.34*	.25*
Collaborativeness	.00	.35*	.22*	-.09	.48*	.27*
Innovation	.03	.33*	.21*	-.09	.48*	.35*
Study 3: Abd-Elsamie, 1998 (400 Egyptian students)						
Order	-.06	.07	—	—	—	—
Student involvement	-.13*	.12*	—	—	—	—
Achievement orientation	-.13*	.15*	—	—	—	—
Teacher led	.08	.00	—	—	—	—
Teacher support	-.04	.11*	—	—	—	—
Collaborativeness	.00	.03	—	—	—	—
Task orientation	-.07	.09	—	—	—	—

TABLE 7.7 (continued)

Correlations Between Approaches to Learning and Actual and Preferred Classroom Environment (School Level)[a]

	Actual Environment			Preferred Environment		
	Surface Approach	Deep Approach	Achieving Approach	Surface Approach	Deep Approach	Achieving Approach
Study 4: Wong & Watkins, 1998 (356 Hong Kong students)						
Enjoyable	-.13*	.16*	.13*	-.14*	.10	.04
Order	.01	.16*	.12	-.05	.15*	.11
Student involvement	-.01	.11	.14*	-.08	.16*	.14*
Achievement orientation	.01	.16*	.13*	-.04	.15*	.11
Teacher involvement	-.02	.22*	.14*	-.05	.15*	.14*
Collaborativeness	-.10	.21*	.07	-.09	.14*	.03
Study 5: Watkins & Akande, 1993 (323 Nigerian students)						
Teacher support	.03	.16*	--	.04	.23*	--
Task orientation	.03	-.26*	--	-.04	-.19*	--
Rule clarity	.17*	-.28*	--	.01	-.18*	--
Innovation	-.22*	.06	--	.03	.02	--
Study 6: Watkins & Hattie, 1990 (1274 Australian students)						
Opportunity to learn	.29*	.45*	.45*	--	--	--
Like teachers	.28*	.41*	.35*	--	--	--
Enjoyable	.21*	.50*	.37*	--	--	--
Study 7: Ramsden, Martin, & Bowden, 1989 (1475 Australian students)						
Teacher support	-.11*	.22*	.17*	--	--	--
Achievement orientation	.20*	.10*	.18*	--	--	--
Independent learning	.00	.25*	.22*	--	--	--
Clear goals	-.06	.22*	.23*	--	--	--
Preparation for higher ed.	-.10	.25*	.22*	--	--	--

[a]Studies 1 to 5 involved the LPQ and versions of the Classroom Environment Scale (CES; Moos & Trickett, 1974); Study 6 the Quality of School Life Scale (Williams & Batten, 1981) and HIS; and Study 7 the LPQ and School Experience Questionnaire (SEQ; Ramsden et al., 1989).

TABLE 7.8

Correlations Between Approaches to Learning Scales and Measures of the
Actual Classroom Learning Environment (University Students)[a]

	Surface Approach	Deep Approach	Achieving Approach
Study 1: Ho, 1998 (1658 Hong Kong students)			
Good teaching	-.12*	.13*	.30*
Clear goals	-.36*	.22*	.39*
Appropriate workload	-.34*	-.06	.10
Appropriate assessment	-.25*	-.03	-.09
Emphasis on independence	-.24*	.18*	.28*
Study 2: Wilson, Lizzio, & Ramsden, 1997 (2130 Australian students)			
Good teaching	-.34*	.24*	--
Clear goals	-.29*	.12*	--
Appropriate workload	-.48*	.07*	--
Appropriate assessment	-.47*	.21*	--
Emphasis on independence	-.29*	.19*	--
Generic skills	-.20*	.37*	--
Study 3: Trigwell & Prosser, 1991 (74 Australian students)			
Good teaching	-.13	.00	--
Clear goals	-.18	-.03	--
Appropriate workload	-.50*	.00	--
Appropriate assessment	-.42*	.13	--
Emphasis on independence	-.16	.08	--
Study 4: Eley, 1992 (152 Australian students)			
Teaching support	-.21*	.40*	.15
Emphasis on achievement	.28*	.18	.21*
Structure & cohesiveness	-.08	.34*	.23*
Metacognitive focus	-.13	.42*	.20*
Independence in learning	-.23*	.42*	.23*
Support for higher education	-.07	.48*	.27*
Study 5: Ropo, 1993 (181 Finnish students)			
Dissatisfaction with teaching	--	.17	.04
Importance of teaching	--	.20*	-.02
Inadequate requirements	--	.17	.04

[a]Studies 1 to 3 involve the ASI and Course Experience Questionnaire (CEQ; Ramsden, 1992);
Study 4, the SPQ, and an adaptation of the SEQ; and Study 6, a version of the ASI, and the
Perception of Instruction Scale (Ropo, 1993).

cross-cultural validity of several relationships that are at the heart of recent Western research into factors influencing student learning.

In particular, the results indicate the personality variables of self-esteem and locus of control are related to the approach to learning a student will adopt in both Western and non-Western countries, and at both school and university levels. Of course, researchers need to be careful making causal deductions from correlational evidence, and there clearly is a need for further longitudinal research to determine causality. But the results are consistent with theoretical positions that deeper approaches to learning are more likely to occur when the students are more confident in their capacity to learn and accept responsibility for their own learning (Biggs, 1987; Schmeck, 1988). I postulate that these conditions are necessary but not sufficient conditions for improving student learning strategies in any culture. Thus, attempts to improve the quality of student learning in non-Western countries could try to adapt recently developed Western methods for improving self-esteem and locus of control (see, for instance, Hattie, 1992).

There are also intriguing nuances in these meta-analytic findings that may be chance findings but that may also be clues that could lead to a greater understanding of the mechanisms involved. For example, is there a reason why the relationship between self-esteem and a deep approach is particularly strong for Western university students? Why is locus of control more highly associated with a surface approach and self-esteem with deep and achieving approaches? Perhaps this indicates that it is necessary for study strategy counselors to encourage the student to adopt an internal locus of control first, then focus on changing self-esteem (which is consistent with how Hattie, 1992, argued self-esteem enhancement interventions should be structured anyway).

The average correlations obtained here between approaches to learning and academic achievement are disappointing, even if they are in the expected direction and fairly consistent over culture and educational levels. However, it has long been recognized although a deep approach to learning is necessary to lead to a high-quality learning outcome, such an approach is not always rewarded by the assessment system (Biggs, 1987; Marton & Säljö, 1976; Schmeck, 1988). In particular, capable, cue-conscious students who perceive that course assessment rewards quantity rather than quality of knowledge are likely to adopt superficial learning strategies (Scouller, 1998; Tang & Biggs, 1996; Thomas, P., & Bain, 1984). These latter three studies indicated that multiple-choice questions are particularly likely to have that effect. Because the assessment system is under the control of teachers or other educators, it is up to them to convince students that higher quality learning outcomes will be rewarded by higher grades.

These findings also indicate a relationship between the learning environ- ment as perceived by the students and the approach to learning they are likely to adopt. Although the database is not as large or as compact as the others presented in this chapter, such relationships seem to hold across cultures and educational levels. More specifically it seems that, consistent with the previous discussion, superficial learning strategies are likely to be associated with courses perceived as having too heavy a workload and being poorly assessed. On the other hand, deep level learning outcomes are likely to be associated with students feeling involved in their classes and being supported by their teachers in both Western and non-Western contexts.

As well as allowing some insights into student learning in different cultures, the data presented in this chapter are relevant to the learning strategy–style debate discussed in greater depth elsewhere in this book. These data give cross-cultural support for both personality and contextual influences on how students learn. Thus, it appears it is necessary to take both these factors into account, and any theoretical position that focuses on one at the expense of the other can never be more than a partial explanation of how students learn.

ACKNOWLEDGEMENTS

This chapter is a considerably enlarged and revised version of a paper presented at 15th Congress of the International Association for Cross- Cultural Psychology, Bellingham, WA, August 3–8, 1998. The writer would like to thank Hotma Ria, Ros Murray-Harvey, Juan Carlos Torre Puente, Larry Bollen, Zhang Li Fang, Andreas Helmke, Gao Ling Biao, and Parill Stribling for providing unpublished data.

REFERENCES

Abd-Elsamie, M. A. (1998). *Anxiety level and classroom as perceived by pupils in relation to learning styles*. Unpublished master's thesis, Zagazig University, Egypt.

Abouserie, R. (1995). Self-esteem and achievement motivation as determinants of students' approaches to studying. *Studies in Higher Education, 20,* 19–26.

Albaili, M. A. (1995). An Arabic version of the Study Process Questionnaire: Reliability and validity. *Psychological Reports, 77,* 1083–1089.

Altbach, P., & Selvaratnam, V. (Eds.). (1989). *From dependence to autonomy: The develop- ment of Asian universities*. Dordrecht, the Netherlands: Kluwer.

Beckwith, J. (1991). Approaches to learning, their context and relationship to assessment performance. *Higher Education, 22,* 17–30.

Berry, J. (1989). Imposed emics-derived etics. The operationalisation of a compelling idea. *International Journal of Psychology, 24,* 721–735.

Biggs, J. B. (1987). *Student approaches to learning and studying.* Melbourne. Australia: Australian Council for Educational Research.

Biggs, J. B. (1992). *Why and how do Hong Kong students learn?* Education Paper, No. 14, University of Hong Kong, Faculty of Education.

Biggs, J. B. (1993). What do inventories of students' learning processes really measure? A theoretical review and clarification. *British Journal of Educational Psychology, 63,* 3–19.

Biggs, J.B. & Watkins, D. (Eds.). (1995). *Classroom learning: Educational psychology for the Asian teacher.* Singapore: Prentice Hall.

Bowden, J. (1988). Achieving change in teaching practice. In P. Ramsden, (Ed.), *Improving learning: New perspectives.* London: Kogan Page.

Brown, J. S., Collins, A., & Duguid, P. (1989). Situated cognition and the culture of learning. *Educational Research, 18,* 32–42.

Busato, V., Prins, F. J., Elshout, J., & Hamaker, C. (1998). Learning styles: A cross-sectional and longitudinal study in higher education. *British Journal of Educational Psychology, 68,* 427–441.

Chan, I. (1990). *The relationship between motives, learning strategies, attributions for success and failure and level of achievement among secondary school students in Hong Kong.* Unpublished master's thesis, University of Hong Kong.

Chan, Y. Y. G., & Watkins, D. (1994). Classroom environment and approaches to learning: An investigation of the actual and preferred perceptions of Hong Kong secondary school students. *Instructional Science, 22,* 233–246.

Dahlin, B., & Watkins, D. (1997). Assessing study approaches in Sweden: A cross-cultural perspective. *Psychological Reports, 81,* 131–136.

Drew, P. Y. (1998). Towards a model of learning outcomes for Hong Kong tertiary students. Unpublished Ph.D. thesis, University of Hong Kong.

Drew, P. Y., & Watkins, D. (1998). Affective variables, learning approaches and academic achievement: A casual modeling investigation with Hong Kong Chinese tertiary students. *British Journal of Educational Psychology, 68,* 173–188.

Dunkin, M. J. & Biddle, B. J. (1974). *The study of teaching.* New York: Holt, Rinehart, & Winston.

Ehindero, O. J. (1990). A discriminant function analysis of study strategies, logical reasoning ability and achievement across major teaching undergraduate curricula. *Research in Education, 44,* 1–11.

Eley, M. (1992). Differential adoption of study approaches within individual students. *Higher Education, 23,* 231–254.

Enriquez, V. (1982). *Decolonising the Filipino psyche.* Quezon City, Philippines: Philippine Psychology Research House.

Entwistle, N. J., Hanley, M., & Hounsell, D. (1979). Identifying distinctive approaches to studying. *Higher Education, 8,* 365–380.

Entwistle, N. J. & Ramsden, P. (1983). *Understanding student learning.* London: Croom Helm.

Fogarty, G. J. & Taylor, J. A. (1997). Learning styles among mature-age students: Some comments on the Approaches to Studying Inventory (ASI-S). *Higher Education Research & Development, 16,* 321–330.

Fraser, B. J. (1986). *Classroom environment.* London: Croom Helm.

Fraser, B. J., Walberg, H. J., Welch, W. W., & Hattie, J. A. (1987). Synthesis of educational productivity research. *International Journal of Educational Research, 11,* 145–252.

Gao, L. B. (1998). *Conceptions of teaching held by school physics teachers in Guangdong, China and their relations to student learning.* Unpublished doctoral dissertation, University of Hong Kong.

Glass, G. V., McGaw, B., & Smith, M. L. (1981). *Meta-analysis in social research.* Beverly Hills, CA: Sage.

Gonzalez, A. (1989). The Western impact on Philippine higher education. In P. Altbach & V. Selvaratnam (Eds.), *From dependence to autonomy: The development of Asian universities.* Dordrecht, the Netherlands: Kluwer.

Gordon, C., Lim, L., McKinnon, D., & Nkala, F. (1996). *Learning approach control orientation, and self-efficacy of beginning teacher education students.* Paper presented at the conference of the Australian Association for Educational Research, Melbourne.

Hattie, J. A. (1992). *The self-concept.* Hillsdale, NJ: Lawrence Erlbaum Associates.

Hattie, J., & Watkins, D. (1988). Preferred classroom environment and approach to learning. *British Journal of Educational Psychology, 58,* 345–349.

Hedges, L. V., & Olkin, I. (1985). *Statistical methods for meta-analysis.* San Diego, CA: Sage.

Helmke, A., & Vo, T., (1998). *A comparison of the learning strategies of German and Vietnamese students.* Unpublished data.

Ho, A. (1998). *Changing teachers' conceptions of teaching.* Unpublished doctoral dissertation, University of Hong Kong.

Ho, I. T. (1992). *Causal attributions and learning strategies of Hong Kong students.* Unpublished master's thesis, University of Hong Kong.

Ho, I. T., Salili, F., Biggs, J. B., & Hau, K. T. (1999). The relationship among causal attributions, learning strategies and level of achievement: A Hong Kong Chinese study. *Asia Pacific Journal of Education, 19,* 44–58.

Hong, J. (1998). *Conceptions of learning of law students: A phenomenographic approach.* Unpublished doctoral dissertation, University of Hong Kong.

Hui, C. H. & Triandis, H. C. (1985). Measurement in cross-cultural psychology: A review and comparison of strategies. *Journal of Cross-Cultural Psychology, 16,* 131–152.

Kember, D. (1996). The intention to both memorise and understand: Another approach to learning? *Higher Education, 31,* 341–354.

Kember, D., & Gow, L. (1991). A challenge to the anecdotal stereotype of the Asian student. *Studies in Higher Education, 16,* 117–128.

Kim, V., & Berry, J. W. (Eds.). (1993). *Indigenous psychologies: Research and experience in cultural context.* London: Sage.

Ma, K. H. (1994). *The relationship between achievement in and attitude towards science, approach to learning and classroom environment.* Unpublished master's thesis, University of Hong Kong.

Marsh, H. W. (1990). *Self-Description Questionnaire 1 manual.* University of Western Sydney, Australia: Macarthur.

Marton, F. (1981). Phenomenography: Sescribing conceptions of the world around us. *Instructional Science, 10,* 177–200.

Marton, F., Dall'Alba, G., & Beaty, E. (1993). Conceptions of learning. *International Journal of Educational Research, 19,* 277–300.

Marton, F., Hounsell, D., & Entwistle, N. J. (Eds.). (1984). *The experience of learning.* Edinburgh, Scotland: Scottish Academic Press.

Marton, F., & Ramsden, P. (1988). What does it take to improve learning? In P. Ramsden, (Ed.), *Improving learning: New perspectives.* London: Kogan Page.

Marton, F., & Säljö, R. (1976). On qualitative differences in learning - I: Outcome and process. *British Journal of Educational Psychology, 46,* 4–11.

Mischel, W. (1968). *Personality and assessment.* New York: Wiley.

Moos, R. H. & Trickett, E. J. (1974). *Classroom Environment Scale manual*. Palo Alto, CA: Consulting Psychologist Press.

Moreno, V., & DiVesta, F. J. (1991). Cross-cultural comparisons of study habits. *Journal of Educational Psychology, 83*, 231–239.

Mpofu, E., & Oakland, T. (1998). *Predicting school achievement in Zimbabwean multiracial schools using Biggs' Learning Process Questionnaire*. Paper presented at the conference of the International Association of Cross-Cultural Psychology, Bellingham, WA.

Murray-Harvey, R., & Keeves, J. (1994). *Student learning processes and progress in higher education*. Paper presented at the annual meeting of the American Educational Research Association, New Orleans, LA.

Newstead, S. E. (1992). A study of two "quick-and-easy" methods of assessing individual differences in student learning. *British Journal of Educational Psychology, 62*, 299–312.

Nunnally, J. C. (1978). *Psychometric theory* (2nd ed.). New York: McGraw-Hill.

Omokhodion, J. O. (1989). Classroom observed: The hidden curriculum in Lagos, Nigeria. *International Journal of Educational Development, 9*, 99–110.

Pintrich, P., & DeGroot, E. (1990). Motivational and self-regulated learning components of classroom academic performance. *Journal of Educational Psychology, 82*, 33–40.

Pintrich, P., Smith, D. A. F., Garcia, T., & McKeachie, W. J. (1993). Predictive validity and reliability of the Motivated Strategies for Learning Questionnaire. *Educational and Psychological Measurement, 53*, 801–813.

Pokay, P., & Blumenfeld, P. (1990). Predicting achievement early and late in the semester: The role of motivation and use of learning strategies. *Journal of Educational Psychology, 82*, 41–50.

Provost, S., & Bond, N. (1997). Approaches to studying and academic performance in a traditional psychology course. *Higher Education Research & Development, 16*, 309–320.

Ramsden, P. (1988). *Improving learning: New perspectives*. London: Kogan Page.

Ramsden, P. (1992). *Learning to teach in higher education*. London: Routledge.

Ramsden, P., Martin, E., & Bowden, J. (1989). School environment and sixth form pupils' approaches to learning. *British Journal of Educational Psychology, 59*, 129–142.

Richardson, J. T. E. (1994). Cultural specify of approaches to studying in higher education: A literature survey. *Higher Education, 27*, 449–468.

Richardson, J., Landbeck, R., & Mugler, F. (1995). Approaches to study in higher education: A comparison study in the South Pacific. *Educational Psychology, 15*, 417–431.

Ropo, E. (1993). Studying technology: An investigation of approaches to studying and perceptions of teaching in a Finnish university of technology. *Higher Education, 25*, 111–132.

Rose, R. J., Hall, C. W., Bollen, L. M., & Webster, R. E. (1996). Locus of control and college students' approaches to learning. *Psychological Reports, 79*, 163–171.

Russell, D. (1982). The Causal Dimensional Scale: A measure of how individuals perceive causes. *Journal of Personality and Social Psychology, 42*, 1137–1145.

Sadler-Smith, E. (1997). "Learning Style'" Frameworks and instruments. *Educational Psychology, 17*, 51–63.

Schmeck, R. (Ed.). (1988). *Learning strategies and learning styles*. New York: Plenum.

Schmeck, R., Ribich, F., & Ramanaiah, N. V. (1977). Development of a self-report inventory for assessing individual differences in learning process. *Applied Psychological Measurement, 1*(3), 413–431.

Scouller, K. (1998). The effect of assessment method on students' learning approaches: Multiple choice question examination versus assignment essay. *Higher Education, 35*, 453–472.

Slavin, R. E. (1987). Ability grouping and student achievement in elementary schools: A best-evidence synthesis. *Review of Educational Research, 57*, 293–336.

Struyf, E., Waeytens, K., Lens, W., & Vandenberghe, R. (1997). *The goal orientation and level of processing of secondary school students*. Paper presented at EARLI conference, Athens, Greece.

Tang, C., & Biggs, J. (1996). How Hong Kong students cope with assessment. In D. Watkins & J. Biggs (Eds.), *The Chinese learner: Cultural, psychological, and contextual influences* (pp. 159–182). Hong Kong/Melbourne: Comparative Education Research Centre/Australian Council for Educational Research.

Thomas, P., & Bain, J. (1984). Contextual differences in learning approaches: The effects of assessment. *Human Learning, 3*, 227–240.

Thomas, T. A. (1984). *An investigation into the influence of anxiety and the effectiveness of treatments involving positive coping skills*. Unpublished bachelor's honor's thesis, University of Sydney, Sydney, Australia..

Torre Puente, J. C. & Muñoz, San Roque, I. . (1997). *Learning approaches and self-efficacy beliefs in high school students*. Paper presented at Congress of Pedro Povedoi Ecuador, Madrid, Spain.

Triandis, H. C. (1972). *The analysis of subjective culture*. New York: Wiley.

Trigwell, K., & Prosser, M. (1991). Improving the quality of student learning: The influence of learning context and approaches to learning on learning outcomes. *Higher Education, 22*, 251–266.

Vermunt, J. (1992). *Learning styles and regulation of learning in higher education*. Amsterdam/Lisse, Netherlands: Swets & Zeitlinger.

Walberg, H. J. & Haertel, G. D. (1992). Educational psychology's first century. *Journal of Educational Psychology, 84*, 6–19.

Watkins, D. (1982). Identifying the study process dimensions of Australian university students. *Australian Journal of Educational Research, 26*, 76–85.

Watkins, D. (1987). Academic locus of control: A relevant variable at tertiary level? *Higher Education, 16*, 221–229.

Watkins, D. (1998). Assessing approaches to learning: A cross-cultural perspective. In B. Dart & G. Boulton-Lewis (Eds.), *Teaching and learning in higher education* (pp. 124–144). Melbourne, Australia: Australia Council for Educational Research.

Watkins, D., & Akande, A. (1996). *The approach to learning of African students*. Unpublished data.

Watkins, D., & Akande, A. (1993). Preferred and actual learning environments and the approach to learning of Nigerian students. *Journal of Social Psychology, 133*, 105–109.

Watkins, D., & Akande, A. (1994). Approaches to learning of Nigerian secondary school children: Emic and etic perspectives. *International Journal of Psychology, 29*, 165–182.

Watkins, D., & Biggs, J. (Eds.) (1996). *The Chinese learner: Cultural, psychological, and contextual influences*. Hong Kong/Melbourne: Comparative Education Research Centre/Australian Council for Educational Research.

Watkins, D., & Dhawan, N. (1999). *The self-concepts and approaches to learning of Indian students*. Unpublished data.

Watkins, D., & Hattie, J. (1981). The learning processes of Australian university students: Investigations of contextual and personological factors. *British Journal of Educational Psychology, 51*, 384–393.

Watkins, D., & Hattie, J. (1990). Individual and contextual differences in the approaches to learning of Australian secondary school students. *Educational Psychology, 10*, 333–342.

Watkins, D., Hattie, J., & Astilla, E. (1986). Approaches to studying by Filipino students: A longitudinal investigation. *British Journal of Educational Psychology, 56*, 357–362.

Watkins, D., & Ismail, M. (1994). Is the Asian learner a rote learner? A Malaysian perspective. *Contemporary Educational Psychology, 19*, 483–488.

Watkins, D., & Juhasz, A. (1994). *The approach to learning of Lithuanian students.* Unpublished data.

Watkins, D., & Mboya, M. (1999). *The approach to learning and academic achievement of African students.* Unpublished data.

Watkins, D.., & Regmi, M. (1994). *The learning strategies of Nepalese students.* Unpublished data.

Watkins, D., & Regmi, M. (1990). An investigation of the approach to learning of Nepalese tertiary students. *Higher Education, 29,* 459–469.

Watkins, D., & Regmi, M. (1992). How universal are student conceptions of learning? A Nepalese investigation. *Psychologia, 35,* 101–110.

Watkins, D., & Regmi, M. (1995). Assessing approaches to learning in non-Western cultures: A Nepalese conceptual validity study. *Assessment and Evaluation in Higher Education, 20,* 203–212.

Watkins, D., Regmi, M. & Astilla, E. (1991). The Asian-learner-as-a-rote-learner stereotype: Myth or reality? *Educational Psychology, 11,* 21–34.

Watkins, D., & Sethi, R. (in press). Assessing the learning processes of Mexican and Euro-American students. *Psychological Reports.*

Williams, T., & Batten, M. (1981). *The Quality of School Life Scale.* Hawthorne, Australia: Australian Council for Educational Research.

Wilson, K., Lizzio, A., & Ramsden, P. (1997). The development, validation, and application of the Course Experience Questionnaire. *Studies in Higher Education, 22,* 33–53.

Wilson, K. L., Smart, R. M., & Watson, R. J. (1996). Gender differences in approaches to learning in first year psychology students. *British Journal of Educational Psychology, 66,* 59–72.

Wittrock, M. (Ed.). (1986). *Handbook of research on teaching* (3rd Ed.). New York: Macmillan.

Wong, M. (1998). *Self-concept and approach to learning among high and low ability-grouped Hong Kong students.* Unpublished master's thesis, University of Hong Kong.

Wong, N. Y. (1995). *The relationship between Hong Kong student's perception of their mathematics classroom environment and approaches to learning.* Unpublished doctoral dissertation, University of Hong Kong.

Wong, N. Y., Lin, W. Y., & Watkins, D. (1996). Cross-cultural validation of models of approaches to learning: An application of confirmatory factor analysis. *Educational Psychology, 16,* 317–327.

Wong, N. Y. & Watkins, D. (1998). A longitudinal study of the psychosocial environment and learning approaches in the Hong Kong classroom. *Journal of Educational Research, 91,* 247–254.

8

Thinking Styles Across Cultures: Their Relationships With Student Learning

Li-fang Zhang
The University of Hong Kong
Robert J. Sternberg
Yale University

Traditionally, many psychologists and educators have believed that students' academic successes and failures are due mainly to individual differences in abilities. However, how can it be that one teacher considers a student to be unintelligent and a second teacher considers the same student to be intelligent? How can it be that one student does a mediocre job on a multiple-choice test and the same student produces an outstanding individual project? These common phenomena in educational institutions of all levels cannot be explained by the traditional view of students' successes and failures. Instead, these phenomena require a new explanation.

Since the beginning of the movement of cognitive styles in the late 1960s and early 1970s, investigators have been studying the roles of thinking and learning styles in student learning. The primary goal of this chapter is to address the two questions raised above through presenting the findings generated by our initial interest in the contribution of thinking styles to academic achievement beyond abilities. Furthermore, to understand the nature of thinking styles, we examined the relationships of thinking styles to student characteristics (personological and situational) and to an aspect of the affective domain, that is, students' self-esteem, as well as to their learning approaches (sometimes called learning styles).

DEFINITION AND THEORETICAL FOUNDATIONS

What is a thinking style? How is a thinking style different from an ability? A style is a preferred way of thinking or of doing things. A style is not an ability, but rather a preference in the use of the abilities one has (Sternberg, 1997). Many different theories of thinking styles have been proposed, and it would not be possible to review all of them here. We review, therefore, only selected theories.

Some theories are of psychological or interest types. For example, Myers (1980; Myers & McCaulley, 1988) proposed a series of psychological types based on Jung's (1923) theory of types. According to Myers, there are 16 types, resulting from all possible combinations of two ways of perceiving—sensing versus intuition; two ways of judging—thinking versus feeling; two ways of dealing with self and others—introversion versus extraversion; and two ways of dealing with the outer world—judgment versus perception. Holland (1973) proposed a theory of 6 types of career interests. The 6 types are realistic, investigative, artistic, social, enterprising, and conventional. Gregorc (1985) proposed 4 main types of styles, based on all possible combinations of two dimensions: concrete versus abstract and sequential versus random. Renzulli and Smith (1978) suggested various learning styles, with each corresponding to a method of teaching (e.g., projects, drill and recitation, and discussion). Kolb (1976, 1984) discussed two dimensions of learning style: perceiving and processing. The first dimension describes concrete versus abstract thinking; the second dimension describes an information-processing activity: active versus reflective. These two dimensions form a model describing 4 types of learning styles. These are: divergent (a divergent learner perceives information concretely and processes it reflectively), convergent (a convergent learner perceives information abstractly and processes it actively), assimilating (an assimilating learner perceives information abstractly and processes it reflectively), and accommodating (an accommodating learner perceives information concretely and processes it actively).

Some other theories of styles are not general theories of styles, but rather theories of specific aspects of cognitive-stylistic functioning (Grigorenko & Sternberg, 1995). For example, Kagan (1976) studied differences between impulsive and reflective individuals and Witkin (1978) examined the differences between field-independent and field-dependent individuals.

More recently, Sternberg (1988, 1990, 1994, 1997) proposed a more general theory of thinking styles. This theory, called the theory of mental self-government, is the primary theoretical foundation for the series of studies reported here.

Theory of Mental Self-Government

Sternberg's (1988, 1990, 1994, 1997) theory of mental self-government addresses people's thinking styles, which may be used in many settings, including university, home, and community. At the heart of this theory is the notion that people need somehow to govern or manage their everyday activities. There are many ways of doing so; whenever possible, people choose styles of managing themselves with which they are comfortable. Still, people are at least somewhat flexible in their use of styles and try with varying degrees of success to adapt themselves to the stylistic demands of a given situation. Thus, an individual with one preference in one situation may have a different preference in another situation. Moreover, styles may change with time and with life demands. Thinking styles are at least in part socialized (Sternberg, 1994, 1997), suggesting that, to some extent, they can be modified by the environment in which people reside. The theory of mental self-government describes 13 thinking styles that fall along five dimensions of mental self-government: (a) functions, (b) forms, (c) levels, (d) scopes, and (e) leanings of government as applied to individuals.

Functions

As in government, there are three functions in human beings' mental self-government: legislative, executive, and judicial. An individual with a legislative style enjoys being engaged in tasks that require creative strategies. An individual with an executive style is more concerned with implementation of tasks with set guidelines. An individual with a judicial style focuses on evaluating the products of others' activities.

Forms

Also as in government, a human being's mental self-government takes four forms: monarchic, hierarchic, oligarchic, and anarchic. An individual with a monarchic style enjoys being engaged in tasks that allow a complete focus on one thing at a time. On the contrary, an individual with a hierarchic style likes to distribute attention to several tasks that are prioritized. An individual with an oligarchic style also likes to work toward multiple objectives during the same period, but may not enjoy setting priorities. Finally, an individual with an anarchic style enjoys working on tasks that would allow flexibility as for what, where, when, and how one works, and eschews systems of almost any kind.

Levels

As with governments, human beings' mental self-government is at two levels: local and global. An individual with a local style enjoys being engaged in tasks that require work with concrete details. On the contrary, an individual with a global style pays more attention to the overall picture of an issue and to abstract ideas.

Scope

Mental self-government can deal with internal and external matters. An individual with an internal style enjoys engaging in tasks that allow one to work independently. In contrast, an individual with an external style likes engaging in tasks that provide opportunities for developing interpersonal relationships.

Leanings

Finally, in mental self-government, there are two leanings: liberal and conservative. An individual with a liberal style enjoys engaging in tasks that involve novelty and ambiguity, whereas a conservative person adheres to the existing rules and procedures in performing tasks.

The theory of mental self-government possesses several characteristics. First, styles it specifies fall along five dimensions, rather than one. Second, styles are viewed as falling along continua rather than as being dichotomous. Third, the theory of mental self-government yields a profile of styles for each individual, rather than merely the identification of a single style. Finally, styles are not viewed as "good" or "bad" in themselves. However, we believe that, in the context of student learning, some thinking styles should be considered as more effective than others. In our view, effective thinking styles among students are thinking styles that are more likely to enable students to adapt to new situations and to solve creatively the problems both of the present and of the future. For example, a student with an effective thinking style should prefer to use his or her abilities in a creative and norm-challenging way, and with a sense of priority.

To investigate the relationships of thinking styles to students' learning approaches, in two of our studies we examined the relationships between the constructs in the theory of mental self-government and those in Biggs' (1987, 1992, 1995) theory of students' approaches to learning. To understand the relationship of thinking style to affective domains, we investigated the relationship between thinking styles and Coopersmith's (1967) concept of self-esteem.

Biggs' Theory of Approaches to Learning

Early work in learning approaches can be found in the frequently cited deep-surface distinction in approaches to learning initiated by Marton (1976) and Entwistle (1981, 1988). Biggs (1987) added a third approach— the achieving approach—to this early work. Therefore, according to Biggs, there are three common approaches to learning: surface, deep, and achieving. Students who take the surface approach to learning are driven by extrinsic motivation and thus adopt a learning strategy that results in a reproduction of what is taught to meet the minimum requirements. Students who take a deep approach to learning are driven by their genuine interests in learning and take on a strategy that will ensure the achievement of a real understanding of what is learned. Students who take an achieving approach are driven by the motivation to beat their peers academically and take on a learning strategy that will ensure the maximization of their grades.

Self-Esteem

According to Coopersmith (1967), self-esteem refers to one's value judgment of one's worthiness. This judgment expresses the degree of approval or disapproval of oneself. It indicates the extent to which an individual believes him- or herself capable, significant, and successful. Work demonstrating the importance of self-esteem in educational settings has been well documented. For example, it has been shown that self-esteem is related to achievement (e.g., Leondari, Syngollitou, & Kiosseoglou, 1998), interpersonal relationships (e.g., Chiu, 1987), and cognitive styles (e.g., Bosacki, Innerd, & Towson, 1997). In one of our studies, the relationship between self-esteem as measured by the Self-Esteem Inventory—Adult Form SEI-A—(Coopersmith, 1981) and thinking styles was investigated.

GENERAL METHODS, RESEARCH FINDINGS, AND DISCUSSIONS

General Methods

Students and preservice and in-service teachers from five universities participated in the studies. The universities were one from Hong Kong, one from the United States, and three from mainland China. Whereas the universities from Hong Kong and mainland China are four of the research-oriented higher educational institutions in the People's Republic of China, the one from the United States is one of the "Big Ten" universities in the midwest.

Students from two secondary schools in Hong Kong also participated in the studies. Both schools were band-one secondary schools. In Hong Kong, secondary schools are classified into five bands, with the top 20% of primary school graduates being admitted to band-one secondary schools, based on their academic achievement (see Yung, 1997, for details).

The total number of participants was 3,043, including 2,909 (1,223 male, 1,678 female, and 8 unspecified) university students (including preservice and in-service teachers) and 134 (93 male and 41 female) secondary-school students.

One measure of thinking styles, one measure of learning approaches, and one measure of self-esteem as well as scores on academic achievement and on students' self-rated abilities were used in the studies. The first measure, the Thinking Styles Inventory (TSI), was employed in all studies because the central goal of the studies was to examine the nature of thinking styles postulated in the theory of mental self-government. The second measure, the SPQ, was used in two studies that aimed at examining the nature of thinking styles in relation to student learning process in higher education. The third measure, the Coopersmith (1981) SEI, was used in studying the relationship between thinking styles and self-esteem among two cross-validation samples. Furthermore, an informational questionnaire was used in most studies to elicit data regarding student characteristics, both personological (e.g., age, sex, socio-economic status) and situational (e.g., number of hobbies, leadership experience, and work and travel experience the participants have had).

The TSI

The TSI (Sternberg & Wagner, 1991) is a self-report test consisting of 65 items falling into 13 scales, with five items per scale. For each item, the participants are asked to rate themselves on a 7-point scale, with 1 indicating the statement does not describe them at all, and 7 indicating the statement characterizes them extremely well. In 1996, the TSI was translated and back translated between English and Chinese. The 13 scales correspond to the 13 types of thinking styles illustrated in the theory of mental self-government. Table 8.1 shows some sample items in English, one from each of the 13 scales.

TABLE 8.1

Sample Items From the Thinking Styles Inventory and the Study Process Questionnaire

Sample Items	Scale Type
Thinking Styles Inventory	
I like tasks that allow me to do things my own way.	Legislative
I like situations in which it is clear what role I must play or in what way I should participate.	Executive
I like to evaluate and compare different points of view on issues that interest me.	Judicial
I like to complete what I am doing before starting something else.	Monarchic
When undertaking some task, I like first to come up with a list of things the task will require me to do and to assign an order of priority to the items on the list.	Hierarchic
I usually know what things need to be done, but I sometimes have trouble deciding in what order to do them.	Oligarchic
When working on a written project, I usually let my mind wander and my pen follow up on whatever thoughts cross my mind.	Anarchic
Usually when I make a decision, I don't pay much attention to details.	Global
I like problems that require engagement with details.	Local
I like to be alone when working on a problem.	Internal
I like to work with others rather than by myself.	External
I like to do things in new ways, even if I am not sure they are the best ways.	Liberal
In my work, I like to keep close to what has been done before.	Conservative
Study Process Questionnaire	
I choose my courses largely with a view to the job situation when I graduate rather than because of how much they interest me.	Surface Motive
I find that studying gives me a feeling of deep personal satisfaction.	Deep Motive
I want top grades in most or all of my courses so that I will be able to select from among the best positions available when I graduate.	Achieving Motive
I think browsing around is a waste of time, so I only study seriously what's given out in class or in the course outlines.	Surface Strategy
While I am studying, I think of real life situations to which the material that I am learning would be useful.	Deep Strategy
I summarize suggested readings and include these as part of my notes on a topic.	Achieving Strategy
Coopersmith Self-Esteem Inventory	
I'm a lot of fun to be with.	Like me
I often wish I were someone else.	Unlike me

The TSI has been shown to be reliable and valid for U.S. samples (see Grigorenko & Sternberg, 1995, 1997). The internal-consistency reliabilities of the scales ranged from the high .50s to the low .80s. Factor analyses were generally, although not completely, supportive of the structure of the theory. For example, in Sternberg's 1994 study, five factors accounted for 77% of the variance in the data, each roughly corresponding to one of the five dimensions delineated in the theory of mental self-government.

The theory tested by the TSI also has demonstrated good external validity. Sternberg (1994) investigated the correlates of the TSI with other tests, both of styles and of abilities. For example, with the MBTI, 30 of 128 correlation coefficients were statistically significant, and with the Gregorc Style Delineator (Gregorc, 1982), 22 of 52 were significant. These correlations went well beyond the levels that would be expected by chance. Thus, Sternberg (1997) suggested that various style measures partition a similar space of the intelligence–personality interface, but in different ways. On the contrary, the correlation of the TSI with the SAT was not significant. Thus, styles are different from intelligence.

Further, results from U.S. research have shown some value of the theory and have generated several implications for teaching and learning in educational settings. In one such study, Sternberg and Grigorenko (1995) identified significant relationships between teaching styles and grade taught, duration of teaching experience, and subject area taught. Findings from a second study suggested significant relationships of students' learning styles with such background information as students' socioeconomic status (as measured by the parental educational and occupational level) and birth order (Sternberg & Grigorenko, 1995). Findings from a third study indicated that teachers inadvertently favored those students whose thinking styles were similar to their own (Sternberg & Grigorenko, 1995). Recently, Grigorenko and Sternberg (1997) found that certain thinking styles contribute significantly to prediction of academic performance over and above prediction of scores on ability tests. Their study also indicated that students with particular thinking styles do better on some forms of evaluation than on others.

SPQ

The SPQ is a self-report test consisting of 42 items. This questionnaire has six subscales, with seven items on each subscale. For each item, the respondents are asked to rate themselves on a 5-point scale anchored by 1, which indicates the statement is never or rarely true of them, and 5, which indicates the statement is always or almost always true of them. The six subscales are: surface-motive, surface-strategy, deep-motive, deep-strategy, achieving-motive, and achieving-strategy. Therefore, the three scales based on the three approaches to learning are surface (motive and strategy), deep (motive and strategy), and achieving (motive and strategy). "Motive" concerns why students choose to learn, whereas "strategy" pertains to how students go about their learning (see also Table 8.1 for sample items).

Numerous studies using the SPQ have been conducted in many parts of the world (e.g., Albaili, 1995; Bolen, Wurm, & Hall, 1994; Kember & Gow, 1990; Murray-Harvey, 1994; Watkins, 1998; Watkins & Akande, 1992; Watkins & Regmi, 1990). Scale internal consistencies from most studies ranged from the mid .50s to the low or mid .70s for the six subscales and from the low .70s to the low .80s for the three scales (for details, see Albaili, 1995; Watkins, 1998).

Two types of validity statistics have been obtained for the SPQ—the internal and the external. The internal validity data are obtained through examining the internal structure of the instrument. Some studies resulted in three factors (surface, deep, and achieving, e.g., Bolen, et al., 1994; O'Neil & Child, 1984), which supported Biggs' original argument, whereas other studies resulted in a two-factor (surface and deep) model (e.g., Niles, 1995; Watkins & Dahlin, 1997). The two-factor model is consistent with the model proposed separately by Marton (1976) and Entwistle (1981).

External validity is obtained through examining the SPQ against other instruments assumed to be based on similar constructs with the SPQ. It has been shown that the SPQ assesses similar constructs as Entwistle's (1981) ASI (Wilson, Smart, & Watson, 1996) and Cantwell and Moore's (1996) Strategic Flexibility Questionnaire (Cantwell & Moore, 1998). However, Kember and Gow's (1990) factor analysis of the SPQ and of the ASI yielded two factorial structures that are slightly different.

Coopersmith SEI-A

The SEI-A (Coopersmith, 1981) is a self-report inventory composed of 25 items. After reading each statement, the respondents are required to choose "like me" or "unlike me," with "like me" indicating the statement describes how they usually feel and "unlike me" indicating the statement does not describe how they usually feel. Statements are phrased in both positive and negative ways. For example, indicating "like me" to the statement, "Things usually do not bother me," would result in earning scores in self-esteem; meanwhile, indicating "unlike me" to the statement, "I give in very easily," also would result in earning scores on the self-esteem scale. Responses to the 25 items result in a total self-esteem score. The current study used a translated and back-translated Chinese version. The internal-consistency reliability coefficients are .80 and .77, respectively, for the two samples involved in the current study. These reliability coefficients are comparable to those of Coopersmith's norm sample (r = .81 for the 20–34 age group).

Although limited psychometric data are available for the adult form of the inventory, the data available indicate the SEI-A has good internal reliabilities. Furthermore, factor analysis has shown that the inventory is heterogeneous (for example, Ahmed, Valliant, & Swindle, 1985, extracted four factors) rather than homogeneous. The inventory's external validity has been obtained by its relationship to the Buss-Durkee Scale of Guilt (Buss & Durkee, 1957) and the Minnesota Multiphasic Personality Inventory (MMPI; Dahlstorm, Welch, & Dahlstorm, 1979). It was found that participants' self-esteem scores were significantly negatively correlated with their scores on the guilt scale and negatively correlated with the MMPI psychasthenia scale.

Research Findings and Discussions

Introduction to the Studies

Since 1996, a series of studies have been conducted on university students (seven studies) from mainland China, Hong Kong, and the United States and on secondary-school students (two studies) in Hong Kong. With no exceptions, all studies examined the reliability (see Table 8.2 for reliability data for all samples) and validity of the TSI. In addition, the nine studies were designed to achieve four major goals centered around thinking styles. The first was to examine the relationships between thinking styles and academic achievement (Studies 1 and 2). The second goal was to investigate the relationships between thinking styles and learning approaches (Studies 3 and 4). The third goal was to explore the relationships between thinking styles and student characteristics (Studies 5 - 8). The fourth goal was to investigate the relationship of thinking styles to self-esteem (Study 9).

Thinking Styles and Academic Achievement: Studies 1 and 2

Study 1.   Our initial interest in thinking styles was to identify the role that thinking styles play in academic achievement among university

TABLE 8.2

Internal Consistency Reliability Coefficients Alpha of the TSI Subscales for Seven Studies

Study	1			2	3			4	5	6	7	8	9A	9B
Country	H.K.	M.C.	U.S.	H.K.	H.K.	M.C.	U.S.	U.S.	H.K.	H.K.	A.C.	H.K.	H.K.	H.K.
Institution	H.E.	H.E.	H.E.	S.E.	H.E.	H.E.	H.E.	H.E.	H.E.	H.E.	H.E.	S.E.	H.E.	H.E.
N	646	215	67	68	854	215	67	65	88	151	96	65	400	394
TSI subscales														
Legislative	.72	.65	.77	.77	.71	.65	.77	.84	.66	.70	.74	.75	.73	.72
Executive	.64	.61	.84	.77	.66	.61	.84	.77	.71	.63	.64	.66	.67	.68
Judicial	.71	.62	.71	.78	.72	.62	.71	.75	.70	.71	.79	.78	.71	.75
Global	.57	.60	.68	.62	.58	.60	.68	.65	.61	.58	.52	.58	.59	.64
Local	.42	.49	.63	deleted[a]	.48	.49	.63	.59	.58	.53	.49	.10	.45	.44
Liberal	.78	.81	.86	.82	.80	.81	.86	.83	.80	.85	.87	.85	.78	.81
Conservative	.69	.74	.83	.80	.72	.74	.83	.86	.87	.89	.77	.70	.77	.72
Hierarchical	.75	.78	.84	.82	.76	.78	.84	.76	.79	.81	.81	.76	.75	.76
Monarchic	.46	.43	.43	.57	.48	.43	.43	.61	.59	.56	.30	.39	.48	.44
Oligarchic	.63	.66	.66	.68	.64	.66	.66	.65	.82	.79	.67	.35	.65	.66
Anarchic	.43	.13	.54	.59	.44	.13	.54	.48	.54	.46	.33	.47	.53	.37
Internal	.78	.67	.76	.76	.77	.67	.76	.76	.75	.76	.80	.79	.76	.76
External	.74	.72	.64	.74	.74	.72	.64	.75	.76	.80	.63	.84	.75	.79

Note. M.C. = Mainland China, S.E. = Secondary Education, H.E. = Higher Education. [a]Deleted due to low reliability.

207

students across cultures. This interest resulted in our first study. In this investigation, we examined the relationships of thinking styles to selected student characteristics as well as to achievement, controlling for students' self-rated abilities—analytical, creative, and practical—based on Sternberg's (1985) triarchic theory of intelligence. Because of the different grading systems used in the three cultures, the achievement measure used for each sample was different. For the U.S. sample, the cumulative grade-point average was used. For the Mainland Chinese sample, the average scores of students' university entrance examinations were used. For the Hong Kong sample, the participants' scores on the Advanced Level Tests (A-Level Tests), which serve as university entrance examination scores in Hong Kong, were used.

In this study, 67 American students (1 9 male and 48 female) 215 Mainland Chinese students (114 male and 101 female), and 646 Hong Kong students (268 male and 378 female) were involved.

The results of this study not only indicated the TSI (the Chinese version was used with the Hong Kong and Mainland China groups) was reliable (see Table 8.2) and valid in all three cultures (the inventory was, for the first time, tested among U.S. university students), but also manifested various relationships of thinking styles to other constructs. In all three cultures, certain thinking styles showed statistically significant predictive validity for academic achievement beyond the participants' self-rated abilities (see Table 8.3). However, the pattern of statistical prediction varied from culture to culture.

For the Hong Kong sample, the types of thinking styles that facilitated academic achievement were those that required conformity (e.g., conservative), orientation toward a sense of order (e.g., hierarchical), and preference for working independently (internal). On the contrary, styles that allow self-directed and norm-challenging ways of performing tasks (legislative and liberal styles) and a preference for working in groups (external) were negatively associated with students' academic achievement. The local thinking style was negatively related to achievement. For the U.S. sample, like the Hong Kong sample, the hierarchical thinking style facilitated academic achievement; furthermore, the local thinking style was negatively correlated with academic achievement. Unlike the results from both Hong Kong and the United States, the results from the Mainland Chinese group indicated the executive thinking style had a negative predictive validity for academic achievement beyond that provided by self-rated abilities. The finding that the executive thinking style was negatively correlated with academic achievement among the Mainland Chinese group challenged the traditional view that Chinese students are more conforming

TABLE 8.3

Incremental Variance of Thinking Styles: R^2, β Weights, and Fs (Hong Kong: $N = 646$; Mainland China: $N = 192$; U.S.: $N = 67$)

Achieve.	CC_a	CH_a	CI	CT_a	GE	MS_a	PH_a	UE_a	UT_b	GPA_c
N	634	324	72	72	141	79	351	638	192	67
R^2_{Ability}	.03	.04	.05	.05	.09	.05	.04	.03	.12	.03
R^2_{Total}	.06	.08	.18	.28	.13	.12	.06	.06	.14	.18
R^2_{Style}	.03	.04	.13	.23	.04	.07	.02	.03	.02	.15
$β_{\text{Style 1}}$	$.12^{**}_{\text{Jud}}$	$.14^{**}_{\text{Con}}$	$.32^{***}_{\text{Global}}$	$-.26^{*}_{\text{Leg}}$	$-.19^{*}_{\text{Liberal}}$	$-.26^{*}_{\text{Local}}$	$-.14^{***}_{\text{Ext}}$	$-.17^{***}_{\text{local}}$	$-.13^{*}_{\text{Exe}}$	$-.29^{**}_{\text{Local}}$
$β_{\text{Style 2}}$	$-.14^{*}_{\text{Local}}$	$.12^{***}_{\text{Hier}}$	$.24^{*}_{\text{Con}}$	$-.45^{***}_{\text{Jud}}$				$.09^{*}_{\text{Ana}}$		$.44^{***}_{\text{Hier.}}$
$β_{\text{Style 3}}$				$.30^{**}_{\text{Hier}}$				$.12^{**}_{\text{Inter}}$		
F	7.43***	5.44***	3.01**	4.27***	4.93***	2.52*	5.80***	7.30***	7.41***	2.76*
df	(5, 628)	(5, 318)	(5, 66)	(6, 65)	(4, 136)	(4, 74)	(4, 346)	(6, 631)	(4, 192)	(5, 61)

Note. Jud = judicial, Con = conservative, Hier = hierarchical, Ana = anarchic, Inter = internal, Ext = external; CC=Chinese language and culture, CH = chemistry, CI = Chinese history, CT = Chinese literature, GE = Chinese literature, GE = geography, MS = mathematics and statistics, PH = physics, UE = use of English, UT = university entrance examination, GPA = grade point average; $_a$Hong Kong sample, $_b$Mainland Chinese sample, $_c$American sample.

*p < .05. **p < .01. ***p < .001.

in their thinking than are Western students (e.g., Ho, D. Y. F., 1996; Jones, Rozelle, & Chang, 1990; Pratt, 1991; Westwood, Tang, & Kirkbride, 1992). Instead, this finding was in line with some of the more recent research evidence suggesting that Asian learners (including Mainland Chinese students) are not rote learners (e.g., Biggs, 1990; Gow & Kember, 1990; Kember & Gow, 1991; Niles, 1995; Watkins, Regmi, & Estela, 1991).

Whereas we did not identify any gender differences in the U.S. and Mainland Chinese groups, we found in the Hong Kong group that male students had higher achievement if they preferred the judicial style (that is, being analytical) and that female students had lower achievement if they preferred the judicial style. Moreover, females students' achievement scores were significantly negatively correlated with the legislative and liberal thinking styles. (Detailed results for the Hong Kong sample has been reported in Zhang & Sternberg, in press).

Study 2.   This study was conducted among Hong Kong secondary-school students by a master's degree student who was an in-service teacher (Tso) in May 1998. Participants were 68 Form 3 (Grade 9) students (35 boys and 33 girls) from a band-one school. Apart from investigating the reliability and validity of the TSI, Tso examined the relationships between thinking styles and academic achievement in 10 school subjects and their average performance in the 10 subjects. The items in the local-style scale were eliminated from the analysis because of their low reliability coefficients. A few more items also were deleted from the monarchic, anarchic, and judicial scales because of their low reliability coefficients. The resulting reliability correlations ranged from .57 to .82, with a median of .76. As in a few other studies illustrated in this chapter, the validity of the TSI was indicated by the interscale correlations that were, in general, in the predicted directions. Some examples of correlations are: (a) conservative with executive ($r = .77$), (b) liberal with conservative ($r = -.40$), (c) liberal with executive ($r = -.40$), and (d) internal with external ($r = -.36$). It was found that students' term average was significantly and negatively correlated with the liberal style ($r = -.25, p < .05$). In addition, there were seven significant correlations that involved four school subjects and five thinking styles. These correlations varied across school subjects. In general, however, creativity-relevant thinking styles (legislative and liberal) as well as the judicial style had significant negative relationships with academic achievement (for example, $r = -.26$ for judicial style with art; $r = -.24$ for judicial style with biology; $r = -.36$ for liberal with art; $r = -.25$ for liberal style with Chinese language). On the contrary, thinking styles that required conformity (conservative) and respect for authority (executive) were positively and significantly related to academic achievement (for example, $r = .30$ for executive style and computer literacy; $r = .31$ for conservative style with computer literacy).

Discussion of Studies 1 and 2. The major value of the preceding two studies, apart from providing information about reliability and validity of the TSI in cross-cultural contexts, was that the results showed that thinking styles contributed to academic achievement (beyond abilities in higher educational institutions) in both higher education and secondary education. This finding is consistent with previous research evidence regarding the effect of cognitive styles on academic achievement (e.g., Bishop-Clark, 1995; Grigorenko & Sternberg, 1997; Kim & Michael, 1995; Saracho, 1991). Furthermore, there were gender and cultural differences in terms of the ways thinking styles were related to achievement.

These findings have at least three implications for teachers. First, teachers should realize the reason some students do not do well in school may not be due to their lack of academic abilities, but to a mismatch between students' thinking styles and those rewarded by their learning environment. Second, teachers should be aware of the kinds of thinking styles they are encouraging among their students and be aware of the styles they are punishing. Third, teachers should be well informed about gender and cross-cultural differences in thinking styles so they can better accommodate individual differences among students.

Thinking Styles and Learning Approaches: Studies 3 and 4

Whereas the first two studies focused on the relationships between thinking styles and the outcomes of learning, the next two studies focused on the relationships between thinking styles and the process of learning. In these two investigations, we studied the relationships between the constructs underlying the TSI based on the theory of mental self-government and those assessed by the SPQ based on Biggs' (1987, 1992) theory of learning approaches.

Study 3. Our participants for this study were 854 (362 male and 492 female) entering students (702 undergraduate freshmen, 66 students pursuing their postgraduate certificates, and 86 pursuing their master's degree) from the University of Hong Kong, 215 (114 male and 101 female) undergraduate freshmen from two universities in Mainland China, and 67 (19 male and 48 female) U.S. university students. The participants responded to the SPQ and the TSI as well as to a demographic questionnaire. Note that the same participants from Mainland China and the United States for Study 1 also responded to the SPQ. Therefore, the data for Study 1 on the TSI for the Mainland Chinese and American samples were used again in this investigation.

Results indicated that both the TSI and the SPQ were reliable and valid for assessing the respective constructs in all three samples of students. The alpha estimates for the 13 scales of the TSI are essentially comparable to those obtained by Sternberg (1994) in his investigation of U.S. school participants and those by Zhang (1999) and Zhang and Sachs (1997) in their study of Hong Kong university participants (see also Table 8.2).

The alpha coefficients for the six subscales of the SPQ ranged from .65 to .80, with a median of .73 for Hong Kong students; from .64 to .74, with a median of .70 for Mainland Chinese students; and from .59 to .77, with a median of .68 for the U.S. students. The alpha coefficients for the surface, deep, and achieving scales were .80, .82, and .83, respectively, for the Hong Kong sample; .78, .78, and .76 for the Mainland Chinese sample; and .71, .81, and .83 for the U.S. sample. These alpha estimates of internal consistency are in line with both those obtained by Biggs (1987) in his original study of the Australian sample and those obtained by other authors such as Albaili (1995) and Watkins (1998).

The validity of the TSI and that of the SPQ were examined by a scale intercorrelation matrix and a principal component factor analysis with a varimax rotation, respectively, for each of the three samples. Most of the scale intercorrelations for the TSI were in the expected directions. For example, the correlations between the executive and conservative scales were .65 for the Hong Kong sample, .66 for the Mainland Chinese sample, and .87 for the U.S. sample, respectively; the correlations between the legislative and liberal scales were .43 for the Hong Kong sample, .50 for the Mainland Chinese sample, and .70 for the U.S. sample, respectively; the correlation between the internal and external scales were -.23 for the Hong Kong sample, -.28 for the Mainland Chinese sample, and -.33 for the U.S. sample, respectively.

For all samples, two-factor solutions were identified in the SPQ. The first factor corresponded to the deep approach and the second to the surface approach. These two factors accounted for 72.9% of the variance in the data for the Hong Kong sample, 67.5% for the Mainland Chinese sample, and 68.6% for the U.S. sample.

The correlation matrix of the scales from the two instruments revealed the following relationships. First, students who reported a surface approach to learning employed an executive thinking style, but not judicial or liberal thinking styles. Second, students who reported a deep approach to learning employed judicial and liberal styles. We find it interesting that whereas the deep-approach learners from Mainland China and the United States did not use the executive thinking style, those from Hong Kong used the executive thinking style. This finding may indicate that the deep-approach learners in Hong Kong dealt and with their learning tasks strategically. That is, they aimed at a deep understanding of what they learned. In the meantime, they also followed their teachers' instructions closely. It also may mean that students took a deep approach in performing some tasks but took a surface approach in performing other tasks. When Pask (1976) discovered that some of his research participants could act as both a comprehension learner (holist) and an operation learner (serialist), he referred those learners as "versatile." Therefore, these "strategic" Hong Kong learners may be what Pask called the versatile learners.

Third, an interesting variation across the three samples also was found between students' approaches to learning and their levels of thinking (global and local). For the Hong Kong sample, regardless of their level of mental functioning, global or local, students used both deep and surface approaches to learning. For the Mainland Chinese sample, although there was no relationship between the levels of thinking and the deep-learning approach, local thinkers employed both surface and achieving strategies in their learning. For the U.S. sample, although global thinkers indicated deep and achieving motivation, the local thinkers used a surface learning strategy (see Table 8.4).

Study 4. In this study we validated further the relationship between thinking styles and learning approaches by computing zero-order correlations of the scales from the two inventories. Furthermore, we investigated the relationships of both inventories to another variable, namely, students' extracurricular experience. The participants were 65 (14 male and 51 female) U.S. university students. The statistical correlations between the scales in the two inventories confirmed the results from the previous study. That is, the more effective thinking styles (e.g., legislative, judicial, liberal, and hierarchical) were significantly positively related to the deep approach, but significantly negatively related to the surface approach. By contrast, the less effective thinking styles (e.g., executive and conservative) were significantly positively correlated with the surface approach, but significantly negatively correlated with the deep approach. Moreover, most of the correlations were greater in magnitude than were those from the previous study. These correlations are also presented in Table 8.4.

The nature of thinking styles was revealed further by the results from stepwise multiple-regression analyses, with student characteristics being the independent variables and the scales of thinking styles and learning

TABLE 8.4

Pearson Correlation Matrix for the Scales in the Study Process Questionnaire and Thinking Styles Inventory
($N = 854$ for Hong Kong; $N = 215$ for Mainland China; $N_1 = 67$ for U.S.; $N_2 = 65$ for U.S.)

Scale	SM H.K.	SM N.J.	SM U.S.-1	SM U.S.-2	DM H.K.	DM N.J.	DM U.S.-1	DM U.S-2	AM H.K.	AM N.J.	AM U.S.-1	AM U.S.-2	SS H.K.	SS N.J.	SS U.S.-1	SS U.S.-2	DS H.K.	DS N.J.	DS U.S.-1	DS U.S.-2	AS H.K.	AS N.J.	AS U.S.-1	AS U.S.-2
Leg	.04	-.09	-.09	-.19	.28**	.24**	.41**	.49**	.21**	.20	.16	.23	-.02	-.12	-.13	-.10	.25**	.33**	.39**	.48**	.10	.02	.27	.30
Exe	.24**	.23**	.20	.44**	.17**	.08	.20	.04	.20**	.20	.43**	.28	.26**	.34**	.43**	.39**	.17**	-.04	-.01	.03	.20**	.20	.26	.14
Jud	-.00	-.02	-.09	-.09	.39**	.31**	.42**	.48**	.17**	.15	.33**	.20	-.13**	-.11	.05	-.03	.38**	.49**	.33**	.36**	.26**	.18	.47**	.20
Global	.17**	.05	.12	.04	.24**	.04	.33**	.20	.18**	.13	.37**	.14	.13**	.02	.10	.00	.25**	.13	.19	.18	.13**	.00	.11	.06
Local	.17**	.18	.00	.16	.24**	.15	.02	.40**	.21**	.14	.18	.27	.17**	.23**	.29	.10	.26**	.10	-.04	.43**	.30**	.23**	.38**	.45**
Liberal	.07	-.15	.01	-.24	.37**	.31**	.41**	.50**	.20**	.08	.17	.01	-.03	-.31**	-.22	-.26	.37**	.53**	.37**	.45**	.19**	.18	.26	.37**
Con	.25**	.36**	.22	.39**	.07	.00	.15	-.04	.19**	.19	.36**	.23	.36**	.47**	.41**	.42**	.07	-.16	-.07	-.05	.19**	.07	.24	.02
Hier	-.01	-.13	-.06	-.08	.32**	.35**	.44**	.49**	.13**	.23**	.34**	.38**	-.04	-.14	.08	-.10	.36**	.39**	.34**	.52**	.39**	.49**	.44**	.47**
Mon	.22**	.20	.20	.17	.28**	.23**	.14	.20	.26**	.30**	.30	.43**	.22**	.18	.18	.34**	.24**	.21	.05	.15	.29**	.31**	.13	.32
Oli	.18**	.23**	.12	.29	.13**	.23**	.16	.14	.24**	.24**	.36**	.19	.19**	.23	.48**	.27	.13**	.14	.06	.09	.12	.25**	.17	-.02
Ana	.04	.14	-.11	-.17	.25**	.26**	.46**	.45**	.10	.28**	.31	.21	.08	.08	.02	-.03	.24**	.27**	.38**	.50**	.18**	.30**	.45**	.36**
Internal	.07	-.02	-.26	-.01	.24**	.13	.33**	.22	.24**	.36**	.29	.14	.05	-.12	.02	.11	.20**	.30**	.22	.12	.07	.10	.15	.12
External	.02	-.02	.12	-.01	.22**	.22**	.28	.43**	.02	-.06	.14	.09	-.02	.02	.07	-.06	.24**	.09	.10	.45**	.20**	.22**	.44**	.20

Note. SM =surface motivation, DM = deep motivation, AM = achieving motivation; SS = surface strategy, DS = deep strategy, AS = achieving strategy; Leg = legislative, Exe = executive, Jud = judicial, Con = conservative, Hier = Hierarchical, Mon = monarchic, Oli = Oligarchic, Ana = anarchic. N.J. = Nanjing.
**$p < .01$.

214

approaches being the dependent variables. Results indicated that effective thinking styles from the theory of mental self-government were related to the same student characteristics (e.g., larger number of hobbies and more leadership and work experience) as were the deep-approach scales from Biggs' model. By the same token, the less effective thinking styles were related to the same student characteristics (smaller number of hobbies and less leadership and work experience) as were the surface scales. For example, some of the results were as follows:

1. Students' hobbies accounted for 17% of the variance ($\beta = .42$, p $< .001$) in their scores on the legislative thinking scale.
2. Their leadership experience accounted for 7% of the variance ($\beta = .27$, p $< .05$) in their scores on the conservative scale.
3. Their hobbies accounted for 8% of the variance ($\beta = .28$, p $< .05$) in their scores on the deep-motive scale.

Discussion of Studies 3 and 4.   The major contribution of these two studies was that they examined the nature of thinking styles in the theory of mental self-government against a theory of student learning process. We found that certain thinking styles and learning processes and approaches were correlated in predictable ways. This relationship was confirmed by the identical way thinking styles and learning approaches were related to particular student characteristics. The question that arises is, "What is the major implication of this finding for teachers?" The answer is that teachers could make use of the relationship between the thinking styles constructs and the learning approaches constructs. For example, teachers could encourage effective thinking styles (e.g., judicial, legislative, and liberal) by allowing students to give their own opinions on the subjects they learn and to choose their own materials of study or projects. Given the opportunities to think for themselves and to work on their favorite projects, students will inevitably take a deep approach to learning. By the same token, teachers also could teach and assign learning tasks that would encourage a deep approach to learning, namely, a true understanding of learning materials. Students who take a deep approach to learning will inevitably employ thinking styles that will allow them to think more creatively and come up with norm-challenging ideas.

Thinking Styles and Student Characteristics: Studies 5 to 8

Study 5.   In this study (Zhang & Sachs, 1997), 88 (30 male and 58 female) university students (pre- and in-service teachers) in Hong Kong responded to the TSI (English version). Two major findings emerged. First, the scales of the TSI were reasonably reliable and factor analysis of the scales was fairly encouraging. Specifically, the alpha coefficients for the 13 scales ranged from .53 to .87, with a median of .70; three factors accounted for 65.6% of the variance (see Zhang & Sachs, 1997, for details). Second, results of this study also supported one of the assumptions underlying the theory of mental self-government. This assumption is that thinking styles are socialized. Thus, students with different characteristics (who were thus socialized differently) presumably should show different thinking styles. This study found significant group differences in certain thinking styles based on variables such as age, sex, college major, subject area taught, and college class levels. A first example is that male participants scored significantly higher on the global thinking style than did their female counterparts. A second example is that student teachers with more teaching experience were more hierarchical and less legislative than those with less teaching experience.

Study 6. In this study (Zhang, 1999), 151 (57 male, 88 female, 6 unspecified) participants from the University of Hong Kong responded to the TSI (English version). Among these participants, 80 were from the Faculty of Education and 71 were from the School of Business. Results again indicated that the thinking styles evaluated by the TSI can be identified among the participants. The alpha coefficients ranged from .46 (the only one below .50) to .89, with a median of .71. A principal-axis factor analysis resulted in five factors, each roughly corresponding to one of the five dimensions described in the theory of mental self-government. These five factors accounted for 78% of the variance in the data. Moreover, students with more extracurricular experience (e.g., work experience as indicated by the length of working experience and travel experience as indicated by the number of cities and countries to which the participants had traveled) scored significantly higher on the scales of the legislative and liberal thinking styles than did those with less work and travel experience (see Zhang, 1999, for details).

Study 7. In this study, 96 (29 male and 67 female) university freshmen from Shanghai responded to the TSI (Chinese version) and to a series of demographic questions, including those about parental educational levels (a measure of socioeconomic status). The reliability coefficients of the 13 scales ranged from .30 (one of the three alpha coefficients below .50) to .87, with a median of .67. The validity of the TSI was manifested through the correlation coefficients in the expected directions, ranging from statistically insignificant to statistically significant at the .001 level. For example, whereas the correlation coefficient between the legislative style and liberal style was .61 ($p < .001$) and that between the executive style and conservative style was .60 ($p < .001$), the correlation between the global and local styles was -.04 (nonsignificant) and that between the liberal and conservative styles was -.10. These reliability and validity statistics, although not as impressive as they were for the other studies described in this chapter, were considered adequate to allow an examination of the relationship between thinking styles and selected student characteristics. The following results also were obtained:

1. Students with more hobbies employed the legislative style more than those with fewer hobbies ($R^2 = .07$, ß $= .27$, $p < .05$).
2. Male students employed the judicial thinking style more than did the female students ($R^2 = .06$, ß $= .24$, $p < .05$).
3. Students from higher socioeconomic families thought more globally than did their counterparts ($R^2 = .09$, ß $= .31$, $p < .01$).
4. Students who had done more traveling employed the external thinking style more than did those who had less traveling experience ($R^2 = .11$, ß $= .34$, $p < .01$).

Study 8.   This study, like Study 2, was conducted by a master's degree student, an in-service teacher, among secondary-school students in Hong Kong (May, 1998). Sixty-six (58 male and 8 female) students (41 Form 2—Grade 8 and 25 Form 6—Grade 12) participated in this study. The average age of the participants was 16. Results indicated that 9 of the 13 reliability coefficients were above .50 (ranging from .58 to .85). The remaining four reliability coefficients ranged from .10 (local scale) to .47 (anarchic scale). The particularly low alpha coefficient for the local scale, as H. K. Ho (1998) explained, might be attributed to the fact that students did not understand the meaning of the items included in this scale. Many participants asked for clarification regarding items in the local scale during the administration of the survey.

Again, validity was examined through zero-order correlations of the scales. Results suggested reasonable validity of the TSI in a Hong Kong school context. Some examples of the correlations are: (a) legislative with liberal ($r = .43$), (b) executive with conservative ($r = .71$), (c) conservative with liberal ($r = -.17$), and (d) internal with external ($r = -.36$). Of the student characteristics examined in relation to thinking styles, socioeconomic status and birth order were the two of major interest (see also Sternberg & Grigorenko, 1995). Consistent with Sternberg and Grigorenko's finding, this study found that participants' socioeconomic status as measured by the size of their housing accommodation is negatively related to the conservative, oligarchic, and local styles. As Sternberg and Grigorenko and H. K. Ho pointed out, this finding can be explained by the notion that people from lower socioeconomic families may tend more toward authoritarianism. However, whereas Sternberg and Grigorenko found a positive correlation between socioeconomic status and the legislative style, this study identified a positive correlation between socioeconomic status and the judicial style. H. K. Ho attributed this positive relationship to the frequent discussions and evaluations about current issues in Hong Kong (which are analytical in nature) to which higher socioeconomic status students were more likely to be exposed. With regard to birth order, whereas Sternberg and Grigorenko identified a positive relationship between later borns and the legislative style, this study found a statistically significant positive relationship between earlier borns and the legislative style. As H. K. Ho explained in his project, in Hong Kong, older children are expected to take care of the younger ones. There are many situations in which the older children are required to handle problems independently. "As a result, their creativity may develop out of necessity" (H. K. Ho, 1998).

Discussion of Studies 5 to 8.   Apart from providing reliability and validity data regarding the TSI (both Chinese and English versions) in Chinese contexts (Hong Kong and Mainland China), the preceding four studies also demonstrated the relationship between certain thinking styles and various student characteristics. Across the four studies, these student characteristics included age, birth order, sex, college major, subject area taught, college class level, socioeconomic status, and traveling and working experiences. The findings of significant group differences in thinking styles based on these characteristics, again, supported the contention that styles are socialized (e.g., Hale, 1983; Hunt, 1964; Saracho, 1993; Shipman, 1973; Sternberg, 1988, 1997; Steward & Steward, 1974). That is, one's thinking styles can be shaped by one's experiences. Based on this assumption, students with different characteristics, personological or situational, should have different thinking styles. For example, students from higher socioeconomic status families are brought up and socialized differently from those from lower socioeconomic status families, which leads to different styles of thinking.

What is the significance of the findings regarding the relationship between thinking styles and student characteristics? How can teachers use this information in the enhancement of teaching and learning? Because styles are socialized, they are modifiable (Sternberg, 1988, 1997). Therefore, teachers can cultivate students' thinking styles. We argue this information could assist teachers in creating a learning environment that is more conducive to effective teaching and learning in at least four ways.

First, teachers could use a variety of teaching methods (such as lecturing, facilitating group discussion and activities, and using cooperative learning) so that all students, regardless of their preferred ways of using their abilities, can benefit from teaching. Second, teachers could use a variety of assessment methods (such as multiple-choice test, short essays, individual projects, and group projects) so that all students, no matter what their dominant thinking styles, can have the opportunity to succeed. Third, teachers could teach students to achieve an understanding of different thinking styles so that students could become more aware of how they are using their abilities. Fourth, teachers could enhance teaching and learning by enriching students' extracurricular experience. Considerable research has indicated that students' extracurricular experiences may have a strong positive effect on educational outcomes, including on creative thinking (e.g., Astin, 1989; Hattie, Marsh, Neill, & Richards, 1997; see also Zhang, 1999, for details). Terenzini, Pascarella, and Blimling (1996) asserted that "students' out-of-class experiences appear to be far more influential in students' academic and intellectual development than many faculty and student affairs administrators think" (p.157).

Thinking Styles and Self-Esteem

Study 9.   Whereas the previous studies were aimed at examining the relationships of thinking styles to achievement, learning process, and students' demographic attributes and their experiences outside the classroom, respectively, this study aimed at investigating the relationship of thinking styles to self-esteem. The TSI and the SEI-A (Coopersmith, 1981) were administered to 794 university students in Hong Kong. For cross-validation, the participants were randomly assigned to two samples. The first sample (N = 400) consisted of 165 male students and 235 female students. The second sample (N = 394) consisted of 184 male students and 208 female students (2 students did not indicate their gender[s]).

The relationship between thinking styles and self-esteem is manifested in Sternberg's (1994) argument that thinking style is at the interface between intelligence and personality. Self-esteem is an important aspect of personality and, therefore, should be related to thinking styles. The more effective thinking styles (e.g., legislative, judicial, hierarchical, and liberal) were expected to be significantly positively related to self-esteem, and less effective thinking styles (e.g., executive and conservative) were expected to be significantly negatively related to self-esteem. Results from both samples generally, although not completely, supported our prediction. The hypothesis that the more effective thinking styles were significantly positively correlated with self-esteem was fully supported. For example, for the validation sample, the correlations of self-esteem score with legislative, judicial, hierarchical, liberal, and external styles were .15 ($p < .01$), .12 ($p < .05$), .25 ($p < .01$), .22 ($p < .01$), and .27 ($p < .01$), respectively. For the cross-validation sample, the correlations of self-esteem score with the legislative, judicial, hierarchical, liberal, and external styles were .11 ($p < .05$), .25 ($p < .01$), .32 ($p < .01$), .13 ($p < .05$), and .36 ($p < .01$), respectively. However, the hypothesis that the executive and conservative thinking styles should be significantly negatively correlated with self-esteem scores was only partially supported. For the validation sample, the correlation coefficients were: (a) executive with self-esteem ($r = -.02$, nonsignificant) and (b) conservative with self-esteem ($r = -.10$, $p < .05$). For the cross-validation sample, the correlation coefficients were: (a) executive with self-esteem ($r = .08$, nonsignificant) and (b) conservative with self-esteem ($r = -.04$, nonsignificant).

Discussion of Study 9.   The major value of this study is that it empirically verified the relationship between thinking styles and one of the important affective domains, that is, self-esteem. This verification supported the argument that thinking styles should be related to personality (e.g., Sternberg, 1994). In the past, research also has been done to study the relationship between cognitive styles and self-esteem. For example, Bosacki et al. (1997) noted that their hypothesis that field independence and self-esteem correlated negatively for girls and positively for boys was confirmed. However, research on this relationship is limited.

The current finding also makes practical sense. That is, students who have higher self-esteem should automatically be more confident about what they do. This self-confidence leads them to be self-instructed and self-directed (legislative style), and to perform their tasks in a nontraditional way (liberal style). Students with higher self-esteem also would be comfortable with what they do to the extent that they prioritize their tasks (hierarchical style).

What is the implication of this finding for teachers? Again, teachers could make use of the relationship between thinking styles and self-esteem. For example, teachers could use different strategies (e.g., giving students the opportunity to shine and to succeed in both academic and nonacademic situations) to enhance students' self-esteem, which could in turn lead to students' use of the more effective thinking styles. In other words, when students are confident in what they do, they think more creatively and deal with their learning tasks in ways with which they are comfortable. Alternatively, teachers could allow for a variety of thinking styles in learning (e.g., using different instructional styles and different assessment formats). As a result of being allowed to use different thinking styles, students may achieve better performance, which would, in turn, promote students' self-esteem.

GENERAL DISCUSSION, CONCLUSIONS, AND RECOMMENDATIONS

The major contribution of the studies presented is that they have shown that thinking styles as defined by the theory of mental self-government do matter in several important ways. First, thinking styles contributed to academic achievement above self-rated abilities. Second, thinking styles are closely related to students' learning approaches. Third, thinking styles have significant relationships with students' characteristics, including age, birth order, gender, socioeconomic status, number of hobbies, leadership experience, and working and traveling experience. Fourth, thinking styles are statistically related to self-esteem. These relationships are summarized in Fig. 8.1, which represents an amalgam of all the studies presented. Furthermore, we found that the thinking styles can be identified in all three cultures under investigation. However, these thinking styles work differently across cultures. For example, whereas creative-relevant thinking styles were negatively related to achievement in one culture (such as in Hong Kong), the executive style (i.e., conforming style) was negatively related to achievement in another culture (such as in Mainland China). To conclude, this series of studies has enhanced the understanding of the importance of thinking styles among university and secondary-school students. All these findings, as discussed earlier at the end of each group of studies, have direct implications for teachers in their enhancement of teaching and learning.

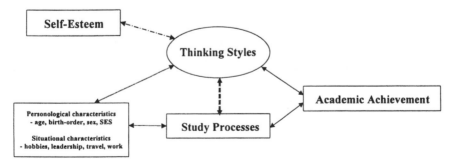

FIG. 8.1.   Thinking styles related to academic achievement, study process, self-esteem, and student's background.

When Riding (1997) discussed the nature of cognitive styles, he raised several questions that need to be clarified regarding the "style" construct. Based on Sternberg's theory of thinking styles, the studies presented in this chapter answered some of the questions. For example, data from these studies have answered, to some extent, the following questions:

1. "What is the interaction between other sources and style?" (p. 45)
2. "Are there cultural differences in style?" (p. 45)
3. "What is the interaction between other experiences and style?" (p. 46).

The work presented in this chapter also examined the relationship of thinking styles to learning outcomes and learning processes, as well as to an important aspect of affective domains, that is, self-esteem. However, there are other questions raised by Riding that are left unanswered. For example, what are the origins of thinking styles? Are they inborn or can they be nurtured? Although we believe in the argument that styles are socialized and thus can be nurtured, we have not conducted any experimental research that examines how socialization factors work. Although we attribute the evidence that thinking styles work differently across cultures to different cultural values, we have not examined exactly how thinking styles are influenced by cultural values. Furthermore, although we believe that thinking styles may also draw on genetic endowment, we do not have any scientific evidence. Also, what are the mechanisms for developing effective thinking styles? Although we have proposed such strategies as using a variety of instructional styles and adopting a variety of assessment methods to allow for different styles, we have not done any experiments that are aimed at identifying ways of developing effective thinking styles.

Another question that is worth further investigating is the nature of thinking styles in relation to other theories of styles or of learning approaches. For example, what are specific ways in which thinking styles and learning approaches overlap and differ from each other? In chapter 4 of this book, Biggs addresses the differences between the two on a conceptual level. Results from two of the studies in this chapter indicate an overlapping between thinking styles and learning approaches on a statistical level. Therefore, it seems that further research is needed to examine the similarities and differences between the two constructs.

Answers to all three questions would enhance the knowledge of the field as well as provide useful guidelines for teachers to follow in their effort to improve the effectiveness of teaching and learning. To gain a better understanding of the thinking styles defined by the theory of mental self-government, there are at least two types of research that need to be conducted. First, we need to go beyond cross-sectional studies. That is, longitudinal studies are required to capture the socialization process of people's thinking styles. Second, we need to go beyond quantitative investigations. That is, much qualitative work needs to be done. A true understanding of a theoretical construct requires both quantification and a deep understanding of what goes through people's minds.

REFERENCES

Ahmed, S. M. S., Valliant, P. M., & Swindle, D. (1985). Psychometric properties of Coopersmith Self-Esteem Inventory. *Perceptual and Motor Skills, 61,* 1235–1241.

Albaili, M. A. (1995). An Arabic version of the Study Process Questionnaire: Reliability and validity. *Psychological Reports, 77*(3), 1083–1089.

Allen, G. L., Woodard, E. A., Jones, R. J., Terranova, M., & Morgan, B. B. (1990). Measures of learning rate and scholastic aptitude as predictors of performance in training-oriented academic courses. *The Journal of General Psychology, 117* (3), 277–293.

Allen, W. R. (1992). The color of success: African-American college student outcomes at predominantly White and historically Black public colleges and universities. *Harvard Educational Review, 62*(1), 26–44.

Astin, A. W. (1989). Student involvement: A developmental theory for higher education. In G. D. Kuh, J. B. Bean, D. Hossler, & F. K. Stage (Eds.), *ASHE reader on college students* (pp. 226–236). Needham Heights, MA: Ginn Press.

Biggs, J. B. (1987). *Student approaches to learning and studying.* Hawthorn, Australia: Australian Council for Educational Research.

Biggs, J. B. (1990, July). *Asian students' approaches to learning: Implications for teaching overseas students.* Paper presented at the Eighth Australian Leaning and Language Conference, Queensland University of Technology.

Biggs, J. B. (1992). *Why and how do Hong Kong students learn? Using the Learning and Study Process Questionnaires* (Education Paper No. 14). Hong Kong: The University of Hong Kong, Faculty of Education.

Biggs, J. B. (1995). Learning in the classroom. In J. Biggs and D. Watkins (Eds.), *Classroom learning: Educational psychology for the Asian teacher* (pp.147–166). Singapore: Prentice-Hall.

Bishop-Clark, C. (1995). Cognitive style, personality, and computer programming. *Computers in Human Behavior, 11*(2), 241–260.

Bolen, L. M., Wurm, T. R., & Hall, C. W. (1994). Factorial structure of the Study Process Questionnaire. *Psychological Reports, 75*(3), 1235–1241.

Bosacki, S., Innerd, W., & Towson, S. (1997). Field independence–dependence and self-esteem in preadolescents: Does gender make a difference? *Journal of Youth and Adolecence, 26*(6) 691–703.

Buss, A., & Durkee, A. (1957). An inventory for assessing different kinds of hostility. *Journal of Consulting Psychology, 21,* 343–349.

Carter, G., & Jones, M. G. (1994). Relationship between ability-paired interactions and the development of fifth graders' concepts of balance. *Journal of Research in Science Teaching, 31*(8), 847–856.

Ceci, S. J. (1986, 1987). *Handbook of cognitive, social, and neurological aspects of learning disabilities* (Vols. 1 & 2). Hillsdale, NJ: Erlbaum.

Chiu, L. H. (1987) Sociometric status and self-esteem of American and Chinese school children. *The Journal of Psychology*, 121(6) 547–522.

Coopersmith, S. (1967). *The antecedents of self-esteem*. San Francisco: Freeman.

Coopersmith, S. (1981). *Manual of the Coopersmith Self-Esteem Inventory*. Palo Alto, CA: Consulting Psychologists Press.

Dahlstorm, W. G., Welch, G. S., & Dahlstorm, L. E. (1979). *An MMPI handbook: Vol. 1. Clinical interpretation*. Minneapolis, MN: University of Minnesota Press.

Dev, P. C. (1997). Intrinsic motivation and academic achievement: What does their relationship imply for the classroom teacher? *Remedial and Special Education*, 18(1), 12–19.

Dunkin, M. J., & Biddle, B. J. (1974). *The study of teaching*. New York: Holt, Rinehart & Winston.

Fuertes, J. N., Sedlacek, W. E., & Liu, W. M. (1994). Using the SAT and noncognitive variables to predict the grades and retention of Asian American university students. *Measurement and Evaluation in Counseling and Development*, 27, 74–84.

Gow, L., & Kember, D. (1990). Does higher education promote independent learning? *Higher Education*, 19, 307–322.

Gregorc, A. F. (1985). *Inside styles: Beyond the basics*. Maynard, MA: Gabriel Systems.

Grigorenko, E., & Sternberg, R. J. (1995). Thinking styles. In D. Saflofske & M. Zeidner (Eds.), *International handbook of personality and intelligence*. New York: Plenum.

Grigorenko, E., & Sternberg, R. J. (1997). Styles of thinking, abilities, and academic performance. *Exceptional Children*, 63, 295–312.

Hale, J. (1983). Black children: Their roots, culture and learning styles. In O. N. Saracho & B. Spodek (Eds.), *Understanding the multicultural experience in early childhood education* (pp. 17–34). Washington, DC: National Association for the Education of Young Children.

Hattie, J., Marsh, H. W., Neill, J. T., & Richards, G. E. (1997). Adventure education and outward bound: Out-of-class experiences that make a lasting difference. *Review of Educational Research*, 67(1) 43–87.

Ho, D. Y. F. (1996). Filial piety and its psychological consequences. In M. H. Bond (Ed.), *The handbook of Chinese psychology* (pp. 155–165). Hong Kong: Oxford University Press.

Ho, H. K. (1998). *Assessing thinking styles in the theory of mental self-government: A mini validity study in a Hong Kong secondary school*. Unpublished manuscript. The University of Hong Kong.

Holland, J. L. (1973). *Making vocational choices: A theory of careers*. Englewood Cliffs, NJ: Prentice-Hall.

Horn, C., Bruning, R., Schraw, G., & Curry, E. (1993). Paths to success in the college classroom. *Contemporary Educational Psychology*, 18, 464–478.

Hunt, J. (1964). How children develop intellectually. *Children*, 11, 83–91.

Jones, A. P., Rozelle, R. M., & Chang, W. C. (1990). Perceived punishment and reward values of supervisor actions in a Chinese sample. *Psychological Studies*, 35(1), 1–10.

Jung, C. (1923). *Psychological types*. New York: Harcourt Brace.

Kagan, J. (1976). Commentary on reflective and impulsive children: Strategies of information processing underlying differences in problem solving. *Monographs of the Society for Research in Child Development*, 41, (5, Serial No. 168).

Kember, D., & Gow, L. (1990). Cultural specificity of approaches to study. *British Journal of Educational Psychology*, 60, 356–363.

Kember, D., & Gow, L. (1991). A challenge to the anecdotal stereotype of the Asian students. *Studies in Higher Education*, 16(2) 117–128.

Kim, J., & Michael, W. B. (1995). The relationship of creativity measures to school achievement and preferred learning and thinking style in a sample of Korean high school students. *Educational and Psychological Measurement, 55*(1), 60–74.

Kolb, D. A. (1976). *Learning Style Inventory: Technical manual.* Englewood Cliffs, NJ: Prentice-Hall.

Kolb, D. A. (1984). *Experiential learning: Experience as a source of learning and development.* Englewood Cliffs, NJ: Prentice-Hall.

Kreitler, S., Zigler, E., Kagan, S., Olsen, D., Weissler, K., & Kreitler, H. (1995). Cognitive and motivational determinants of academic achievement and behavior in third and fourth grade disadvantaged children. *Journal of Educational Psychology, 65*, 297–316.

Kwok, D. C., & Lytton, H. (1996). Perceptions of mathematics ability versus actual mathematics performance: Canadian and Hong Kong Chinese children. *British Journal of Educational Psychology, 66*, 209–222.

Leondari, A., Syngollitou, E., & Kiosseoglou, G. (1998). Academic achievement, motivation, and future selves. *Educational Studies, 24*(2) 153–163.

Marton, F., & Booth, S. A. (1997). *Learning and awareness.* Mahwah, NJ: Lawrence Erlbaum Associates.

Mboya, M. M. (1993). Self-concept of academic ability: Relations with gender and academic achievement. *Perceptual and Motor Skills, 77*, 1131–1137.

Murray-Harvey, R. (1994). Learning styles and approaches to learning: Distinguishing between concept and instruments. *British Journal of Educational Psychology, 64*(3), 373–388.

Myers, I. B. (1980). *Gifts differing.* Palo Alto, CA: Consulting Psychologists Press.

Niles, F. S. (1995). Cultural differences in learning motivation and learning strategies: A comparison of overseas and Australian students at an Australian university. *International Journal of Intercultural Relations, 19*(3) 369–385.

Pask, G. (1976) Styles and strategies of learning. *British Journal of Educational Psychology, 46*, 128–148.

Pratt, D. D. (1991). Conceptions of self within China and the United States: Contrasting foundations for adult education. *International Journal of Intercultural Relations, 15*(3), 285–310.

Renzulli, J. S., & Smith, L. H. (1978). *Learning Styles Inventory.* Mansfield Center, CT: Creative Learning Press.

Riding, R. (1991a). *Cognitive style analysis.* Birmingham, England: Learning and Training Technology.

Riding, R. (1991b). *Cognitive style analysis user manual.* Birmingham, England: Learning and Training Technology.

Riding, R. J. (1997). On the nature of cognitive style. *Educational Psychology, 17*(1 & 2), 29–49.

Saracho, O. N. (1991). Teacher expectations and cognitive style: Implications for students' academic achievement. *Early Child Development and Care, 77*, 97–108.

Saracho, O. N. (1993). Sociocultural perspectives in the cognitive styles of young students and teachers. *Early Child Development and Care, 84*, 1–17.

Shipman, V. C. (1973). *Disadvantaged children and their first school experiences: Interim report.* Princeton, NJ: Educational Testing Services.

Sternberg, R. J. (1985). *Beyond IQ: A triarchic theory of human intelligence.* New York: Cambridge University Press.

Sternberg, R. J. (1988). Mental self-government: A theory of intellectual styles and their development. *Human Development, 31*, 197–224.

Sternberg, R. J. (1990). *Metaphors of mind: Conceptions of the nature of intelligence.* New York: Cambridge University Press.

Sternberg, R. J. (1994). Thinking styles: Theory and assessment at the interface between intelligence and personality. In R. J. Sternberg and P. Ruzgis (Eds.), *Intelligence and personality* (pp. 169–187). New York: Cambridge University Press.

Sternberg, R. J. (1997). *Thinking styles.* New York: Cambridge University Press.

Sternberg, R. J., & Grigorenko, E. (1995). Styles of thinking in the school. *European Journal for High Ability, 6,* 201–219.

Steward, M. S., & Steward, D. S. (1974). Effect of social distance on teaching strategies of Anglo-American and Mexican-American mothers. *Developmental Psychology, 10,* 797–807.

Terenzini, P. T., Pascarella, E. T., & Blimling, G. S. (1996). Students' out-of-class experiences and their influence on learning and cognitive development. *Journal of College Student Development, 37,* 149–162.

Tso, S. M. (1998). *Correlational study of thinking styles and academic achievement.* Unpublished manuscript, The University of Hong Kong.

Watkins, D. (1998). Assessing approaches to learning: A cross-cultural perspective on the Study Process Questionnaire. In B. Dart and G. Boulton-Lewis (Eds.), *Teaching and learning in higher education* (pp.124–144). Melbourne, Australia: Australian Council for Educational Research.

Watkins, D., & Akande, A. (1992). Assessing the approaches to learning of Nigerian students. *Assessment and Evaluation in Higher Education, 17,* 11–20.

Watkins, D., & Dahlin, B. (1997). Assessing study approaches in Sweden. *Psychological Reports, 81,* 131–136.

Watkins, D., & Regmi, M. (1990). An investigation of the approach to learning of Nepalese tertiary students. *Higher Education, 20,* 459–469.

Watkins, D., Regmi, M., & Estela, A. (1991). The Asian-learner-as-rote-learner stereotype: Myth or reality? *Educational Psychology, 2(1)* 21–34.

Westwood, R. I., Tang, S. F., & Kirkbride, P. S. (1992). Chinese conflict behavior: Cultural antecedents and behavioral consequences. *Organizational Development Journal, 19(2),* 13–19.

Witkin, H. A. (1978). *Cognitive styles in personal and cultural adaptation: The 1977 Heinz Werner lectures.* Worcester, MA: Clark University Press.

Yung, K. K. (1997). What happens to the attainment of our bottom 20% of students at the end of their nine-year compulsory education? *Educational Research Journal, 12(2),* 159–173.

Zhang, L. F. (1999). Further cross-cultural validation of the theory of mental self-government. *Journal of Psychology, 133(2)* 165–181.

Zhang, L. F., & Sachs, J. (1997). Assessing thinking styles in the theory of mental self-government: A Hong Kong validity study. *Psychological Reports, 81,* 915–928.

Zhang, L. F., & Sternberg, R. J. (1998). Thinking styles, abilities, and academic achievement among Hong Kong university students. *Educational Research Journal, 13(1),* 41–62.

9

Experiential Learning Theory: Previous Research and New Directions

David A. Kolb
Richard E. Boyatzis
Charalampos Mainemelis
Case Western Reserve University

Experiential learning theory (ELT) provides a holistic model of the learning process and a multilinear model of adult development, both of which are consistent with what we know about how people learn, grow, and develop. The theory is called *experiential learning* to emphasize the central role that experience plays in the learning process, an emphasis that distinguishes ELT from other learning theories. The term experiential is used therefore to differentiate ELT both from cognitive learning theories, which emphasize cognition over affect, and behavioral learning theories, which deny any role for subjective experience in the learning process.

Another reason the theory is called experiential is its intellectual origins in the experiential works of Dewey, Lewin, and Piaget. Taken together—Dewey's philosophical pragmatism, Lewin's social psychology, and Piaget's cognitive-developmental genetic epistemology—form a unique perspective on learning and development (Kolb, 1984).

THE EXPERIENTIAL LEARNING MODEL AND LEARNING STYLES

Experiential learning theory defines learning as "the process whereby knowledge is created through the transformation of experience. Knowledge results from the combination of grasping and transforming experience" (Kolb 1984, p. 41). The ELT model portrays two dialectically related modes of grasping experience —*concrete experience* (CE) and *abstract conceptualization* (AC)—and two dialectically related modes of transforming experience —*reflective observation* (RO) and *active experimentation* (AE). According to the four-stage learning cycle depicted in Fig. 9.1, immediate or *concrete experiences* are the basis for observations and *reflections*. These reflections are assimilated and distilled into *abstract concepts* from which new implications for action can be drawn. These implications can be *actively tested* and serve as guides in creating new experiences.

A closer examination of the ELT model suggests that learning requires abilities that are polar opposites, and that the learner must continually choose which set of learning abilities he or she will use in a learning situation. In grasping experience, some of us perceive new information through experiencing the concrete, tangible, felt qualities of the world, relying on our senses and immersing ourselves in concrete reality. Others perceive, grasp, or take hold of new information through symbolic representation or abstract conceptualization—thinking about, analyzing, or systematically planning, rather than using sensation as a guide. Similarly, in transforming or processing experience some of us carefully watch others who are involved in the experience and reflect on what happens, whereas others jump right in and start doing things. The watchers favor reflective observation, whereas the doers favor active experimentation.

Each dimension of the learning process presents us with a choice. Because it is virtually impossible, for example, to simultaneously drive a car (CE) and analyze a driver's manual about the car's functioning (AC), we resolve the conflict by choosing. Because of our hereditary equipment, our particular past-life experiences, and the demands of our present environment, we develop a preferred way of choosing. We resolve the conflict between concrete or abstract and between active or reflective in some patterned, characteristic ways. We call these patterned ways *learning styles*.

The LSI and the Four Basic Learning Styles

In 1971 Kolb developed the LSI to assess individual learning styles. Although individuals tested on the LSI show many different patterns of

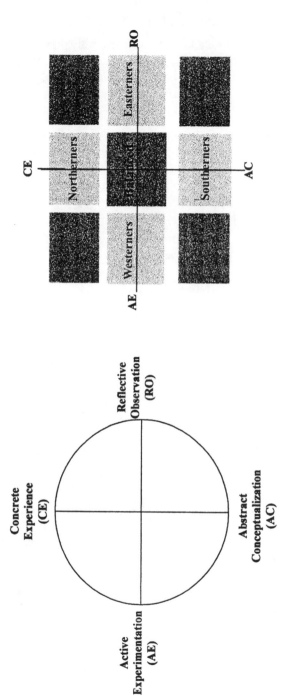

FIG. 9.1.   The experiential learning cycle and basic learning styles.

scores, research on the instrument has identified four statistically prevalent learning styles: diverging, assimilating, converging, and accommodating (Fig. 9.1). The following summary of the four basic learning styles is based on both research and clinical observation of these patterns of LSI scores (Kolb, 1984, 1999a, 1999b).

Diverging. The diverging style's dominant learning abilities are CE and RO. People with this learning style are best at viewing concrete situations from many points of view. It is labeled diverging because a person with this style performs better in situations that call for generation of ideas, such as a "brainstorming" session. People with a diverging learning style have broad cultural interests and like to gather information. Research shows they are interested in people, are imaginative and emotional, have broad cultural interests, and specialize in the arts. In formal learning situations, people with the diverging style prefer to work in groups, listening with an open mind, and receiving personalized feedback.

Assimilating. The assimilating style's dominant learning abilities are AC and RO. People with this learning style are best at understanding a wide range of information and putting it into concise, logical form. Individuals with an assimilating style are less focused on people and more interested in ideas and abstract concepts. Generally, people with this style find it more important that a theory have logical soundness than practical value. The assimilating learning style is important for effectiveness in information and science careers. In formal learning situations, people with this style prefer readings, lectures, exploring analytical models, and having time to think things through.

Converging. The converging style's dominant learning abilities are AC and AE. People with this learning style are best at finding practical uses for ideas and theories. They have the ability to solve problems and make decisions based on finding solutions to questions or problems. Individuals with a converging learning style prefer to deal with technical tasks and problems rather than with social issues and interpersonal issues. These learning skills are important for effectiveness in specialist and technology careers. In formal learning situations, people with this style prefer to experiment with new ideas, simulations, laboratory assignments, and practical applications.

Accommodating. The accommodating style's dominant learning abilities are CE and AE. People with this learning style have the ability to learn from primarily "hands-on" experience. They enjoy carrying out plans and involving themselves in new and challenging experiences. Their tendency may be to act on "gut" feelings rather than on logical analysis. In solving problems, individuals with an accommodating learning style rely more heavily on people for information than on their own technical analysis. This learning style is important for effectiveness in action-oriented careers such as marketing or sales. In formal learning situations, people with the accommodating learning style prefer to work with others to get assignments done, to set goals, to do field work, and to test different approaches to completing a project.

Factors That Shape and Influence Learning Styles

The above patterns of behavior associated with the four basic learning styles are shown consistently at various levels of behavior. During the last three decades researchers have examined the characteristics of learning styles at five levels of behavior: personality types, early educational specialization, professional career, current job role, and adaptive competencies. We briefly summarize these research findings in Table 9.1 and discuss them in this chapter.

Personality Types. ELT follows Jung (1977) in recognizing that learning styles result from individuals' preferred ways for adapting in the

TABLE 9.1

Relations Between the Basic Learning Styles and Five Levels of Behavior

Behavior Level	Diverging	Assimilating	Converging	Accommodating
Personality types	Introverted Feeling	Introverted Intuition	Extraverted Thinking	Extraverted Sensation
Educational specialization	Arts, English History Psychology	Economics Mathematics Sociology Chemistry	Engineering Physical Sciences	Business Management
Professional career	Social service Arts Communication	Sciences Research Information	Technology Economics Environment	Organizations Business
Current jobs	Personal jobs	Information jobs	Technical jobs	Executive jobs
Adaptive competencies	Valuing skills	Thinking skills	Decision skills	Action skills

world. Jung's extraversion–introversion dialectical dimension as measured by the MBTI correlates with the active–reflective dialectic of ELT as measured by the LSI, and the MBTI feeling thinking dimension correlates , with the LSI CE–AC dimension. The MBTI sensing type correlates with the LSI accommodating learning style, and the MBTI intuitive type correlates with the LSI assimilating style. The MBTI feeling types correlate with the LSI diverging learning styles, and the MBTI thinking types correlate with the LSI converging style.

The above discussion implies the accommodating learning style is the *extraverted sensing* type, and the converging style is the *extraverted thinking* type. The assimilating learning style corresponds to the *introverted intuitive* personality type, and the diverging style corresponds to the *introverted feeling* type. Myers' (1962) descriptions of these MBTI types are similar to the corresponding LSI learning styles as described by ELT (see also Kolb, 1984, pp. 83–85).

Educational Specialization.   Early educational experiences shape people's individual learning styles by instilling positive attitudes toward specific sets of learning skills and by teaching students how to learn. Although elementary education is generalized, there is an increasing process of specialization that begins at high school and becomes sharper during the college years. This specialization in the realms of social knowledge influences individuals' orientations toward learning, resulting in particular relations between learning styles and early training in an educational specialty or discipline.

People with undergraduate majors in the arts, history, political science, English, and psychology have diverging learning styles, whereas those majoring in more abstract and applied areas such as physical sciences and engineering have converging learning styles. Individuals with educational backgrounds in business and management have converging learning styles, and those with backgrounds in economics, mathematics, sociology, and chemistry have assimilating learning styles.

Professional Career Choice.   A third set of factors that shape learning styles stems from professional careers. One's professional career choice not only exposes one to a specialized learning environment, but it also involves a commitment to a generic professional problem, such as social service, that requires a specialized adaptive orientation. In addition, one becomes a member of a reference group of peers who share a professional mentality and a common set of values and beliefs about how one should behave professionally. This professional orientation shapes learning style through habits acquired in professional training and through the more immediate normative pressures involved in being a competent professional.

Research over the years has shown that social service (i.e., psychology, nursing, social work, public policy) and arts and communications professions (i.e., theater, literature, design, journalism, media) comprise people who are heavily or primarily diverging in their learning style. Professions in the sciences (i.e., biology, mathematics, physical sciences) or the information or research fields (i.e., educational research, sociology, law, theology) are comprised of people with an assimilating learning style. Professions in technology (i.e., engineering, computer sciences, medical technology), economics, and environment science (i.e., farming, forestry) comprise people with converging learning styles. Finally, professions in organizations (i.e., management, public finance, educational administration) and business (i.e., marketing, government, human resources) comprise people with accommodating learning styles.

Current Job Role. The fourth level of factors influencing learning style is the person's current job role. The task demands and pressures of a job shape a person's adaptive orientation. Executive jobs, such as general management, that require a strong orientation to task accomplishment and decision making in uncertain emergent circumstances require an accommodating learning style. Personal jobs, such as counseling and personnel administration, that require the establishment of personal relationships and effective communication with other people demand a diverging learning style. Information jobs, such as planning and research, that require data gathering and analysis, as well as conceptual modeling, have an assimilating learning style. Technical jobs, such as bench engineering and production, that require technical and problem-solving skills require a converging learning style.

Adaptive Competencies. The fifth and most immediate level of forces that shapes learning style is the task or problem on which the person is currently working. Each task requires a corresponding set of skills for effective performance. The effective matching of task demands and personal skills results in an adaptive competence. The accommodating learning style encompasses a set of competencies that can best be termed *acting skills*: leadership, initiative, and action. The diverging learning style is associated with *valuing skills*: relationship, helping others, and sense making. The assimilating learning style is related to *thinking skills*: information gathering, information analysis, and theory building. Finally, the converging learning style is associated with *decision skills*: quantitative analysis, use of technology, and goal setting (Kolb, 1984).

AN OVERVIEW OF RESEARCH ON ELT AND
THE LSI: 1971–1999

What has been the effect of ELT and the LSI on scholarly research? Because ELT is a holistic theory of learning that identifies learning style differences among different academic specialties, it is not surprising to see that ELT and LSI research is highly interdisciplinary, addressing learning and educational issues in several fields. Since the first publications in 1971 (Kolb, 1971; Kolb, Rubin & McIntyre, 1971) there have been many studies of the ELT and LSI. The most recent update of the *Bibliography of Research on Experiential Learning Theory and the Learning Style Inventory* (A. Kolb & D. A. Kolb, 1999) includes 1004 entries.

Table 9.2 shows the distribution of these studies by field and publication period. The field classification categories are: education (including k–12, higher education, and adult learning), management, computer and information science, psychology, medicine, nursing, accounting, and law. Studies were also classified as early (1971–1984) or recent (1985–2000). In

TABLE 9.2

Early and Recent ELT/LSI Research by Academic Field and Publication

ELT/LSI Research	Early Period (1971-1984)	Recent Period (1985-1999)	Total (1971-1999)
By academic field			
Education	165	265	430
Management	74	133	207
Computer Science	44	60	104
Psychology	23	78	101
Medicine	28	44	72
Nursing	12	51	63
Accounting	7	15	22
Law	1	4	5
Total	354	650	1004
By publication type			
Journal articles	157	385	542
Doctoral dissertations	76	133	209
Books and Chapters	43	58	101
Other	78	74	152
Total	354	650	1004

Note. The data are from *Bibliography of Research on Experiential Learning Theory and the Learning Style Inventory*, by A. Kolb and D. A. Kolb, 1999, Cleveland, OH: Case Western Reserve University, Department of Organizational Behavior. Copyright © 1999. Adapted with permission.

addition to being the midpoint of the 29 year history of the work, the division makes sense in that the most comprehensive statement of ELT, *Experiential Learning*, was published in 1984, and the original LSI was first revised in 1985.

Table 9.2 also shows the distribution of the 1004 studies according to the publication type. More than 50% of the studies were published in journals and about another 20% were doctoral dissertations. Of the studies, 10% were either books or book chapters, and the remaining 150 studies were conference presentations, technical manuals, working papers, and master theses. Numbers should be considered approximate because a few recent citations have yet to be verified by abstract or full text. Also, classification by field is not easy because many studies are interdisciplinary. However, the bibliography probably gives a fair representation of the scope, topics, and trends in ELT and LSI research. The following is a brief overview of research activity in the various fields.

Education

The education category includes the largest number of ELT and LSI studies. The bulk of studies in education are in higher education (excluding professional education in the fields identified below). K–12 education accounts for a relatively small number, as does adult learning alone. However, in many cases adult learning is integrated with higher education. Several studies in the education category have been done in other cultures: United Kingdom, Canada, Australia, Finland, Israel, Thailand, China, Melanesia, Spain, Malta, and American Indian.

Many of the studies in higher education use ELT and the LSI as a framework for educational innovation. These include research on the matching of learning style with instructional method and teaching style and curriculum and program design using ELT (e.g., Claxton & Murrell, 1987). Several publications assess the learning style of various student, faculty, and other groups.

Other work includes theoretical contributions to ELT, ELT construct validation, LSI psychometrics, and comparison of different learning style assessment tools. In adult learning there are publications on ELT and adult development, moral development, and career development. The work of Sheckley and colleagues on adult learning at the University of Connecticut is noteworthy (e.g., Allen, Sheckley, & Keeton 1992; Travers, 1998). K–12 education research has been primarily focused on the use of ELT as a framework for curriculum design, particularly in language and science. (e.g., Hainer, 1992; McCarthy, 1996)

Management

ELT and LSI research was first published in management, and there has continued to be substantial interest in the topic in the management literature. Studies can be roughly grouped into four categories: management and organizational processes, innovation in management education, theoretical contributions to ELT including critique, and psychometric studies of the LSI. Cross-cultural ELT and LSI research has been done in Poland, New Zealand, Australia, Canada, United Kingdom, and Singapore. In the management and organization area, organizational learning is a hot topic. Dixon's (1999) book, *The Organizational Learning Cycle,* is an excellent example.

Another group of studies has examined the relationship between learning style and management style, decision making, and problem solving. Other work has measured work-related learning environments and investigated the effect of a match between learning style and learning environment on job satisfaction and performance. ELT has been used as a framework for innovation in management education, including research on matching learning styles and learning environments, program design, and experiential learning in computerized business games (e.g., Boyatzis, Cowen, & Kolb, 1995; Lengnick-Hall & Sanders, 1997).

Other education work has been on training design, management development, and career development. Another area of research has been on the development and critique of ELT. Most psychometric studies of the LSI in the early period were published in management, whereas recent psychometric studies have been published in psychology journals. Hunsaker (1981) reviewed the early studies in management and concluded, "The LSI does not demonstrate sufficient reliability to grant it the predictive reliability that such a measurement instrument requires. The underlying model, however, appears to receive enough support to merit further use and development" (p. 151).

Computer and Information Science

The LSI has been used widely in computer and information science, particularly to study end-user software use and end-user training (e.g., Bostrom, Olfman, & Sein, 1990; Davis & Bostrom, 1993). Of particular interest for this book on individual differences in cognitive and learning styles is the debate about whether these differences are sufficiently robust to be taken in account in the design of end-user software and end-user computer training. Other studies have examined the relationship between learning style and problem solving, decision making, on-line search behavior, and performance in computer training and computer-assisted instruction.

Psychology

Studies in psychology have shown a large increase over time, with 77% of the studies in the recent period. Many of these recent studies were on LSI psychometrics. The first version of the LSI was released in 1976 and received wide support for its strong face validity and independence of the two ELT dimensions of the learning process (Katz, 1986; Marshall & Meritt, 1985). Although early critique of the instrument focused on the internal consistency of scales and test-retest reliability, a study by Ferrell (1983) showed that the LSI version 1 was the most psychometrically sound among four learning instruments of that time. In 1985, version 2 of the LSI was released and improved the internal consistency of the scales (Sims, Veres, Watson, & Buckner, 1986; Veres, Sims, & Shake, 1987). Critiques of this version focused on the test-retest reliability of the instrument, but a study by Veres, Sims, and Locklear (1991) showed that randomizing the order of the LSI version 2 items resulted in dramatic improvement of test-retest reliability. This finding led to experimental research and finally to the latest LSI revision, LSI version 3 (Kolb, 1999a). The LSI version 3 has significantly improved psychometric properties, especially test-retest reliability (see Kolb, 1999b).

Other research includes factor analytic studies of the LSI, construct validation studies of ELT using the LSI, and comparison of the LSI with other learning style and cognitive style measures. Another line of work uses ELT as a model for personal growth and development, including examination of counselor–client learning style match and its effect on counseling outcomes. Notable here is the work of Hunt and his colleagues at the Ontario Institute for Studies in Education (Hunt, 1987, 1992).

Medicine

Most studies in medicine focus on learning style analysis in medical education specialties: residency training, anesthesia education, family medicine, surgical training, and continuing medical education. Of significance here is the research by Baker and associates (e.g., Baker, et al., 1988; Baker, Reines, & Wallace, 1985). Also, Curry (1999) has conducted several studies comparing different measures of learning styles. Other research has examined clinical supervision and patient-physician relationships, learning style and student performance on examinations, and the relationship between learning style and medical specialty career choice.

Nursing

ELT and LSI research has also increased dramatically, with 81% of the nursing studies in the recent period. In 1990 Laschinger reviewed the experiential learning research in nursing and concluded, "Kolb's theory of experiential learning has been tested extensively in the nursing population. Researchers have investigated relationships between learning style and learning preferences, decision-making skills, educational preparation, nursing roles, nursing specialty, factors influencing career choices and diagnostic abilities. As would be expected in a human service profession, nursing learning environments have been found to have a predominantly concrete learning press, matching the predominating concrete styles of nurses . . . . Kolb's cycle of learning which requires the use of a variety of learning modalities appears to be a valid and useful model for instructional design in nursing education" (p. 991).

Accounting

There has been considerable interest in ELT and LSI research in accounting education, where there have been two streams of research activity. One is the comparative assessment of learning style preferences of accounting majors and practitioners, including changes in learning style over the stages of career in accounting and the changing learning style demands of the accounting profession, primarily due to the introduction of computers. Other research has focused on using ELT to design instruction in accounting and studying relationships between learning style and performance in accounting courses.

In 1991 Stout and Ruble reviewed ELT and LSI research in accounting education. Reviewing the literature on predicting the learning styles of accounting students, they found mixed results and concluded that low predictive and classification validity for the LSI was a result of weak psychometric qualities of the original LSI and response-set problems in the LSI Version 2. They tentatively recommended the use of the randomized version proposed by Veres et al. (1991). They wrote, "Researchers who wish to use the LSI for predictive and classification purposes should consider using a scrambled version of the instrument," and noted that "it is important to keep in mind that assessing the validity of the underlying theoretical model (ELT) is separate from assessing the validity of the measuring instrument (LSI). Thus, for example, the theory may be valid even though the instrument has psychometric limitations. In such a case, sensitivity to differences in learning styles in instructional design may be warranted, even though assessment of an individual's learning style is problematic" (p. 50).

Law

We are now seeing the beginning of significant research programs in legal education. An example is the program developed by Reese (1998) using learning style interventions to improve student learning at the University of Denver Law School.

Evaluation of ELT and the LSI

There have been two recent comprehensive reviews of the ELT and LSI literature, one qualitative and one quantitative. In 1991 Hickcox extensively reviewed the theoretical origins of ELT and qualitatively analyzed 81 studies in accounting and business education, helping professions, medical professions, post secondary education, and teacher education. She concluded that, overall, 61.7% of the studies supported ELT, 16.1% showed mixed support, and 22.2% did not support ELT.

In 1994 Iliff conducted a meta-analysis of 101 quantitative studies culled from 275 dissertations and 624 articles that were qualitative, theoretical, and quantitative studies of ELT and the LSI. Using Hickcox's (1991) evaluation format, he found that 49 studies showed strong support for the LSI, 40 showed mixed support, and 12 showed no support. About half of the 101 studies reported sufficient data on the LSI scales to compute effect sizes via meta-analysis. Most studies reported correlations he classified as low ($<$ .5) and effect sizes fell in the weak (.2) to medium (.5) range for the LSI scales. In conclusion, Iliff suggested that the magnitude of these statistics is not sufficient to meet standards of predictive validity.

Most of the debate and critique in the ELT and LSI literature has centered on the psychometric properties of the LSI. Results from this research have been of great value in revising the LSI in 1985 and again in 1999. Other critique, particularly in professional education, has questioned the predictive validity of the LSI. Iliff (1994) correctly noted that the LSI was not intended to be a predictive psychological test like IQ, GRE, or GMAT. The LSI was originally developed as a self-assessment exercise and later used as a means of construct validation for ELT. Tests designed for predictive validity typically begin with a criterion such as academic achievement and work backward in an atheoretical way to identify items or tests with high criterion correlations. Even so, even the most sophisticated of these tests rarely rises above a .5 correlation with the criterion. For example, although Graduate Record Examination Subject Test scores are better predictors of first-year graduate school grades than either the General Test score or undergraduate grade-point average, the combination of these three measures only produces multiple correlations with grades ranging from .4 to .6 in various fields (Anastasi & Urbina, 1997). Although researchers in the professions are understandably searching for measures with high predictive validity to aid in decision making, a more realistic approach than relying on any single measure is to rely on prediction from new multitrait multimethod techniques such as structural equation modeling (e.g., Coover 1993; Travers, 1998; White & Manolis, 1997).

Construct validation is not focused on an outcome criterion, but on the theory or construct the test measures. Here, the emphasis is on the pattern of convergent and discriminant theoretical predictions made by the theory. Failure to confirm predictions calls into question the test and the theory. "However, even if each of the correlations proved to be quite low, their cumulative effect would be to support the validity of the test and the underlying theory" (Selltiz, Jahoda, Deutsch, & Cook, 1960, p. 160). Judged by the standards of construct validity, ELT has been widely accepted as a useful framework for learning-centered educational innovation, including instructional design, curriculum development, and lifelong learning. Field and job classification studies viewed as a whole also show a pattern of results consistent with the ELT structure of knowledge theory described in Table 9.1.

Recent critique has been more focused on the theory than on the instrument examining the intellectual origins and underlying assumptions of ELT from what might be called a postmodern perspective, where the theory is seen as individualistic, cognitivist, and technological (e.g. Holman, Paulican & Thorpe, 1997; Hopkins, 1993; Vince, 1998).

NEW DIRECTIONS IN ELT: FROM SPECIALIZED TO BALANCED LEARNING STYLES

To date most ELT-related research has examined conditions of extreme learning specialization; a new direction for ELT is the empirical testing of its theoretical propositions with regard to integrated learning. Integrated learning is conceptualized as an idealized learning cycle or spiral, where the learner "touches all the bases"—experiencing, reflecting, thinking, and acting—in a recursive process that is responsive to the learning situation

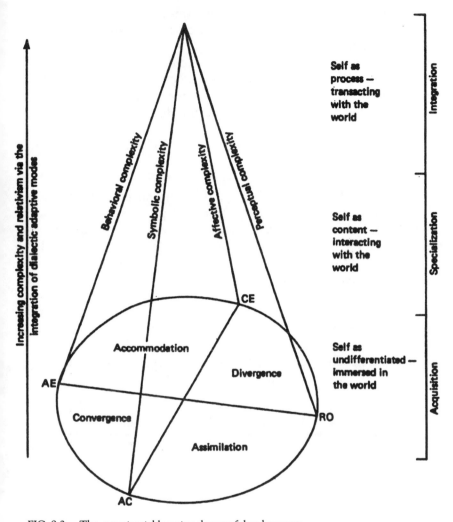

FIG. 9.2.   The experiential learning theory of development.

Note: From Experiential Learning: Experience as the source of Learning and Development (p. 141), by D. A. Kolb, 1984, Englewood Cliffs, NJ: Prentice-Hall. Copyright © 1984 by David A. Kolb. Reprinted with permission.

and what is being learned. The theory argues this development in learning sophistication results from the integration of the dual dialectics of the learning process as shown in Figure 9.2.

In developmental terms, there are three orders of learning styles as shown in Table 9.3. The first includes the specialized or basic learning styles described earlier: diverging, assimilating, converging, and accommodating. People with a basic learning style resolve the dialectics of the learning process by specializing in some modes at the expense of others. These learning styles correspond to the base of the ELT developmental cone portrayed in Fig. 9.2.

The second-order learning styles represent learning orientations that integrate one of the two dialectics of the learning process, therefore combining the abilities of two basic learning styles. Abbey, Hunt, and Weiser (1985) and Hunt (1987) called these learning styles northerner, easterner, southerner, and westerner (see also Kolb, 1984, chap. 6). The names correspond to the spatial location of these learning styles in the two-dimensional LSI cycle.

The northerner learning style integrates the RO--AE dialectic, and specializes in CE. It combines the characteristics and abilities of the diverging and accommodating styles. People with the easterner learning style are flexible in the CE–AC dimension, but specialize in RO. They combine learning skills associated with the diverging and assimilating

TABLE 9.3

Learning Modes and First, Second, and Third-Order Learning Styles.

Learning Styles	Developed Modes	Underdeveloped Modes
	First-order learning styles	
Diverging	CE, RO	AC, AE
Assimilating	AC, RO	CE, AE
Converging	AC, AE	CE, RO
Accommodating	CE, AE	AC, RO
	Second-order learning styles	
Northerner	CE, RO, AE	AC
Easterner	CE, AC, RO	AE
Westerner	CE, AC, AE	RO
Southerner	AC, RO, AE	CE
	Third-order learning styles	
Balanced Profiles	CE, AC, RO, AE	None

Notes. CE = concrete experience, AC = abstract conceptualization, RO = reflective observation, AE = active experimentation. For the spatial location of the four modes in the ELT learning cycle, see Fig. 9.1.

styles. Southerners combine elements from the assimilating and converging styles, being flexible in the RO–AE dimension and specializing in AC. Westerners integrate the CE–AC learning modes, but specialize in AE (Hunt, 1987). The four second-order learning styles correspond to the middle part of the developmental cone shown in Fig. 9.2.

The third-order learning styles have three balanced learning profiles that correspond to the apex of the ELT developmental cone shown in Fig. 9.2. All three balanced profiles are manifestations of integrated learning in the sense that people with these styles learn in a holistic way, effectively using the abilities associated with all four learning modes. The slight difference between the three balanced profiles is that the first emphasizes the CE–AC dimension more than the RO–AE dimension, whereas the inverse is true for the second profile. The third balanced profile equally emphasizes both dimensions.

What do researchers know about these second- and third-order styles? Not much, because the few related studies, although inspiring, have been unsystematic. One of the reasons the systematic empirical investigation of balanced learning profiles has not occurred is that past research has relied exclusively on the LSI. It is only recently that a system of commensurate instruments was developed to assess the full range of ELT constructs. The commensurate ELT instruments include, apart from the LSI, the Adaptive Style Inventory (ASI) and the Learning Skills Profile (LSP). These instruments have been designed to be theoretically commensurate and methodologically diverse to reduce spurious common-method variance among them.

The second new direction, therefore, is the comprehensive assessment of the ELT constructs through the LSI, ASI, and LSP. This broadens the research focus to include not only learning preferences, but also flexibility and skills. The ASI (Boyatzis & Kolb, 1993) uses a paired comparison method to rank learning preferences for the four learning modes in eight personalized learning contexts. It measures adaptive flexibility in learning: the degree to which one changes learning style to respond to different learning situations in his or her life. Earlier studies found that adaptive flexibility is positively related to higher levels of ego development on Loevinger's instrument (Kolb & Wolfe, 1981). Individuals with high adaptive flexibility are more self-directed, have richer life structures, and experience less conflict in their lives (Kolb, 1984).

The LSP (Boyatzis & Kolb, 1991, 1995) used a modified Q-sort method to assess level of skill development in four skill areas related to the four learning modes: interpersonal skills (CE), information skills (RO), analytical skills (AC) and behavioral skills (AE). Several recent studies have used the LSP in program evaluation (Ballou, Bowers, Boyatzis, & Kolb, 1999;

Boyatzis, Cowen, & Kolb, 1995) and learning needs assessment (Boyatzis & Kolb, 1995, 1997; Rainey, Hekelman, Glazka, & Kolb, 1993; Smith 1990).

Taken together, the LSI, ASI, and LSP provide greater flexibility in testing the constructs of ELT and in learning more about balanced learning profiles. Most recently, Mainemelis, Boyatzis, and Kolb (1999) employed the three instruments to test a fundamental ELT hypothesis: The more balanced people are in their learning orientation on the LSI, the greater will be their adaptive flexibility on the ASI. They used two indicators of a balanced learning profile: the LSI scores on the abstract–concrete and active–reflective dimensions. The results supported their hypotheses, showing that people with balanced learning profiles in both dimensions are more sophisticated (adaptively flexible) learners. The magnitude of the correlations was stronger for the balanced profile on the abstract–concrete dimension, a fact that deserves further investigation. Other results supported these corollary predictions that individuals with specialized LSI learning styles will show greater level of skill development in the commensurate skill quadrant of the LSP.

The study also produced some findings unexpected or contrary to Mainemelis et al.'s predictions. For example, although they predicted that specialized learning styles would show less adaptive flexibility on the ASI, the results showed this was true only for the abstract learning styles but not for the concrete styles; the latter are positively related to adaptive flexibility. Finally, although the authors expected that the more balanced one's learning style is on the LSI, the greater level of skill development he or she will show on the LSP, the results suggested that skill development is more related to specialization in learning style than to balance.

Although this recent research has largely supported the ELT constructs with regard to integrated learning, Mainemelis et al. concluded that, to assess effectively the characteristics of balanced learning styles, much more work is needed—from further mathematical analysis of the LSI scores and ASI formulae, to clinical observation of integrated learning orientations. These new research directions, coupled with the growing dissemination of ELT in various academic disciplines, bring ELT back to its basics: the creative exploration of the links among experience, learning, and development across the social spectrum.

In the emerging, networked world of information-based economies, learning is becoming more important than productivity in determining a person's or an organization's adaptation, survival, and growth (Kelly, 1999). Increasingly complex and service-oriented jobs demand flexibility as a requirement for sanity and success. We believe that ELT helps us understand learning and flexibility at a deeper, yet more comprehensive, level than previously. It also provides guidance for applications to helping people improve their learning and designing better processes in education and development. For those with an interest in learning organizations, it provides a theory and assessment methods for the study of individual differences while addressing learning at many levels in organizations and society.

REFERENCES

Abbey, D. S., Hunt, D. E., & Weiser, J. C. (1985). Variations on a theme by Kolb: A new perspective for understanding counseling and supervision. *The Counseling Psychologist, 13*, 477–501.

Allen, G. J., Sheckley, B. G., & Keeton, M. T. (1993, Winter). Adult learning as recursive process. *The Journal of Cooperative Education, 28*, 56–67.

Anastasi, A., & Urbina, S. (1997). *Psychological testing.* Englewood Cliffs, NJ: Prentice-Hall.

Baker, J. D., III., Cooke, J. E., Conroy, J.M., Bromley, H. R., Hollon, M. F., & Alpert, C. C. (1988). Beyond career choice: The role of learning style analysis in residency training. *Medical Education, 22*, 527–532.

Baker, J. D., III, Reines, H. D., & Wallace, C. T. (1985). Learning style analysis in surgical training. *American Surgeon, 51*, 494–496.

Ballou, R., Bowers, D., Boyatzis, R. E., & Kolb, D. A. (1999). Fellowship in lifelong learning: An executive development program for advanced professionals. *Journal of Management Education, 23*, 338–354.

Bostrom, R. P., Olfman, L., & Sein, M. K. (1990). The importance of learning style in end-user training. *MIS Quarterly, 14*, 101–119.

Boyatzis, R. E., Cowen, S. S., & Kolb, D. A. (Eds.). (1995). *Innovation in professional education: Steps in a journey from teaching to learning.* San Francisco: Jossey-Bass.

Boyatzis, R. E., & Kolb, D. A. (1991). *Learning Skills Profile.* (Available from TRG Hay/McBer, Training Resources Group, 116 Huntington Avenue, Boston, MA 02116, trg_mcber@haygroup.com)

Boyatzis, R. E., & Kolb, D. A. (1993). *Adaptive Style Inventory: Self scored inventory and interpretation booklet.* Available from TRG Hay/McBer, Training Resources Group, 116 Huntington Avenue, Boston, MA 02116, trg_mcber@haygroup.com)

Boyatzis, R. E., & Kolb, D. A. (1995, March-April). From learning styles to learning skills: The Executive Skills Profile. *Journal of Managerial Psychology, 10*, 3–17.

Boyatzis, R. E., & Kolb, D. A. (1997). Assessing individuality in learning: The Learning Skills Profile. *Educational Psychology, 11*(3–4), 279–295.

Claxton, C. S., & Murrell, P. M. (1987). *Learning styles: Implications for improving educational practices.* (ASHE-ERIC/Higher Education Report No. 4). Washington, DC: George Washington University.

Coover, F. D. (1993). Computer self-efficacy in professional nurses: An analysis of selected factors using latent variable structural equation modeling [CD-ROM]. Abstract from: ProQuest File: Dissertation Abstracts Item: 9233004

Curry, L. (1999). Cognitive and learning styles in medical evaluation. *Academic Medicine, 74*, 409–413.

Davis, S. A., & Bostrom, R. P. (1993). Training end user: An experiential investigation of the roles of the computer interface and training methods. *MIS Quarterly, 17*, 61–85.

Dixon, N. (1994/1999). *The organizational learning cycle. How we can learn collectively.* United Kingdom: McGraw-Hill.

Ferrell, B. G. (1983). A factor analytic comparison of four learning styles instruments. *Journal of Educational Psychology, 75*(1), 33–39.

Hainer, E.V. (1992). Cognitive and learning styles of high school students: Implications for ESL curriculum development. In J. M. Reid (Ed.), *Learning styles in the ESL/EFL classroom* (pp. 48–62). New York: Heinle & Heinle.

Hickcox, L. K. (1991). *An historical review of Kolb's formulation of experiential learning theory.* Unpublished doctoral dissertation, University of Oregon, Corvallis.

Holman, D., Pavlica, K., & Thorpe, R. (1997). Rethinking Kolb's theory of experiential learning in management education: The contribution of social constructionism and activity theory. *Management Learning, 28,* 135–148.

Hopkins, R. (1993). David Kolb's experiential learning-machine. *Journal of Phenomenological Psychology, 24,* 46–62.

Hunsaker, J. S. (1981). The experiential learning model and the Learning Style Inventory: An assessment of current findings. *Journal of Experiential Learning and Simulation, 2,* 145–152.

Hunt, D. E. (1987). *Beginning with ourselves.* Cambridge, MA: Brookline.

Hunt, D. E. (1992). *The renewal of personal energy.* Toronto, Canada: Ontario Institute for Studies in Education.

Iliff, C. H. (1994). *Kolb's Learning Style Inventory: A meta-analysis.* Unpublished doctoral dissertation, Boston University.

Jung, C. *Psychological Types* R. F. C. Hull, trans., *Collected Works of C. G. Jung,* Vol 6. Bollington Series XX, Princeton University Press (1977).

Katz, N. (1986). Construct validity of Kolb's Learning Style Inventory, using factor analysis and Guttman's smallest space analysis. *Perceptual and Motor Skills, 63,* 1323–1326.

Kelly, K. (1999). *New rules for a new economy: 10 radical strategies for a connected world.* New York: Viking Press.

Kolb, D. A. (1971). Individual learning styles and the learning process (Working Paper #535–71). Sloan School of Management, Massachusetts Institute of Technology.

Kolb, D. A. (1984). *Experiential learning: Experience as the source of learning and development.* Englewood Cliffs, NJ: Prentice-Hall.

Kolb, D. A. (1999a). *Learning Style Inventory,* version 3. Available from TRG Hay/McBer, Training Resources Group, 116 Huntington Avenue, Boston, MA 02116, trg_mcber@haygroup.com)

Kolb, D. A. (1999b). *Learning Style Inventory*—version 3: Technical specifications. Available from TRG Hay/McBer, Training Resources Group, 116 Huntington Avenue, Boston, MA 02116, trg_mcber@haygroup.com)

Kolb, A., & Kolb, D. A. (1999). *Bibliography of research on experiential learning theory and the Learning Style Inventory.* Department of Organizational Behavior, Weatherhead School of Management, Case Western Reserve University, Cleveland, OH.

Kolb, D. A., Rubin, I. M., & McIntyre, J. (Eds.). (1971). *Organizational psychology: An experiential approach.* Englewood Cliffs, NJ: Prentice-Hall.

Kolb, D. A., & Wolfe, D. (1981). Professional education and career development: A cross-sectional study of adaptive competencies in experiential learning. Report No. NIE G-77–0053). East Lansing, MI: National Center for Research on Teacher Learning. (ERIC Document Reproduction Service No. ED 209 493 CE 030 519.

Laschinger, H. K. (1990). Review of experiential learning theory research in the nursing profession. *Journal of Advanced Nursing, 15,* 985–993.

Lengnick-Hall, C. A., & Sanders, M. M. (1997). Designing effective learning systems for management education: Student roles, requisite variety, and practicing what we teach. *Academy of Management Journal, 40*, 1334–1368.

Mainemelis, C., Boyatzis, R. E., & Kolb, D. A. (1999). Learning styles and adaptive flexibility: Testing experiential learning theory (Working Paper 99–7). Department of Organizational Behavior, Weatherhead School of Management, Case Western Reserve University, Cleveland, OH.

Marshall, J. C. & Merritt, S. L. (1985). Reliability and construct validity of alternate forms of the Learning Style Inventory. *Educational and Psychological Measurement, 45*, 931–937.

McCarthy, B. (1996). About learning. Excel. Barrington, IL 60010.

Myers-Briggs, I. (1962). *The Myers-Briggs Type Indicator manual.* Princeton, NJ: Educational Testing Service.

Rainey, M. A., Hekelman, F., Galazka, S. F., & Kolb, D. A. (1993, February). Job demands and personal skills in family medicine: Implications for faculty development. *Family Medicine, 25*, 100–103.

Reese, J. H. (1998). *Enhancing law student performance: Learning styles interventions.* Saratoga Springs, NY: The National Center on Adult Learning.

Selltiz, C., Jahoda, M., Deutsch, M., & Cook, S. (1960). *Research methods in social relations.* New York: Holt.

Sims, R. R., Veres, J. G., Watson, P., & Buckner, K. E. (1986). The reliability and classification stability of the Learning Style Inventory. *Educational and Psychological Measurement, 46*, 753–760.

Smith, D. (1990). *Physician managerial skills: Assessing the critical competencies of the physician executive.* Unpublished doctoral dissertation, Department of Organizational Behavior, Weatherhead School of Management, Case Western Reserve University, Cleveland, OH.

Stout, D. E. & Ruble, T. L. (1991). The Learning Style Inventory and accounting education research: A cautionary view and suggestions for future research. *Issues in Accounting Education, 6*, 41–52.

Travers, N. (1998). *Experiential learning and students' self-regulation.* Saratoga Springs, NY: The National Center on Adult Learning.

Veres, J. G., Sims, R. R., & Locklear, T. S. (1991). Improving the reliability of Kolb's revised LSI. *Educational and Psychological Measurement, 51*, 143–150.

Veres, J. G., Sims, R. R. & Shake, L. G. (1987). The reliability and classification stability of the Learning Style Inventory in corporate settings. *Educational and Psychological Measurement, 47*, 1127–1133

Vince, R. (1998). Behind and beyond Kolb's learning cycle. *Journal of Management Education, 22*, 304–319.

White, J., & Manolis, C. (1997). Individual differences in ethical reasoning among law students. *Social Behavior and Personality, 25*, 19–47.

10

Epilogue: Another Mysterious Affair at Styles

Robert J. Sternberg
Yale University

In *The Mysterious Affair at Styles*, Agatha Christie (1995) created a convoluted murder mystery—the first involving her famous detective Hercule Poirot—with a surplus of suspects and an abundance of reasons why each suspect might be the guilty party. In the end, even those who might think they knew who the murderer was are likely to be surprised.

There is another mysterious affair at styles, this one also involving many suspects. The mystery is why styles research, so active and unified under the "cognitive styles" banner in the middle of the century, seems to be so much less unified and active by the end of the century. Although several research programs are ongoing at the present time, these programs have not experienced the kind of metaphorical centripetal force that creates a unified active field of research. The programs have remained largely isolated, both from each other and from the fields into which they might fit, such as personality or cognition research. Why should research programs on styles have remained largely isolated, both from each other and from mainstream field of research, at the same time that research on trait theories of personality (e.g., Big Five theory) and on psychometric ability theories of the mind (e.g., *g* theory) have thrived? There are many suspects, but I believe one suspect is the main villain, and it does not take Hercule Poirot to ferret out the prime suspect.

Several reasons contributed to this apparent reduction in activity and disunification (see Preface). First, some of the early theories presented styles that were not clearly distinguishable from abilities, on the one hand, or from personality traits, on the other. The result was that the study of styles was easily absorbed into the study of other things so that there seemed to be no need for a distinct area of research on styles, much less one that that merged with either abilities research or personality research. To some, styles research was abilities (or personality) research.

Second, many of the early theories were of isolated styles that made little contact with other psychological literature. Even though the styles were related closely to personality or cognitive traits, the appropriate literatures were not adequately addressed. The styles literatures also have often remained isolated one from another, with styles theorists not citing relevant work by other styles theorists.

Third, the quality of some of the early empirical research was variable. Often, adequate means were not built into the research to provide both convergent and discriminant validation when new styles were proposed.

I believe the major problem for the untimely demise of styles research, however, has been that the styles literature has failed to provide any common conceptual framework and language for researchers to communicate either with each other or with psychologists at large. In the literature on intelligence, g theorists deal with a common conceptual framework using a common language. The theory may be incomplete or it may be wrong, but it provides a common ground to unite a large number of researchers. The same can be said of five-factor theory: It provides a common conceptual framework and language for personality theorists within the trait tradition, and often it is even seen as nothing more than a common language. In contrast, styles theorists use many different conceptual frameworks and speak many different languages. Some researchers talk about surface and deep styles, a few about legislative or executive or judicial styles, a few about concrete or abstract learning styles, and on the list goes. The result is a kind of balkanization of research groups, and balkanization always has led to division and, arguably, deaths of a thousand cuts.

Is a common conceptual framework and language for styles even possible? I believe so, but only if one accepts the notion proposed by Biggs that styles are, in essence, approaches to learning and even to life. The common conceptual framework I propose is through the *psychology of choice and decision making*. One thing all of the styles proposed in this volume have in common is that they represent choices. Individuals have preferences for certain styles. For example, in the Boulton-Lewis, Marton, and Wilss conceptualization of styles, surface and deep styles do not represent abilities nor do they represent personality traits. Rather, they represent choices in the face of environmental stimuli. A student who is genuinely interested in material and who decides to become truly engaged with it does so through a deep-processing style. An individual who is bored, uninterested, or simply otherwise engaged is more likely to choose a surface-processing style. Or, in Entwistle, McCune, and Walker's conceptualization, a student who decides that grades are what counts may adopt a strategic style. In each case, though, any individual could choose any style, and individuals vary their styles to fit the circumstances. A similar argument applies to Riding's, Sternberg's, and Kolb's frameworks. For example, an individual may prefer to be a converger or a diverger, or an assimilator or an accommodator, but the individual does not have to be any one of these and may vary his or her style across tasks and situations. It is this element of choice and decision that distinguishes the styles discussed by the contributors to this book from the styles of the old cognitive styles movement, which much more reflected abilities.

If we view thinking and learning styles as representing informed choices, it becomes more clear why the number and diversity of styles is so large. The number of choices people can make about how to approach the world is extremely large. Nevertheless, a common set of theoretical questions emerges, and these questions might provide a common framework for investigators of styles:

1. *What* is the range of choices people can make? Each theory represented in this volume may be viewed as specifying a part of the range of choices. From this point of view, the theories are not so much competitive as they are complementary, considering different choices people can make.
2. *Why* do people make the choices they do? To what extent are choices a function of: (a) *person characteristics* (e.g., are more creative people more likely to be legislative and more analytical people more likely to be more judicial), (b) *task characteristics* (e.g., are more difficult tasks more likely to be approached in an executive manner simply because the individual lacks the knowledge base to approach them in either a legislative or a judicial way), (c) *situation characteristics* (e.g., are people socialized in some cultures more likely to adopt a surface approach and in other cultures a deep approach, as suggested by the essays of Watkins and of Zhang and Sternberg), (d) interactions among any two or three of these aspects (as discussed by Renzulli in his chapter in this volume).
3. *How* do people implement these choices in their daily lives? This is a question addressed in almost all the chapters. People apply styles to study, to work, and to their personal lives.

Perhaps styles as they now are studied have not integrated well into the literatures on abilities and personality because they do not belong in either place. Conventional cognitive styles did fit well at the interface between abilities and personality, but, arguably, they actually were either abilities or personality traits and so did not need to be studied separately. Current theories of styles have moved away from such redundant attributes, but they are still viewed by many as at the interface between abilities and personality. Perhaps where they belong is in the literature on choice and decision making. They are the part of our approach to problems that represents not some inborn or even environmentally acquired trait or even skill, but simply a choice based on a preference waiting to be analyzed. We can study styles in this way: It is our choice. If we view styles in this more active and less trait-like manner, perhaps we will solve the mystery at Styles. The mystery is that they have become balkanized because they have been placed in the wrong part of the conceptual world of psychology and education. Instead of being viewed in terms of abilities and personality, they need to be viewed in terms of choice and decision making.

REFERENCE

Christie, A. (1995). *The mysterious affair at Styles.* New York: Berkley.

Author Index

Subject Index

D

U